# STUDIES ON VOLTAIRE AND THE EIGHTEENTH CENTURY

## 252

General editor

PROFESSOR H. T. MASON

Department of French
University of Bristol
Bristol BS8 1TE

WILLIAM H. TRAPNELL

# The Treatment of Christian doctrine by philosophers of the natural light from Descartes to Berkeley

THE VOLTAIRE FOUNDATION
AT THE TAYLOR INSTITUTION, OXFORD

1988

© 1988 University of Oxford

ISSN 0435-2866

ISBN 0 7294 0363 7

*British Library cataloguing in publication data*

Trapnell, William H.

The treatment of Christian doctrine by philosophers of the
natural light from Descartes to Berkeley.
— (Studies on Voltaire and the eighteenth century,
ISSN 0435-2866; 252)
1. Christian doctrine.
I. Title   II. Series
230
ISBN 0-7294-0363-7

*Printed in England at The Alden Press, Oxford*

# Contents

# Contents

# Introduction

WE also ride the streetcar that bent the buildings inward over the head of young Einstein.[1] The acceleration of history pinches the sky between faith and reason. The obsolescence of the Newtonian universe resulted in relativity; the obsolescence of the Cartesian universe, in progress; the obsolescence of the Scholastic universe, in culmination ... In reverse order, each successive term in the series increased faith in reason no more than the dependence of reason on faith. In an age of discrimination between the two of them, the temptation to merge them beckoned to Hume.[2] Do faith and reason face two ways in one god? What a threat to believers, who say reason brings us to faith in a truth beyond reason! A threat to unbelievers too, however, for it implies that reason, which they follow exclusively, leads nowhere. The possibility that all knowledge may be illusion haunts them both, and the rest of us as well.

Before Hume thinkers spoke of reason as if they really knew what they were talking about. They argued over its nature without realising that argument alters nature. Most of them analysed it like anatomists dissecting cadavers in search of life. Only a few glimpsed the burgeoning growth of the reflexive conscience. Even fewer realised that fear of illusion is a sympton of intellectual health. As apologists continued to exalt Christian mystery above reason, freethinkers began to engineer a collision between this mystery and reason, both on the assumption that ideas behave to some extent like bodies in a Cartesian plenum or a Newtonian space. They also agreed that reason, in one way or another, comes from God, for atheists peopled the Old Regime less than they frightened it. If he gives us reason, all must have a share and theoretically an equal share. The seventeenth and the eighteenth centuries often referred to the gift as the natural light and the share as common sense. From a historical viewpoint, the noble concept belongs to philosophy and the popular one, to philology.

How ancient is the parallel between reason and light? As ancient as thought itself? Almost, perhaps. Certainly more ancient than Heraclitus who imagined,

1. 'I go to the bottom of the clocktower [in Bern], and get into the tram [Einstein] used to take every day on his way to work as a clerk in the Swiss Patent Office [...] We will take the tram up towards the speed of light to see what the appearances look like. The relativity effect is that things change shape [...] The tops of the buildings seem to bend inwards.' J. Bronowski, *The Ascent of Man* (Boston 1974), p.249.
2. 'Almost all reasoning is [...] reduced to experience [in my *Treatise*]; and the belief, which attends experience, is explained to be nothing but a peculiar sentiment, or lively conception produced by habit.' David Hume, *An abstract of a Treatise of human nature* (1740; rpt. Cambridge 1938), p.24.

in the sixth and fifth centuries B.C., that human souls are part of the logos, a rational, material fire pervading the world and governing its evolution. The Stoics developed this idea into a system. Seminal reason (*logos spermatikos*) generates matter and animates souls, thus forming a world identical in part with God or Nature. Under the influence of Plato, the later Stoics spiritualised and personified the logos. Philo blended the earlier Stoicism into his synthesis of Platonic philosophy and Jewish theology. A fiery ether, the Philonian logos serves as a material intermediary between a transcendent God and his human creatures, whose souls consist of this ether. Although Philo does not say whether he considers it a person, he tends to identify it with Wisdom and the Word, hypostases of God in Hellenistic Judaism. The Stoics had always compared the logos to the sun and its light, but Philo distinguished between the latter two, describing God as the sun and reason as its light, a distinction adopted by Christianity. The spiritualised and personified logos in Stoicism merged with the Jewish Word to form the Son in the prologue of the fourth gospel, whose author apparently did not know of Philo. Just as divine reason (*logos endiathetikos*) emits the divine word (*logos prophorikos*) in Stoicism, God generates the Son eventually incarnated by Jesus. To his Word the author also attributes the Old Testament glory (*shekinah*), a brilliant light manifesting Yahweh's presence: 'The Word was the true light that enlightens all men … [He] lives among us and we saw his glory' (John i.19, 14).[3]

The Neoplatonists adapted the spiritual logos to their metaphysics. According to Plotinus it emanates from Mind and Soul, the second and third hypostases in a subordinationist trinity formed by a serial emanation from the absolutely transcendent One. The Plotinian logos consists of countless logoi shaping matter and enlightening human minds, which are separate from them. Augustine approves of Plotinus's comments on an allusion by Plato to the spiritual light of God, which illuminates our separate souls 'as if God were the sun'.[4] From the *Republic* of Plato himself Augustine borrows the double analogy of vision to understanding and the visual light in the material world to the intellectual light of Ideas. While sunlight illuminates objects so that we can see them, the divine light illuminates ideas so that we can understand them. Yet Augustine neither identifies sunlight with the eye nor the divine light with the soul. The soul cannot even perceive the Ideas by ordinary spiritual contemplation, but only by mystic contemplation, the Christian equivalent of Plotinian ecstasy. Although Augustine does not mention the natural light in so many words, Gilson considers

---

3. Consider as well: 'God is light' (1 John i.5); 'All that is good […] comes down from the Father of all light' (James i.17). These and all further Biblical quotations come from *The Jerusalem Bible* (New York 1966).
4. *The City of God*, trans. Marcus Dods (Grand Rapids 1956), p. 181.

the phrase entirely appropriate for the interpretation of his opinion.[5] The reception of the natural light, Augustine believes, impinges on neither the supernatural order nor the world of the senses, a source of moral contamination. It produces truth of the intelligible rather than the sensual world, thus necessary rather than contingent truth.

This conception of reason went unchallenged in the early Middle Ages when Augustine's authority reigned nearly supreme. In the thirteenth century, however, the Scholastics discovered Aristotle's complete philosophy in texts transmitted by Arab scholars and, in particular, his philosophy of nature, previously unknown to them. They realised to their embarrassment that a pagan had developed a comprehensive metaphysical system the like of which Christians had so far proved incapable of achieving. Reason had obviously wrought this mighty work. Why had God favoured the enemy? The Arabs had answered the question by distinguishing between the truth of reason available to all men, Aristotle included, and the truth of faith, a Moslem privilege. Some Scholastics must have applied this distinction to Christianity by 1240 when, as Sardemann indicates,[6] Guillaume d'Auvergne, archbishop of Paris, condemned it. Unable to find a better explanation for Aristotle's achievement, however, he reversed himself and admitted the two kinds of truth. From Aristotle himself he even derived a further distinction between what amounts to the divine and the natural light. *The natural light of reason* actually appears in Thomas Aquinas, who regards it as the lowest level of access to knowledge, the other two being, in this life, faith and, in the next, contemplation of God.

His friend Bonaventure prefers to speak of four lights, the exterior light which enables us to cultivate the mechanical arts, the inferior light which derives knowledge from the senses, the interior light which produces philosophy, and the superior light which reveals theology. The first three correspond to the natural light of Thomas, who nonetheless accepts Arsitotle's theory that all human knowledge depends on the senses. Faithful to Augustine, Bonaventure separates spiritual truth from and raises it above sensual truth. Implicitly he maintains the dichotomy between the natural light and the divine light, thus keeping the pagan Aristotle in his place. He takes the parallel between light and reason more seriously than most of his predecessors. Physical light, in his

---

5. 'The intellectual mind which Augustine assigns to man as his own and which is therefore created can be called a *natural light*, if we may be allowed to use a phrase which Augustine does not employ but which does no violence to his thought.' Etienne Gilson, *The Christian philosophy of saint Augustine* (New York 1960), p.79.

6. Franz Sardemann, *Ursprung und Entwicklung der Lehre von ... lumen naturale ... bis Descartes* (Kassel 1902). See p.41. Much of the information in my synopsis of the natural light comes from this work.

opinion, multiplies itself and transmits to the objects it illuminates the properties they exhibit. When God created it on the first day, for instance, it gave extension to matter. He also created the self-propagating light of reason and endowed every human soul with it. Only through this light can the soul learn the truth. Bonaventure liked to quote James i.17: everything good and perfect 'comes down from the God of light'. Fashioned from the light of reason and furnished with sense experience, the soul arrives at the first principles of philosophy: a thing is identical to itself, the whole is greater than any of its parts, etc. Thus Bonaventure joined Thomas in accrediting the natural light as a standard concept in medieval philosophy. Together with other useful concepts, it survived the seventeenth-century revolt against a decadent Scholasticism.

Unlike the natural light, common sense inspired no more curiosity before the seventeenth century than its humble reputation suggests. The stratification of ancient society allowed the consideration of the possibility for political, economic or intellectual equality only within a class united by a common interest, such as citizens of a state at war or members of a persecuted sect. Occasionally the solidarity inspired by circumstances affecting an entire community overcame the layers of resentment and disdain between the classes. While these impromptu democracies eroded under the stresses of force and economics, a few ideas survived, such as common consent, public opinion and human reason. Since the validity of the first two depends on the value of the third, superiors naturally belittle the intelligence of inferiors. Yet fabulists, like jesters, enjoyed immunity from the intolerance of the powerful, who expected entertainment from them in the form of satire ostensibly at their expense. Aesop[7] tells of a fox who, having discovered a mask in an actor's house, exclaims, 'What a beautiful head! yet it is of no value, as it entirely wants brains.'[8] According to the moral, this fable suits people magnificent of body and unreasonable (*alogistous*[9]) of mind. Changing the context, the Latin translations replace the adjective *alogistous* by the noun *sensum*, or intelligence, and a negative.[10] In his imitation of this fable Phaedrus[11] made a more significant change when he modified *sensum* by *communem*. Körver[12] states that *sensus communis* rarely means basic human intelligence as it does here. Usually it means either civic responsibility or a faculty coordinating the data from the five senses. The Scholastics used it in

7. Seventh to sixth century B.C.

8. *The Fox and the mask*, trans. George Townsend (London n.d.), p.157.

9. *Corpus fabularum aesopicarum*, ed. Augustus Hausrath (Berlin 1957), p.40-41.

10. *Der lateinische Aesop des Romulus und die Prosa-Fassungen des Phädrus*, ed. Georg Thiele (Heidelberg 1910), p.132-33.

11. First century A.D.

12. Helga Körver, *Common sense: die Entwicklung eines englischen Schlüsselwortes* (Bonn 1967). Much of the information in my synopsis of common sense comes from this work.

the latter connotation, while Shaftesbury and Voltaire ressuscitated the former.[13]

Körver finds an early example of appealing to basic human intelligence to prove a point in *Adversus nationes* by Arnobius: 'Non istud nos soli, sed veritas ipsa dicit et ratio et ille communis qui est cunctis in mortalibus sensus.'[14] Truth and reason are synonyms of the common sense in all mortals. In French *le bon sens* appeared long before *le sens commun*. An apparently late thirteenth-century version of *La Vie de saint Alexis* contains the following sentence: 'Il s'est d'aprendre extremis comme soutil et de boen sens.'[15] Only in 1534 did Rabelais introduce *le sens commun*. Gargantua's father Grandgousier sends Ulrich Gallet to dissuade Picrochole from pursuing the war he has started. The ambassador's eloquence consists in a French imitation of Latin. After reminding Picrochole of Grandgousier's generosity, Gallet asks him whether, in seeking his own ruin, he should attack his best ally. Gallet answers this question himself: 'La chose est tant hors les [bornes] de raison, tant abhorrente de sens commun que à peine peut-elle être par humain entendement conçue.'[16] Here *sens commun* can only mean basic intelligence. The corresponding term in English appears a year later. George Joye and William Tyndale disagreed over the proper interpretation of John v.25: 'The dead will hear the voice of the Son of God.' Tyndale thought these words referred to the resurrection of the flesh, but Joye objected, 'T[yndale] is not so far besides his common senses as to say the dead body heareth Christ's voice.'[17] Joye insisted that the souls will hear his voice and not the bodies. Körver believes this to be the only plural use of *common sense* in the English language. The semantics of *common sense* and especially *good sense* evolved to a large extent in imitation of the French equivalents. The earliest example of *good sense* discovered by Körver occurs in Thomas Rymer's *Reflections on Aristotle's Treatise of poesie* (1674). Descartes, the most influential advocate of good sense on the continent, had been dead for twenty-four years.

The following study examines the significance of good or common sense, the natural light and reason in seventeenth and eighteenth-century Western European thought. Available for whoever wished to use them and for whatever purpose, they necessarily implied no scruples and no allegiance. They were

13. 'Some of the most ingenious commentators [...] make this common sense [...] to signify sense of public weal, and of common interest [etc.].' Anthony of Shaftesbury, *Characteristics of men, manners, opinions, times, etc.* (London 1900), p.70. '*Sensus communis* signifiait chez les Romains non seulement sens commun, mais humanité, sensibilité.' 'Sens commun', *Dictionnaire philosophique* (Paris 1961), p.388.

14. *Adversus nationes libri VII*, ed. C. Marchesi (Turin 1953), p.211.

15. Gaston Paris (ed.), *La Vie de saint Alexis* in *Romania* 8 (1879), p.170.

16. *Œuvres complètes* (Paris 1955), p.93.

17. George Joye, *An apologye made by George Joye to satisfye (if it may be) W. Tyndale* (Birmingham 1882), p.36.

the natural means of intellectual emancipation, but they served those who feared such emancipation as well as those who desired it. Emancipation from what? Every age has its tyranny, which often stems from religions and ideologies. The tyrannies of the seventeenth and eighteenth centuries depended on Christianity and monarchy, which usually interpenetrated and supported each other. Although subsequent history shows that monarchy threatened freedom more than Christianity, the contemporaries had every reason to believe otherwise. After the Reformation and the wars of religion, the Anglican, Lutheran and Calvinist churches were competing with the Catholic to impose their doctrines rather than inspire faith in them. All four clergies laboured more to control minds in this life than to save souls for the next, hence their alliance with the state and recourse to repression. Too often they failed the test of corruption, the subtle distinction between service to the community in justification of privileges and consolidation of privileges by exploitation of the public trust. The lust for power predominated at the expense of brotherly love which, except for lip service, had long been left to a naive minority. Yet strength and weakness converge in corruption. Authority depends on consent, and consent on interest. Church authority stems from acceptance of doctrine. Destroy confidence in the doctrine and the church must either reform or fall. The critical ideas that undermined Old Regime Christianity illustrate the evolution of reason.

Yet most of the writers who expressed them were not seeking this end. A Catholic, Descartes, for instance, avoided the discussion of his faith; an excommunicated Jew, Spinoza sympathised with some Protestants; Leibniz, a Lutheran, may have thought Christianity more useful than true; Locke, an Anglican, privately embraced unitarianism. Theories of the natural light also differed from thinker to thinker. Nearly every proponent of common sense assumed that he conformed to it, that all who respected it would agree with him, that anyone who disagreed deserved no sympathy. The debate nonetheless raised so many issues, attracted so many participants and revealed such a variety of opinions that no comprehensive study could achieve cohesion. Which thinkers therefore suit a study of basic human reason? Those who take an interest in common sense and the natural light qualify as candidates, but those who dedicate themselves to the study of reason itself win the competition, hence the seven philosophers considered here. To test their use of reason, I have chosen some of the Christian doctrines they treat. Original sin, the Trinity, the two natures and the eucharist seem the most vital and vulnerable of these.

At least one Catholic scholar acknowledges that Augustine invented original sin,[18] but the great Father took the elements of this doctrine from Paul and

18. See Athanase Sage A.A., 'Péché originel: naissance d'un dogme', *Revue des études augustiniennes*

Genesis. In the story of the fall, the Hebraic God Yahweh created Adam, the first man, and put him in the oasis of Eden where the tree of the knowledge of good and evil grew. He warned Adam not to eat the fruit from this tree on pain of death. Then he created the first woman and married her to Adam. Though naked, the couple were not ashamed. The slyest of Yahweh's creatures was the serpent, who told the woman she would not die if she ate fruit from the tree of moral knowledge, but the knowledge she acquired would assimilate her to the gods, Yahweh's rivals. He persuaded her to eat the fruit and she in turn persuaded Adam. The knowledge of good and evil they immediately learned inspired shame for their nudity, so that they covered themselves with loin cloths made of fig leaves. When they heard Yahweh walking in the oasis, they hid from him, but he called Adam and discovered what they had done. He punished all three of them: the serpent would have to crawl forever on its belly and the woman's offspring would crush its head under their heels. Eve would suffer pain in giving birth, lust after her husband and have to submit to him. Adam would live a hard life tilling the soil. Seeing that he resembled the gods by his moral knowledge, Yahweh banished him from Eden. The Jews interpreted this legend as proof that all men descend from a couple created by God. Adam had fallen from a state of innocence by disobeying God, who had punished him and his entire posterity by a congenital mortality and peccability. The ancient Hebrews, who believed in no life after death, could imagine permanent retribution by God only through punishment of future generations.

By Jesus's day many Jews and particularly the Pharisees believed in the resurrection of the dead, yet without changing the ancient interpretation of the fall. It is now evident that Paul, the only New Testament author who mentions the fall, agrees with this interpretation. He nonetheless draws a parallel, apparently unauthorised by Jesus, between the two Adams, the old one who brought sin and death into the world and the new one who brought redemption and resurrection. The best attested version of Romans v.6 states that Adam's sin contaminates all men, for all have sinned. Discredited today, another version affirms that all men have participated in Adam's sin. Augustine insists on this version, which appears in the Vulgate. All men, he teaches, inherit the guilt of Adam's sin and, worse, a resulting inclination to further sin known as concupiscence. God punishes them for their genetic participation in Adam's disobedience by inflicting the urge to sin on them. Baptism removes concupiscence, but a weakness in facing temptation remains. Concupiscence therefore condemns all unbaptised people, including infants who die before they can receive the sacrament, to suffer the wrath of God in hell. The excitement of

13 (1967), p.211-48. My unfinished 'Voltaire and original sin' has yielded the summary exposed here.

7

copulation symptomises the concupiscence with which the parents are infecting their offspring. This theory reflects Augustine's own obsession with sex, which he at first indulged and then repressed. He made the typical mistake of assuming that all men faced the same temptation and that his vice epitomised all vice. His ignorance of Greek, the language in which the New Testament had been written, and of Judaism, the essential source of his religion, exposed him to the errors he committed in his polemic against the Pelagians. A more skilful polemicist, Julian of Eclanum, drove him to extremes that would have discredited a lesser saint, extremes like his misinterpretation of Romans v.6 and his condemnation of infants who die unbaptised. The greatest theologian in the history of Christianity nonetheless prevailed and the Church grafted his doctrine of original sin on to the interpretation of the fall it had inherited from Judaism. Only one important modification ensued, the merciful relegation of unbaptised infants to limbus. Otherwise the Reformation and the Counterreformation reaffirmed practically the same doctrine.

The development of the Trinity began with the Hebrew cult of Yahweh,[19] who forbade images of himself and worship of the rival gods around him. Wielding natural forces from a fiery cloud, he enhanced the power of priestly rulers like Moses and disciplined his people by the threat of retaliation against future generations. He inspired their wars on other nations and eventually descended to the ark which they carried with them in their desert wanderings. Once the Hebrews had occupied Palestine, he moved to the Temple in Jerusalem, a central location where they could come and worship him. The sedentary life fostered speculation on national origins and borrowings from sophisticated neighbours, so he became a creator and a God of history. National decline may then have diverted attention from his past to an even more glorious future. He was now eternal, universal, ubiquitous, omniscient, omnipotent and unique. By the time of Jesus, a providential father had evolved from the stern figure of the Old Testament. Hellenism converted the material God into a spiritual being who, eventually eclipsed by Christ, reverted to stern authority. Henceforth he would appear remote and abstract.

The Hebrews thought he had a mighty breath which they called spirit. A similar force moved the prophets to prophesy, but Hellenistic Jews transformed it into a mental faculty of Wisdom. Though still impersonal, it was now immaterial and pervasive. Paul assigned it the task of communicating intimate knowledge of the divinity to believers. The first three gospels retain the archaic version, which evolves from an impersonal to a personal substitute for Christ

19. My *Christ and his 'associates' in Voltairian polemic* (Stanford 1982) has yielded the summary exposed here.

8

in Acts. Though inferior to him, it inspires his followers and occasionally even disciplines them.[20] In John, the risen Christ breathes the impersonal spirit on his disciples while, in an earlier episode, it flows from Jesus's breast like a mysterious fluid. The personal spirit appears as an allegorical figure whom John calls the Paraclete at times and the Spirit of Truth at others. Nowhere in the New Testament does the personal spirit approach equality or consubstantiality with God. His further development nonetheless tends to merge with that of the Trinity.

The second person of the Trinity eventually resulted from the deification of Jesus, which began soon after his death. Practically indifferent to his humanity, Paul considers him a subordinate divinity revealed by the resurrection. The relations between Christ and God interest him no more than those between the two natures. Does he even identify the pre-incarnation Christ with the spirit? Conflicting passages confuse the issue. The author of Hebrews (not Paul) interprets the unaccomplished kingdom of God as a second coming which he anticipates. He describes Christ as a self-sacrificing priest who redeemed the sins of his fellow Jews. Christ represents God perfectly without sharing in his divinity.

The first three (synoptic) gospels mingle Christian propaganda with biographical information about Jesus selected for its apologetic value. Written in Greek by Hellenistic Christians, these gospels divorce Jesus from Judaism. Yet one Aramaic tradition (M) appears in all three and another (Q) in the last two. They often disagree, but they agree that Jesus came from rural Galilee, where a superstitious, archaic and chauvinistic Judaism predominated. Except for his failure to marry, he resembled the other Galilean holy men, who healed the infirm and the insane by removing sin and exorcising devils in the name of God. They also called God their father without claiming divinity for themselves (a blasphemy). Jesus expected that the last judgment of the living and the resurrected dead would soon inaugurate the kingdom of God on earth. He differed from other apocalypticists only by the immediacy of this eschatology. The historical probability of his baptism by John the Baptist served as a pretext for apologetic speculation which each successive gospel takes a step further. Although the intentions vary, the first three describe the descent of the spirit in the form of a dove on Jesus's head and the vocal recognition of Jesus by God as his son. The fourth gospel drops the fact and keeps the apocrypha to establish his subordinate divinity. After his baptism, Jesus drew crowds by healing, exorcising and preaching the kingdom of God. He did not know, he admitted,

---

20. In Acts v.2-5, it executes Ananias and Sapphira for withholding part of their wealth from the Christian community. In Acts ii.3-4, it assumes the form of inverted flames and touches the disciples' heads, inspiring them to speak foreign languages.

9

exactly when it would come, yet he finally dispatched his disciples to the surrounding towns on the assurance that it would arrive before they returned. This prophecy failed and all but a remnant abandoned him.

His fellow Galileans yearned for a messiah to drive the Romans out of Palestine and restore the sovereignty of God. Yet none of the synoptic gospels contain any serious evidence that he ever claimed or acknowledged the title. Nor did his momentary popularity tempt him to play a messianic role. He nonetheless sympathised with the messianic aspirations of the Pharisees and the Zealots, despite the synoptists' attempts to conceal this sympathy. None of their testimony justifies the assumption that he had the slightest urge to alter or abandon his Galilean Judaism. Since his conversion of many Jews had not brought the kingdom of God, he decided to redeem the Jewish nation by his own martyrdom. Once he had sacrificed himself, he thought, the kingdom would come. In keeping with Pharasaic belief, he prophesied that God would raise him from the dead. Peter objected to this prophecy on the grounds, no doubt, that the true messiah cannot die without fulfilling his mission. Jesus rebuked him, not because he contemplated a spiritual messiahship (a Hellenistic myth), but rather because Peter was opposing a prerequisite for the kingdom. Jesus knew that, if he descended on Jerusalem with his remaining followers, the Romans in view of his recent popularity would suspect him of fomenting a messianic revolt. Provoke them and they would crucify him: it had happened before. The fanfare of his arrival in the capital and his raid on the Temple merchants, which he could not have accomplished alone, led to his arrest. Although the evangelists try to shift the blame for his execution to the Romans' Saducee collaborators, the Romans themselves evidently condemned and executed him. According to all four gospels, Pilate asked him whether he was 'the king of the Jews', the Roman equivalent of the messiah. Analysis of the various answers they attribute to him implies that he acknowledged this title no more than the Jewish one. Yet the placard on his cross read 'king of the Jews'. The death of the presumed messiah must have had a staggering impact on his followers. From the trauma of their disappointment and humiliation emerged rumours of appearances to them by Jesus risen from the dead. Comparison of the passages reporting them in the New Testament raises many minor contradictions and, according to Fuller,[21] two major ones: the appearances in Jerusalem conflict with those in Galilee and the appearances of a spiritual figure with those of a bodily one. Few reputable scholars still find any scientific evidence in these reports. They find even less in the gospel testimony to the empty tomb from which Jesus's body disappeared. The absence of any allusion

---

21. Reginald Fuller, *The Formation of the resurrection narratives* (London 1972), p.5.

in the earliest Christian writings to this miracle discredits it.

Paul tends to confuse the pre-incarnation Christ with the spirit, but not John who identifies him with the Hellenistic Word. God generated a Son and Mary conceived him, so that he assumed humanity without losing divinity. Although John made no attempt to explore this relationship, his gospel furnished most of the raw materials for later speculation on the two natures and the Trinity. He almost certainly subordinated the Son to the Father despite the contradictory statements he makes about the relations between them. The propaganda he uses to accredit Jesus's divinity distorts the synoptic figure, but he adds little useful information. Indeed he portrays a pompous and bombastic Jesus of scant historical value. Although conceptions of the Christian divinity varied considerably during the next two centuries, subordinationism characterises them all. Some Fathers recognised only two divine persons, others taught that the incarnation had increased the number from two to three and still others declared three from the beginning. Without abandoning the subordination of the persons, a few even advocated a divine substance common to all three, which Origen regarded as spiritual, and Tertullian as material. By the fourth century, consubstantiality and Origen's theory of eternal generation had persuaded theologians like Alexander of Alexandria that the Father and the Son are equal and coeternal. But an Alexandrian presbyter named Arius objected that sharing substance with the Son weakened the Father. He rejected eternal generation on the grounds that there had to be a time when the Son did not exist. The Father had created a separate and subordinate divinity in his Son. The ensuing dispute resulted in the Council of Nicaea (325), from which Constantine obtained approval of consubstantiality and condemnation of Arianism in an attempt to unite his empire under one faith. The dispute continued, however, as he vacillated between parties and his successors shifted from one to another. Consubstantiality emerged victorious only late in the century when the Arians had split into factions. The consubstantiality of the spirit and his procession from the other persons incited further controversy before they also prevailed. Finally Augustine formulated the definitive Trinity of three persons in one substance. Except for the incarnation, no person acts independently of the others and each consists in the entire divine substance. Another half-century of dispute came to an end at the Council of Chalcedon (451), which decreed two natures, the human and the divine, in the person of Christ. Although epithets applied to one may also apply to the other, they do not mingle. The human nature has its own immortal soul and remains intact, despite its union with the divine. After Augustine had settled the issue of the Trinity, therefore, Chalcedon settled that of the two natures.

The eucharist evolved from the Hellenistic transformation of the Jewish sacrificial tradition originating in the Hebrew cult.[22] The Last Supper which Jesus, a devout Jew, shared with his disciples belonged to this tradition. He almost certainly did not ask them to eat his body and drink his blood[23] in any realistic way, an idea abhorrent to Jews. His Jewish monotheism prevented his Hellenistic followers neither from deifying him after his death nor from initiating communion in the substance of his divinity. Yet they disagreed over the salvific effect of this communion, the reality of Christ's corporeal presence and the sacrificial significance of the ceremony. The sacrament raised little Patristic curiosity before Ambrose, who established the conversion of the bread into Christ's body at the moment of consecration, distinguished the reality of the body from the appearances of bread and confirmed the reactualisation of Christ's sacrifice on the cross. His student Augustine taught that the perceptible sign of bread indicates the spiritual presence of the body, but only to believing communicants. He identifies Christ with the head of the body on the altar, which consists in the mystic union of the predestinate elite, the true church. They offer themselves, Christ offers himself and the entire Trinity offers itself in a re-enactment of the sacrifice on the cross. Augustine discriminates between the perceptible sacrament and the mysterious effect, but he regards this effect as substantial enough to constitute a real presence. Although he condemns Capernaism and Stercoranism, his language sometimes implies a possible toleration of these eucharistic horrors. Despite the location of Christ's physical body in heaven, it is present everywhere and whenever a priest recites the consecration: 'This is my body ... This is my blood.'[24]

Mixing Augustine with Ambrose, Paschase exaggerates his own realism occasionally, his attacks on Stercoranism and Capernaism notwithstanding. At the moment of consecration, Christ transforms the bread into his body by dint of his creative power. The illusory corporeal veil of bread conceals the mystery of the spiritual body, which Paschase equates to the one in heaven. His adversary Ratramn replies that the figure of the corporeal veil conforms to the mystery beneath, thus revealing it indistinctly. He contradicts Paschase's relegation of this figure to mere sensory illusion. Defining the mystery as a substantive power, he denies the identity of the body in heaven with the one on the altar. Since spiritual reality escapes the limits of time and space, however, he believes in the real presence of the heavenly body in the eucharist. In the celebration of the sacrament, he sees another figure, that of the sacrifice on the cross and,

22. My *Voltaire and the eucharist*, Studies on Voltaire 198 (Oxford 1981), has yielded the summary exposed here.
23. For greater concision I will henceforth omit the wine and the blood whenever an allusion to the bread and the body implicates them symmetrically.
24. 1 Corinthians xi.23-25; Mark xiv.22-24; Luke xxii.19-20; Matthew xxvi.26-28.

apparently, the pledge of redemption. The contrast between the predominance of reason in Ratramn and faith in Paschase established a tradition that would continue to characterise eucharistic controversy. A stubborn dialectician, Berengar infuriated his contemporaries by adapting a dynamic symbolism from the forgotten Ratramn, which he later converted into a pure symbolism despite his persistent endorsement of the real presence. In reaction to his criticism, Lanfranc developed Ambrosian metabolism into a primitive transubstantiation and Guitmund of Aversa replaced Lanfranc's destruction and re-creation by direct conversion. Guitmund also introduced concomitance, the multipresence of Christ's whole body in heaven and in every crumb of bread and drop of wine. The conciliar persecution of Berengar for his resistance to these miracles illustrates the continuous triumph of faith over reason in the development of eucharistic dogma. Thomas ascribes to the words of consecration an intrinsic power that does what they say, so the validity of the sacrament does not depend on the integrity of the celebrant. He locates Christ's body in heaven and on the altar at the same time 'by the conversion of another thing into itself.'[25] The substance of bread becomes that of Christ's body, while the accidents of bread subsist by their dependence on the fundamental accident of spatial configuration which the new substance has appropriated. Though not in their normal situation, the accidents of this substance are present by concomitance. Reaffirming the concomitance of Christ's body in the wine as well as the bread, Thomas notes that priests were restricting laymen to communion on bread alone.

The other Scholastics, who accepted transubstantiation too, argued over the manner in which it occurred. Although the nominalist William of Ockham privately believed in impanation, he taught that bread ceases to exist when the body replaces it. A realist, Wyclif objected that cessation and conversion contradict each other, that accidents cannot survive the destruction of substance and, like Berengar and Ratramn, that the senses continue to perceive bread after the consecration. Although he did not produce a coherent doctrine, he defended an unsubstantial real presence and attacked clerical privilege and abuse. Well before the Reformation, he demanded that dogma conform to Scripture. Hus advocated only the orthodox part of Wyclif's theology, but his enemies burned him alive at the Council of Constance on several allegations of heresy including remanance, the Wycliffian subsistence of bread after the consecration. They likewise condemned him on the false charge of inciting his fellow priests to restore the lay cup. Like Hus and Wyclif, Luther censured clerical privilege and abuse, but he also protested against the suppression of

---

25. Thomas Aquinas, *Summa theologiae*, trans. David Bourke and others (New York 1965-1975), 3.75.2.

the lay cup, the sacrificial interpretation of the eucharist, and private mass. Considering the eucharist a testament, he attributes the real presence to the faith of communicants and rejects transubstantiation on philosophical and theological grounds. Instead he prefers impanation, yet without making any final commitment to it. The heavenly and eucharistic bodies are identical in being and nature, but not in form and manner. While Luther insisted on both a spiritual and a bodily presence, Zwingli limited the presence to spirit and Calvin advanced an intermediate solution. All three agreed nonetheless that Scripture must justify doctrine. The Council of Trent condemned the three doctrines without naming their authors. It reaffirmed transubstantiation, the real multi-presence and concomitance. Unable to decide on requests from several rulers for restoration of the lay cup, it left this decision to the pope who granted them a temporary concession. The sacrificial interpretation of the mass appears in one of its most solemn statements. After Trent the Catholics and the Protestants continued to quarrel over transubstantiation and the lay cup.

The treatment of Christian doctrine by philosophers of the natural light will emerge only from analysis of the texts they have written. We cannot ask them why they said what they did, what they meant, how they arrived at it or what they would have said if ... Unless one discussed or debated a point of interest to us with another, we can determine no certain agreement or disagreement between them. Thus the present study avoids such speculation, although the conclusion founds a few conjectures on probabilities established in the preceding chapters. Nor does it seek to determine whether these philosophers were *right* or *wrong*, whatever these words happen to mean. It concerns itself with what they wrote and, insofar as we can tell, what they meant and why they thought so. The project reflects my conviction that much remains to be discovered or rediscovered by analysis of the words they have written. Each of the following chapters examines the natural light in the thought of a particular philosopher and his use of it in consideration of the eucharist, the Trinity, Christ and original sin.

The expedition does not travel upstream in search of sources, but rather downstream in search of confluences, downstream from Descartes to Berkeley.

# Descartes

'JE n'ai jamais présumé que mon esprit fût en rien plus parfait que ceux du commun.'[1] What did Descartes mean? How should we interpret this unjustified and uncharacteristic remark in the *Discours de la méthode* (1637)? Sincere modesty? Scientific detachment? Irony? Elsewhere and even in the same work he takes his obvious superiority over other men for granted. Nor was he a humble genius, despite his reluctance to publish. A gentleman did not cater to the crowd! Yet he had no taste for oblivion either, hence the *Discours*, a brief work written in French for the benefit of polite society and not in Latin, the language of learned specialists. He did not want gentlemen to take him for a pedant. He was thinking of them when he denied that he had an exceptional mind.[2] Boasting of one's intelligence not only seemed undignified but also pretentious. 'La puissance de bien juger,' he continues, 'et de distinguer le vrai d'avec le faux, qui est proprement ce qu'on nomme le bon sens ou la raison, est naturellement égale en tous les hommes' (i.568). He founds this assertion on a psychological observation: everyone considers himself so well endowed with reason that even those most difficult to please in such matters are satisfied with their share. The irony implied does not detract, apparently, from his confidence in the validity of the evidence he advances. Since reason raises us above the beasts, each of us must have it 'tout entière' (i.569). In beasts Descartes sees no more than machines lacking a mind or soul, the same thing in his philosophy. The uniform superiority of men over animals does not exclude the diversity of human intelligence, which 'ne vient pas de ce que les uns sont plus raisonnables que les autres, mais seulement de ce que nous conduisons nos pensées par diverses voies' (i.568). The quality of thought depends on how we cultivate our mind and not on native intelligence, which is equal in all of us. In Scholastic terms, all minds have the same *form* but different *accidents*, so all are *individuals* in the same *species*. While every one inherits this form, each varies according to the accidents it acquires: 'ce n'est pas assez d'avoir l'esprit bon, mais le principal est de l'appliquer bien' (i.568), an allusion to the method

1. René Descartes, *Œuvres philosophiques*, ed. Ferdinand Alquié (Paris 1972-1973), i.568. All further references to this text will appear in parentheses after quotations.
2. The following remark also applies to 1637: 'En 1647, les spectateurs du combat sont les gens du monde; il convient de leur montrer comment la philosophie cartésienne est *naturelle*, comment elle est le simple épanouissement de l'esprit humain, alors que la philosophie scolastique est un ensemble de matériaux qu'on jette pêle-mêle dans la mémoire, qui empêtrent la raison.' Henri Gouhier, *La Pensée religieuse de Descartes* (Paris 1972), p.149.

introduced and recommended by the *Discours*. Thus Descartes does not contradict himself when, on one hand, he declares all men equal in intelligence and, on the other, he implies the superiority of his own mind.[3] Though proud of his method, he doubted the ability of many people to apply it. They yield to the common and customary acceptance of ridiculous and extravagant errors which 'peuvent offusquer [leur] lumière naturelle,[4] et [les] rendre moins capables d'entendre raison' (i.578).

In the *Discours*, Descartes tells how he purged his mind of the errors accumulated from his childhood and education by repudiating all of his knowledge. Only afterwards did he begin to rebuild it on the foundation of clear and distinct certainty, the touchstone of truth in his opinion. He considers this act too difficult for nearly everyone else, since he divides minds into those given to haste and those given to prejudice. Hasty minds lack the patience to develop their thought in an orderly manner. Once they have left the beaten path of conventional thinking, they never succeed in pioneering a straight one in keeping with their own ideas and spend the rest of their lives wandering around in confusion. In proposing an alternative to the first tendency of *précipitation*, Descartes does not discredit the second by calling it *prévention*. He might have followed it himself, he confesses, if his experience had not led elsewhere. Minds subject to this tendency have 'assez de raison, ou de modestie, pour juger qu'ils sont moins capables de distinguer le vrai d'avec le faux, que quelques autres' (i.583). They therefore submit to instruction by others and follow their opinions rather than seek opinions of their own. The passage implies an élite composed of 'others' who, like Descartes, have a higher aptitude for distinguishing truth from error. The contradiction between this aristocracy and the democracy of reason he has already exposed lurks in the words and not in the thought, as his favourite analogies of straying from the beaten path and failing to beat a straight path suggest. The nature of the experience which has turned his mind away from prejudice confirms this suggestion. Varying and conflicting opinions had exasperated him until 'je me trouvai comme contraint d'entreprendre moi-même de me conduire' (i.584). Evidently he was not thinking of the natural

---

3. Leibniz refutes this point in a letter to Eccard (1677): 'I esteem the genius and the discernment of Descartes highly, but he tried to convince the world that the things which he achieved by virtue of his outstanding ability were done solely through the use of a certain unique method which he had established, so that men were drawn to the hope of discovering an art by which mediocre minds could equal an excellent one. In fact, it seems to me that almost no Cartesian has produced anything which even remotely approaches the discoveries of the master.' Gottfried Wilhelm Leibniz, *Philosophical papers and letters* (Dordrecht 1970), p.180.
4. 'Der "Bon sens" ist nichts anderes als das von Descartes oft berufene "natürliche Licht", die dem Menschen innewohnende Vernunft.' Gerhart Schmidt, *Aufklärung und Metaphysik* (Tübingen 1965), p.23.

ability to distinguish between truth and error, but rather the method by which one must exploit this ability.

Other writings which he left unfinished and unpublished confirm his faith in the universality of good sense. The *Studium bonae mentis*, which he wrote between 1620 and 1623, has disappeared. Written before 1629, the *Regulae ad directionem ingenui* contains several passages on the same subject. Rule no. I observes that people devote themselves to what we would call sociology, botany, astronomy, metallurgy and other fields,[5] 'tandis que personne ne songe au bon sens, c'est-à-dire à cette sagesse universelle' (i.78). Yet the other disciplines justify themselves only insofar as they contribute to universal wisdom. The interdependence of all sciences and their dependence upon 'la lumière naturelle de [la] raison' (i.79) persuaded the youthful author of the *Rules* that one need only cultivate this faculty in order to master all the disciplines, obviously an error. Later he would seek the key to universal knowledge in mathematics. Rule VIII declares his intention of exposing a method by which anyone may discover the truth, 'fût-il d'intelligence moyenne' (i.122). Not intelligence, but rather method provides access to knowledge. Needless to say, the *Rules* amount to an early formulation of method.

Descartes's correspondence reveals further information about his conception of the natural light. In a letter to Mersenne (16 Oct. 1639), he disagrees with Herbert of Cherbury[6] over the source of truth: universal consent according to the Englishman and the natural light according to the Frenchman. 'Tous les hommes ayant une même lumière naturelle,' says Descartes, 'ils semblent devoir tous avoir les mêmes notions' (i.145), but almost no one makes proper use of it. Though all whom he and Mersenne know might consent to an error, none of these are aware of the many undiscovered truths accessible to the natural light. The dialectic between equality of intelligence and inequality of method continues in a letter to Dinet[7] prefacing the second edition (1642) of the *Méditations*: 'Je ne crois pas voir plus clair que les autres, mais peut-être cela m'a beaucoup servi; de ce que, ne me fiant pas trop à mon propre génie, j'ai suivi seulement les voies les plus simples et les plus faciles' (ii.1086). In his opinion, therefore, the most thorough exposition of his mature metaphysics had resulted from the simplest and easiest means of investigation, those available to all men. Yet none had exploited them before him. In 1643 he defied the Dutch theologian Voetius, who had attacked his philosophy, to prove it was dangerous

5. '[Il me semble] étrange que tant de gens étudient avec un si grand soin les mœurs humaines, les propriétés des plantes, les mouvements des astres, les transmutations des métaux et autres objets d'étude de ce genre tandis que presque personne ne songe au bon sens' (i.78).
6. The author of *De veritate* (1624).
7. The Jesuit provincial for France.

and perverse: 'je recherche [...] la connaissance des vérités qu'il nous est permis d'acquérir par les lumières naturelles' (iii.30). How could the natural light – he usually preferred the singular – be dangerous and perverse? By October of 1644, public approval of his philosophy had convinced him that this response justified his appeal to the natural light. 'Ceux qui ont le sens commun assez bon', he wrote to Charlet, and who have not committed themselves to Scholasticism, are so inclined to embrace his philosophy that it could scarcely fail to win universal approval one day (iii.536).

No one admired him more than the Palatine Princess Elizabeth, who eagerly submitted to his intellectual and moral guidance. He in turn admired her courage in facing the adversity of exile from her native land. In June of 1644 he wrote to her: 'Il n'y a aucun bien au monde excepté le bon sens qu'on puisse absolument nommer bien, il n'y a aussi aucun mal dont on ne puisse tirer quelque avantage, ayant le bon sens' (iii.579). For better or worse good sense is man's greatest asset and it will enable Elizabeth to make the best of her misfortune. The Lettre-Préface to the French-language edition (1647) of the *Principes de la philosophie* informs the public of the same conviction. After examination of many minds, the author found none so crude or sluggish that it could not think solid thoughts and even learn the highest sciences, if guided 'comme il faut' (iii.778). This remark tells us more about his judgement than his evidence, for he does not seem to have made the kind of investigation he implies here. Yet his life of country seclusion in Holland may have exposed him to casual acquaintances with uncultivated minds of varying potential. Experience had confirmed him in his opinion by 31 March 1649, when he wrote to Chanut, the French ambassador to the court of Christina, Queen of Sweden. His ideas surprise the public at first, he testifies, because they deviate from common wisdom. 'Toutefois, après qu'on les a comprises, on les trouve si simples et si conformes au sens commun, qu'on cesse entièrement de les admirer' (iii.900). People wonder (*admirer*) only at what they cannot fully understand.

He continued to believe that unprejudiced common sense could not fail to recognise the irrefutable truth of his philosophy. He had no better reason for accepting Christina's invitation to come to Sweden and teach it to her. The opportunity to recruit so illustrious a disciple outweighed the danger, which he anticipated,[8] of travel to a country where he would die of pneumonia in 1650. Though unable to complete his instruction of the Queen, he left an incomplete literary model of instruction in his papers and entitled it as follows: *La Recherche de la vérité par la lumière naturelle qui, toute pure et sans emprunter le secours de la*

---

8. 'J'ai beaucoup plus de difficulté à me résoudre à ce voyage que je ne me serais moi-même imaginé' (iii.899): to Chanut in 1649.

*religion ni de la philosophie, détermine les opinions que doit avoir un honnête homme, touchant toutes les choses qui peuvent occuper sa pensée, et [qui] pénètre jusque dans les secrets des plus curieuses sciences* (ii.1105). This title suggests a project more ambitious than useful, a thought that may have occurred to Descartes by the time he had written the thirty-five pages in the Alquié edition. Yet the existing text is a valuable aid to study of the philosopher, despite controversy over the date of composition. Most critics agree that he composed it after the *Méditations*, which it tends to recapitulate in dialogue form.

In the introduction preceding the dialogue he discusses the education of 'un honnête homme' (ii.1105), the equivalent of a gentleman in seventeenth-century France.[9] A gentleman, he declares, has no obligation to read all books and learn Scholastic philosophy. Thorough study of the humanities would waste his time and leave him unprepared for the active life he must lead. 'Les bonnes actions [...] lui devraient être enseignées par sa propre raison, s'il n'apprenait rien que d'elle seule' (ii.1105). Before reason can guide him, however, he will have to free himself of the bias instilled in him by sensory illusion and the authority of tutors during his childhood. Unless he is strong in character, he will need the instruction of a wise man to eliminate bad doctrine, establish a foundation for knowledge and discover the means of access to the highest sciences. The *Recherche de la vérité* teaches these very things according to Descartes. It even reveals 'les véritables richesses de nos âmes' which will enable each of us, without assistance from anyone else, to acquire all the knowledge necessary for the conduct of life and the acquisition of 'toutes les plus curieuses connaissances que la raison des hommes est capable de posséder' (ii.1106). Advertising? Evidently Descartes, who wrote the *Recherche* in French,[10] intended it for the same public as the *Discours*, 'les honnêtes gens qui ne se piquent de rien', as the saying went. He protests that he deserves no greater glory for his discoveries than one who happens upon a treasure while taking a stroll. He expects they will acquire a currency like that of money, which has the same value whether it comes from a peasant's pocket or the royal treasury. This optimism favours Alquié's opinion that Descartes wrote the work in 1641 and not later as others contend.[11]

Three characters participate in the dialogue: Epistémon, a Scholastic; Eudoxe, a Cartesian, and Poliandre 'qui n'a jamais étudié' (ii.1108). The latter two qualify as gentlemen by the author's standards, but Eudoxe has submitted to

9. By *gentleman* I do not mean *gentilhomme*, a nobleman.
10. Only the beginning of the French text subsists. Alquié has translated the rest into French from a Latin translation published in the *Opuscula posthuma* of 1701. See Descartes, *Œuvres*, ii.1102-1104.
11. See his introduction to the *Recherche* in Descartes, *Œuvres*, ii.1102-1104.

the discipline recommended by the introduction and Poliandre has not. Assuming the role of the wise man mentioned there, Eudoxe teaches Poliandre
the new philosophy by Socratic questioning in order to convince Epistémon of
the harmony between this philosophy and the natural light. Though untactful
and overbearing, he obtains dramatic results from the docile Poliandre despite
interference by Epistémon. As in most philosophical dialogues, the author's
doctrine triumphs over weak opposition, yet Eudoxe explains: 'Pour découvrir
les vérités même les plus difficiles [...] il suffit de ce qu'on nomme vulgairement
le sens commun, pourvu toutefois que l'on soit bien conduit' (ii.1128) Once
Poliandre rediscovers several of Descartes's more difficult truths, Eudoxe
applauds 'ce que peut le bon sens bien gouverné' and encourages Poliandre to
show Epistémon 'jusqu'où le bon sens peut aller' (ii.1132). Since Poliandre
follows no authority but common sense and no bias inhibits his reason, he
practically cannot make a mistake or, at least, if he made one, he could not fail
to recognise and correct it. Scholastics like Epistémon, on the other hand, have
so many opinions and prejudices that they can hardly rely on 'la seule lumière
de la nature' (ii.1135). Accustomed to heeding authority, they do not even listen
to the voice of their own reason.

Descartes was opposing Scholasticism rather than Scholastics, for he hoped
to convert them and replace their philosophy by his own.[12] He may have
intended Epistémon as a caricature of the Jesuit Bourdin, who had criticised
the *Méditations* because they conflict with Scholasticism. But Descartes wrote
courteous letters to the Jesuit Scholastics who had taught him at La Flèche and
hinted at the desirability of inserting his philosophy in the curriculum of the
Jesuit schools. He obviously did not think they were insensitive to the natural
light like Bourdin and Epistémon. As we have seen, he believed all men had a
good sense that does not vary in potential, but rather in effect according to
application. When he exhorted his readers to reject authority and think for
themselves, however, he was appealing only to an élite: his fellow gentlemen in
particular, but also ladies like Christina and Elizabeth as well as any other
intellectuals willing to listen. He wasted no tact on intellectuals who were not,
as his replies to their objections demonstrate.[13] Contempt for 'la pluralité des
voix' (ii.905) appears in two letters from 1642. He had long since realised, he
assured Gibieuf, 'que mes pensées ne seraient pas du goût de la multitude'

12. 'L'originalité de Descartes [...] c'est de dissocier hardiment le destin de la scolastique de la
défense de la religion à laquelle elle se raccroche.' Roger Lefèvre, *La Métaphysique de Descartes*
(Paris 1972), p.10.
13. He answers Gassendi's objections to his *Méditations* in the 'Réponses aux cinquièmes
objections', which include the following sentence: 'Encore que vous n'ayez pas tant employé les
raisons d'un philosophe pour réfuter mes opinions que les artifices d'un orateur pour les éluder,
cela ne laisse pas de m'être agréable' (ii.787).

(ii.905). His disapproval of Herbert's faith in universal consent is a symptom of an aristocratic attitude typical of his time and class. He belonged to a Breton family ascending from the bourgeoisie to the nobility of the robe. His writings reflect no greater interest in the classes beneath him than the vague allusion to the humble mentioned above. He resembled most of the thinkers advocating the right to freedom of thought under the Old Regime in that the ultimate significance of his doctrine far exceeded his intentions. If all men have good sense, sound method will give them, and even the humble majority he and his fellow gentlemen ignored, access to the truth.[14] This consequence apparently never crossed his mind.

His philosophy resulted from an exploration of metaphysics which he undertook as if no one had ever preceded him. Truth cannot be guaranteed by the authority of predecessors, he believed, but only by personal conviction. He suspected Scholasticism, which had conditioned his education, of contamination by errors, hence an analogy: if Bourdin thought that some of the apples in a basket were rotten, how would he keep them from spoiling the others? Would he not empty the basket, examine the apples, discard the bad ones and put the good ones back in the basket? Descartes would have liked to see Bourdin empty his Scholastic mind and restore a Cartesian residue. The *Méditations philosophiques*, to which Bourdin had objected, tell how the author purged his own mind of errors by doubting its entire contents. Only this doubt itself remained, for he could scarcely doubt that he was doubting. Nor could he doubt anything unless the doubting thing existed, so that the act of doubting proved his personal existence (*cogito*): 'la lumière naturelle[15] [...] m'a tantôt fait voir que, de ce que je doutais, je pouvais conclure que j'étais' (ii.436). Construing doubt as a kind of thought, he defined himself as a thinking thing. But how could he be sure that his other thoughts were not illusions? Perhaps a deceiving God had instilled them in him. One of the thoughts in his mind, however, could not have come from a deceiving God: though imperfect himself, he conceived of a perfect being, and perfection could not come from imperfection, nor from an imperfect or deceiving God. No, the thought of a perfect being could only come from such a being himself, thus God exists. This is Descartes's first proof of God. He sees nothing in it 'qui ne soit très aisé à connaître par la lumière

14. 'The men of the seventeenth century did not build a new heaven or a new earth. But in appealing to the reason of the man of *bon sens*, in teaching him to look to his own mind for truth, and in carefully training him in the method of finding it, they prepared the instrument that was to bring their own heaven and their own earth tumbling to the ground.' John Randall, *The Career of philosophy from the Middle Ages to the Enlightenment* (New York 1962), p.400.

15. In 1639 he wrote to Mersenne: 'Je distingue deux sortes d'instincts: l'un est en nous en tant qu'hommes et est purement intellectuel; c'est la lumière naturelle ou *intuitus mentis*, auquel seul je tiens qu'on se doit fier; l'autre est en nous en tant qu'animaux' (iii.255).

naturelle' (ii.248). The natural light also persuades him that nothing else can exist without the creator's constant support, no more than 'aucune lumière du soleil ne peut exister sans le soleil' (ii.367). Since Descartes's mind exists, the Creator must be supporting its existence and therefore God exists. This is his second proof of God. To these *a priori* proofs he adds an *a posteriori* proof. The thought of a perfect being excludes the possibility of his inexistence, an imperfection, and so the essence of God necessitates existence. All three proofs of God's existence depend on the initial proof that Descartes's own mind or soul exists.[16]

He wrote 'Dieu est pure intelligence' (i.63) at the beginning of his career and 'Notre âme est une émanation de sa souveraine intelligence' (iii.716) at the end. He probably did not regard souls as consubstantial with God, but rather as similar and inferior in substance,[17] a conception that suits the traditional idea of the natural light. Just as proof of God's existence depends on the existence of a mind that contemplates him, confirmation of the other thoughts in this mind depends on his existence. We must accept all thought inspired by him as necessarily true, for a perfect being cannot deceive us. But how can we recognise them? We need only discriminate truth from error. The natural light which God 'nous a donnée [...] n'aperçoit jamais aucun objet qui ne soit vrai en ce , qu'elle l'aperçoit' (iii.109). It is true as perceived. Descartes calls the spontaneous perception of truth intuition and describes it in Rule III as an indubitable representation 'qui naît de la seule lumière de la raison' (i.87). He identifies it as pure intelligence, by which he means intelligence devoid of sensations from either the senses or the imagination. It results in the instantaneous comprehension of a clear and distinct idea.[18] Clear? Clarity contrasts with obscurity. A clear idea becomes increasingly obscure as its perception fades from memory. It is very obscure when it recalls a perception that never occurred. Distinct? Distinctness contrasts with confusion, an overlapping of concepts. A distinct idea is necessarily clear, but not vice versa, because a clear idea may have some obscure components.[19] The mind acquires intuitive knowledge by discerning what God wants the natural light to reveal: 'L'esprit [...] voit en la lumière de Dieu les choses qu'il lui plaît lui découvrir par une impression directe de la clarté divine sur notre entendement.' (iii.847). Among the truths

16. 'Je ne considère pas l'*esprit* comme une partie de l'âme, mais comme cette âme tout entière qui pense' (ii.797).
17. '*Entre la raison divine créatrice, source de la rationalité de notre raison, et la raison humaine, Descartes reconnaît un intervalle infini.*' Jean-Marc Gabaude, *Liberté et raison* (Toulouse 1970, 1972), i.404.
18. 'J'appelle généralement du nom d'idée tout ce qui est dans notre esprit, lorsque nous concevons une chose, de quelque manière que nous la concevions' (ii.345).
19. See Etienne Gilson (ed.), *Discours de la méthode* (Paris 1966), p.69, n.3.

God commmmunicates to us are essences of eternal truths which he creates himself.[20]

The instantaneous comprehension of a clear and distinct idea in its entirety involves only self-evident truth.[21] Most of the truth accessible to the mind does not qualify as self-evident, so we must rely on deduction to perceive it. Descartes distinguishes between the (self-) evidence of intuition and the (self-) necessity of deduction. The latter consists in a series of intuitions, each following the other. In Rule III he makes the following analogy: 'Nous savons que le dernier anneau de quelque longue chaîne est attaché au premier, même si nous ne voyons pas d'un seul et même coup d'œil l'ensemble des anneaux intermédiaires dont dépend ce rattachement' (i.89). Each intuition in the chain takes place in a separate instant, so that the series of instants covers a period of time. We can concentrate on each successive intuition, but not on the deduction as a whole. The certainty of the knowledge acquired by deduction depends on the remembrance of the intuitions involved. Descartes does not trust memory as much as intuition,[22] so he reduces his reliance on memory to a minimum. He reviews the intuitions in a deduction until he can pass from the first to the last almost in an instant. This operation tends to compress the deduction into a single intuition guaranteeing the logical necessity of the whole. Yet a deduction cannot actually become an intuition, because intuition alone constitutes the natural light.[23]

Good sense, on the other hand, consists of both intuition and deduction. Self-evident truth, the unique object of intuition, is in Descartes's view independent of the senses, which he trusts only in part. They alert us to danger and opportunity, but they cannot tell us the nature of things. The *Principes de la philosophie* urge us to abandon the prejudices of the senses and rely on the pure understanding in which 'les premières notions ou idées, qui sont comme les semences des

20. Martial Gueroult detects a discrepancy here: 'Toutes ces vérités, qui découlent nécessairement de la toute-puissance de Dieu, et auxquelles Dieu lui-même ne peut absolument pas se soustraire, sont des vérités premières situées en quelque sorte *au-delà des vérités éternelles instituées par le libre arbitre divin.* Faisant corps avec l'être même du Tout-Puissant, elles ne peuvent pas ne pas être; elles ne peuvent donc avoir été librement créées; elles sont incréées.' *Descartes selon l'ordre des raisons* (Paris 1953), ii.30.

21. 'Est évident ce dont la vérité apparaît à l'esprit d'une manière immédiate. S'opposent à l'évident: 1. ce qui est faux; 2. ce qui n'est que probable. La règle de l'évidence élimine donc du domaine de la philosophie tout le vraisemblable.' Gilson, p.69, n.1.

22. 'The conclusion, that is, the necessary link or connexion between the last and the first step, or the necessary dependence of the consequent on the logical interconnexions of all its self-evident grounds, is not present to the mind with the self-evidence of an intellectual intuition.' L.J. Beck, *The Method of Descartes* (Oxford 1964), p.91.

23. Descartes uses *intuitus mentis* as a synonym of the natural light in a letter to Mersenne (see n.15). Bernhard Klöpel finds intuition identical with the natural light in *Das Lumen naturale bei Descartes* (Leipzig 1896). See p.30.

vérités que nous sommes capables de connaître, se trouvent naturellement'
(iii.148-49). Rule XII describes them as purely intellectual ideas known to the
mind only by virtue of an innate light, in other words the natural light. Descartes
distinguishes between these ideas and adventitious ideas or sense data and
factitious ideas or illusions of the imagination induced by the will. Although
innate ideas do not contain the full truth available to the pure understanding,
they enable it to attain this truth. The *Notae in programma* (1647) compare them
to children who inherit a tendency to contract their parents' diseases rather
than these diseases themselves. Even an unborn child has innate ideas and,
since his soul must think in order to exist, he is conscious of them. Continuing
to exist requires increasing thought, a consequence accepted by Descartes:
'L'âme humaine, quelque part qu'elle soit, pense toujours, même dans le ventre
de nos mères' (ii.360). Indeed its essence consists in thinking. As if in anticipation
of ridicule by Gassendi and Voltaire, however, he denies that unborn infants
engage in metaphysical contemplation.[24] From conception on, therefore, the
soul never stops thinking, but not even after death? While Descartes usually
shies away from speculation on the immortality of the soul, his letter to Silhon
in 1648 tends to confirm his orthodoxy in this respect. Here he raises the
question of whether the mind can acquire knowledge after separation from the
body. 'En pouvez-vous douter?' (iii.847) he asks Silhon. In support of an
affirmative answer, he cites the soul's ability to acquire knowledge independent
of the senses even when joined to the body.

Descartes gives much attention to the relationship between the mind and the
body, which he tries to explain by locating the mind in the pineal gland. He
chooses this organ, which resembles an upright pear according to the figures
in the 1644 edition of l'*Homme*,[25] because it is the only single and central one
in the head. He supposes it to be flexible so that it can lean in any direction.
The arteries on which it stands supply it with animal spirits, gaseous particles
extracted from the blood. Leaning under the influence of the mind or the
pressure of the spirits, it directs them in a stream towards the openings of nerve
tubes which surround it. The choice of the openings which the stream enters
determines the motor, sensory or mental functions activated. This is what
Williams calls 'the hydraulic transmission system of mechanical changes in the
body'.[26] When the spirits incline the pineal gland, matter affects spirit and,

24. '*Je ne veux pas* [...] *vous demander si vous avez mémoire de ce que vous pensez étant encore dedans*
[*le*] *ventre* [*de votre mère*].' Pierre Gassendi in 'Réponses aux cinquièmes objections', Descartes,
*Œuvres*, ii.714. 'Je ne me sens pas [...] disposé [...] à imaginer que, quelques semaines après ma
conception, j'étais une fort savante âme, sachant alors mille choses que j'ai oubliées en naissant.'
Voltaire, *Lettres philosophiques* (Paris 1964), p.84.
25. By Louis de La Forge, a doctor at La Flèche.
26. Bernard Williams, 'Descartes', *Encyclopedia of philosophy* (New York, London 1967).

when the mind inclines it, spirit affects matter. Unfortunately, this ingenious theory merely begs the question of how spirit and matter communicate with each other. How can the mind cause the pineal gland to lean? How can the inclination of the gland influence the mind? Descartes does not say, but he apparently assumed that gasification is an initial step in the spiritualisation of matter. Perhaps the semantics of *spiritus* – he wrote *L'Homme* in Latin – suggested this naive assumption, for the word means breath, life, inspiration. Semantics may also have persuaded him to locate the ancient common sense, which coordinates all sensations, in the same place as the mind.

He makes a point of discriminating between the jurisdictions of faith and the natural light. In the 'Réponses aux secondes objections' he finds obscure what we believe in, but not what moves us to believe in it. Two kinds of evidence incline us to believe: 'l'une [...] part de la lumière naturelle, et l'autre [...] vient de la grâce divine' (ii.573). Modifying his solution to the problem, he lists three kinds of questions in the *Notae in programma*: (1) those answered by faith alone (the Trinity, the incarnation, etc.); (2) those answered by faith and yet accessible to reason (the existence of God, the difference between the soul and the body, etc.); (3) those answered only by reason (the quadrature of the circle, the philosophical stone, etc.). He generally avoids the first category and even reassures the theologians that he is not overstepping the limits of philosophy.[27] In 1644, for instance, he wrote to Mesland: 'Je m'abstiens le plus qu'il m'est possible des questions de théologie' (iii.75). A sincere but unzealous Catholic, he thought laymen and philosophers should submit to the authority of the Church. Yet how could a thinker as powerful and original as he explicitly and wholeheartedly conform to any doctrine as arbitrary and incoherent as seventeenth-century Catholicism? He could not, of course, and analysis of his writings shows that he did not.

He sets the Trinity above reason, as we have seen, on a level accessible only to faith. In 1640 he wrote to Mersenne that we can know it only by faith, for it 'ne se peut connaître par la lumière naturelle' (ii.306). No mind can understand the Trinitarian persons, according to the 'Réponses aux sixièmes objections', unless faith enlightens it. Even if it understands the persons, however, it cannot distinguish between them, but merely conceive of their mutual relations. Descartes does not discuss the persons when he answers Arnauld's objection

27. 'On présente souvent Descartes comme ayant séparé la philosophie de la religion, afin d'émanciper l'esprit humain de la tutelle du dogme. Les textes ne nous suggèrent rien de semblable. Ce qui frappe, dans sa correspondance comme dans ses livres, c'est la préoccupation, non pas d'affranchir la métaphysique ou la physique du joug de la religion, mais bien plutôt de préserver la religion contre les empiètements de la philosophie.' Jean Laporte, *Le Rationalisme de Descartes* (Paris 1945), p.467-68.

to his description of God as a self-cause in the *Méditations*. The 'Réponses aux quatrièmes objections' only remind Arnauld that theologians do not use cause to explain the generation or procession of the Trinitarian persons. 'Quoique j'aie dit', adds Descartes, 'que Dieu pouvait en quelque façon être dit *la cause de soi-même*, il ne se trouvera pas néanmoins que je l'aie nommé en aucun lieu *l'effet de soi-même*' (ii.686). The latter term implies the inferiority of the Son to the Father, which would implicate him in the heresy of subordinationism. Descartes can exclude cause from Trinitarian relations rhetorically, but not logically, because the generation of the Son by the Father causes him to exist. Sanctified by the Church, the distinction between the generation of the Son and the procession of the Spirit nonetheless tends to justify his evasion of heresy by semantic subtlety. He is skirting one of the most vulnerable weaknesses in the Trinity: how can the three persons be equal when they have unequal powers to produce such persons? Descartes understandably refrains from involving himself in anything so unclear and indistinct.

But Christology confronted him with even more formidable obscurity. In his thesis on Descartes Alquié expressed surprise 'qu'à sa constante affirmation d'un Dieu créateur, [il] ne joigne jamais la moindre réflexion sur le Dieu incarné du christianisme'.[28] Not quite, since Alquié himself edited such a reflexion in the *Œuvres philosophiques* which he published later. The following passage appears in a letter to Chanut in 1647: 'Le mystère de l'incarnation, par lequel Dieu s'est abaissé jusqu'à se rendre semblable à nous, fait que nous sommes capables de l'aimer' (iii.715). Thus Descartes does not distinguish between God the Father and God the Son in a matter concerning the Son as distinct from the Father. A deliberate writer, he probably did not simply forget to call Jesus Christ by name in his only extant allusion to the incarnation. The name does occur in a letter to Mesland (1644), but it only serves as an example of someone doing good works because they are necessary.[29] It seems unlikely that Christ inspired Descartes's interest or enthusiasm.

He concerned himself even less with the fall and original sin. In a rare allusion to the fall he leaves the question of whether Adam had previously been immortal to the theologians.[30] He does not refer to original sin in his philosophical works

---

28. Ferdinand Alquié, *La Découverte métaphysique de l'homme chez Descartes* (Paris 1966), p.255.

29. 'On ne laisse pas de mériter, bien que, voyant très clairement ce qu'il faut faire, on le fasse infailliblement, et sans aucune indifférence, comme a fait Jésus-Christ en cette vie. Car l'homme pouvant n'avoir pas toujours une parfaite attention aux choses qu'il doit faire, c'est une bonne action que de l'avoir, et de faire, par son moyen, que notre volonté suive si fort la lumière de notre entendement, qu'elle ne soit point du tout indifférente' (iii.73-74).

30. 'L'homme est-il immortel avant la chute et comment? Ce n'est pas à un philosophe de s'en enquérir, il faut laisser cela aux théologiens.' Descartes, *Œuvres de Descartes* (Paris 1966), v.127. 'Je ne doute point [...] qu'Adam et Eve n'ont pas ete créés enfants, mais en âge d'homme parfaits. La

and he considers error a trait acquired in childhood. 'Il ne croit pas', concludes Alquié in his edition, 'que le péché ait corrompu la raison' (iii.944). In sum, his opinion of the Trinity is orthodox but perfunctory, his neglect of Christ suggests indifference and his philosophy implies heresy with respect to original sin.

In avoiding these issues, he left little testimony vulnerable to censorship by the guardians of the faith. Yet he did succumb to the temptation of trying to rationalise transubstantiation by means of his philosophy. The Scholastic explanation of the dogma did not satisfy him. In a letter to an unknown correspondent in 1646, he recalled two questions which he had raised earlier in his career: (1) how can the accidents of bread remain in a place where bread no longer exists? (2) how can the body of Christ have the dimensions of this bread? By then, however, he had given his answers to both questions.

He answered the first question in the 'Réponses aux quatrièmes objections', the objections of the Jansenist theologian Antoine Arnauld. After reading the manuscript of the *Méditations*, Arnauld judged the author's philosophy to be in conflict with the Thomist interpretation of transubstantiation. Descartes's philosophy implies that accidents are not real things, but merely modes of substance that will disappear when substance disappears. He attributes the sensually perceptible accidents such as colour, taste and odour to direct or indirect contact with the object perceived. Since their existence depends on this contact, they cannot logically subsist after substance has disappeared. Descartes regards the mentally perceptible accidents of mobility, extension and figure as attributes of substance and therefore inseparable from substance. If substance disappears, they will disappear too. Consequently his theory implies a contradiction of transubstantiation as nearly all Catholic theologians understood it. Arnauld warned that they would take offence.

To avoid offending them is precisely why Descartes was circulating his manuscript in advance of publication. Answering Arnauld with uncharacteristic benevolence, he exposes a theory designed to meet objections like his. His conception of *superficie* or surface relief plays an essential role in this theory. It is the area of contact between two material substances which, like all material substances, cannot penetrate each other in the plenum of his universe. A two-dimensional mode of both substances, it subsists even if a third material substance replaces one of the others, provided the new substance has exactly the same configuration as the old. Descartes considers surface relief extremely irregular, for contact in a plenum necessitates the protrusion of one material substance into the pores of the other. The particles of matter move constantly

religion chrétienne veut que nous croyions ainsi, et la raison naturelle nous persuade absolument cette vérité' (v.178).

and the degree of mobility determines whether a substance qualifies as a solid, a liquid or a gas. The resulting mobility of surface relief causes sensations when sense organs come into direct or indirect contact with it. 'Puisque nul sentiment ne se fait sans contact, rien ne peut être senti que la surface des corps' (ii.875), states Descartes in the 'Réponses aux sixièmes objections'. In transubstantiation the body of Christ replaces the bread on the altar without disturbing the surface relief between the bread and the surrounding air. His blood replaces the surface relief between the wine and the air. Since the surface relief remains the same in both cases, the senses continue to perceive bread and wine.

Descartes quotes the Council of Trent to the effect that, after the substantial conversion of bread into Christ's body, only the species[31] of bread remains. What can species mean, Descartes demands, if not surface relief? Certainly not real accidents, since all real existence is substantial by definition. The Scholastic error of distinguishing between substance and real accidents, Descartes insinuates, resulted in the Lutheran heresy of consubstantiation, the substantial coexistence of bread with Christ's body and of wine with his blood. He contends that real accidents necessitate a second miracle after transubstantiation itself. The subsistence of accidents independent of substance violates both reason and the theological principle that the words of consecration do nothing but what they say. Theologians themselves 'ne veulent pas attribuer à miracle les choses qui peuvent être expliquées par raison naturelle' (ii.702). Descartes thought his theory gave so reasonable an account of transubstantiation that they would eventually abandon the Thomist interpretation and embrace his. None of his polemic against Scholasticism appeared in the first edition of the *Méditations*. Father Mersenne, whom he had entrusted with the publication, removed the final pages in the 'Réponses aux quatrièmes objections' to spare him the wrath of the Scholastics.

In a letter to the Jesuit Mesland (1644), he hinted that he had found an answer for it. He had not divulged his opinion, he said, because 'je m'abstiens, le plus qu'il m'est possible, des questions de théologie' (iii.75). The Council of Trent had warned, he noted, that one can scarcely express the manner of Christ's presence in the eucharist by words. If the public knew his philosophy better, however, he could teach them an explanation of this mystery that would silence the Protestants. Having stirred Mesland's curiosity, he satisfied it in another letter the next year. But first he took further precautions. Unless Mesland thought his opinion entirely compatible with orthodox theology, he must keep it a secret. If, on the other hand, he saw fit to disclose it, he must conceal the author's name. Later he assured Mesland that the opinion was not

31. '*Espèce* signifie: *objet immédiat de la connaissance sensible*, cet objet étant considéré comme un intermédiaire entre la connaissance proprement dite et la réalité connue.' Alquié, *Œuvres*, ii.698, n.1.

an essential part of his philosophy and even asked him to destroy his letter. Did he really expect Mesland to comply with this request? The Jesuit was, in any case, less discreet than Mersenne.

Descartes's theory of how Christ's body conforms to the surface relief of the eucharistic bread derives from his analysis of body. He generally applies this term to a material object whose identity changes with any change in its parts. Remove the slightest particle and such a body is incomplete. Replace one by another and it is no longer the same body. When he speaks of a person's body, however, he does not mean a particular piece and quantity of matter, but rather all the matter united with this person's soul. Even if such a body gains or loses weight, he considers it the same provided it has the same soul. An adult has a bigger body than when he was a child and none of the same parts remain, yet we believe it to be the same because the same soul continues to vivify it. Should we amputate a man's arm or leg, he will not have the same body in the general sense, but he will in the personal sense. Needless to say, Descartes interprets the body of Christ in the personal sense.

He believes transubstantiation, which may take place either naturally or supernaturally, converts a body in the general sense into a part of another body in the personal sense. It takes place naturally, for instance, when we eat ordinary bread and drink ordinary wine, because the particles of these substances dissolve in our stomach, flow into our veins and mingle with our blood. 'Elles se transsubstantient naturellement, et deviennent partie de notre corps' (iii.549). Becoming a part of our body unites them with our soul. If we could isolate them, however, we would find them to be the same as those which previously constituted the bread and the wine. In supernatural transubstantiation, the soul of Christ vivifies particles of bread and wine which his body has not digested. The words of consecration miraculously incorporate them into his body, even though they remain physically separate from its other parts: 'Toute la matière [...] qui est ensemble informée de la même âme humaine, est prise pour un corps humain tout entier'[32] (iii.549). Descartes anticipates the concern of Catholics accustomed to faith in the organic unity of the eucharistic body. He blandly reassures them that the integrity of a human body does not necessitate exterior members or a given quantity of matter. Nor should the physical dispersion of the sacramental body detract from veneration of the eucharist. To

32. 'Descartes [...] avait attribué au corps de Jésus-Christ la même extension et quantité qu'avait le pain. Il a ensuite rayé ce paragraphe *sur la minute* [...] En déduisant cela de ses principes, Descartes constatait seulement qu'en identifiant substance et étendue, il ne pouvait accorder à la substance du corps du Christ que l'étendue qu'occupait auparavant la substance du pain, cette étendue qui était terminee par la substance du pain.' J.-R. Armogathe, *Theologia cartesiana: l'explication physique de l'eucharistie chez Descartes et dom Desgabets* (La Haye 1977), p.75-76. Armogathe shows that the deleted tenet would have contradicted Thomist transubstantiation.

insist, on the other hand, that the transubstantiated hostia contains anything like a human hand or arm would fly in the face of the evidence.

Although the second part of Descartes's theory did not appear in print as the first part did, his letters to Mesland circulated among his followers for a long time after his death. Scholastics hostile to his philosophy soon learned of the entire theory and seized the opportunity to accuse him of heresy. In the ensuing controversy, even a sympathiser like Bossuet refused to defend the second part of the theory from the charge. The idea of a dispersed and biologically unorganised eucharistic body dismayed Catholics whose faith in the resurrection stemmed from the similarity between their own bodies and that of Christ which had actually risen from the dead. This theory doomed the second part of the theory to rejection despite the attempts of a few Cartesians to repair it by modifying the theory. Catholic and Protestant polemicists tacitly agreed that this part tended to harmonise with Calvin's doctrine of the eucharist, thus further discrediting it among Catholics. Less vulnerable to accusations of heresy, the first part of the theory depended on Descartes's physics and particularly his plenum. When his younger contemporary Pascal demonstrated that nature does not abhor a vacuum, he in effect ruined the concept of a surface relief defined by substances fitting tightly together. Ironically, therefore, the Catholics themselves thwarted Descartes's intentions of silencing the Protestants.

Christianity and the Church profited little from the allegiance of the most powerful thinker who lived in the early seventeenth century. This allegiance came more from a sense of honour and duty, if not convenience, than the kind of faith that had built the ancient and medieval Church. The very exemption of theology from philosophical analysis implied fear that it might no longer withstand the test. While Descartes abstained from most of the doctrinal controversies that impassioned his age, he participated in one that offered him an opportunity to illustrate his physics. What motivated his theory of transubstantiation? Hardly Catholic zeal, but rather the hope of persuading the French Jesuits to teach his philosophy in their schools. More clever than profound, they rejected this philosophy when it could have served their interests and embraced it only when another had surpassed it. Their expedient Christianity resulted in the sowing of many a dragon seed. A more faithful alumnus than Voltaire and Diderot, Descartes nonetheless informed Catholics and Christians that God had provided them with direct access to most of the truth available to them. They could not learn this truth from Christ and his Church, but only through God-given reason by the use of a good method.[33] Descartes's deistic

33. 'The natural light [...] indicates how the inquiring human mind can[...] attain the knowledge of God without having to depend solely on revelation or the light of grace.' Stephen Daniel, 'Descartes' treatment of "lumen naturale"', *Studia leibnitiana* 10 (1978), p.99.

proclivity[34] even tempted them to wonder why reason could not reveal all the truth available to them. While the old theology dictated what they should believe, the new philosophy oriented their thought so that they could think for themselves. When thinking for themselves became acting for themselves, they were on the road to freedom, a consequence apparently unforeseen by the philosopher himself.

34. 'Il ne faut pas hésiter de parler d'un véritable théocentrisme de la connaissance chez Descartes. La lumière naturelle de l'esprit émane de Dieu et l'esprit ne trouve le fondement de ses certitudes que dans l'acte où il se reconnaît créé par lui.' Joseph Combes, *Le Dessein de la sagesse cartésienne* (Lyon, Paris 1960), p.93.

# Spinoza

How much does Spinoza owe Descartes? Evidently a great deal, but some would say more than others. While some stress his debt to Descartes, and others his assimilation of medieval Jewish philosophy, that of Maimonides in particular, no one doubts his originality. The mere combination of Cartesian and Jewish heresy drove the synagogue of Amsterdam to excommunicate him in 1656 for fear of Christian reactions. Although he kept his distance from both Judaism and Christianity, he sympathised with the neoprimitive Christianity of the Mennonite and Collegian sects. His philosophy, which he discussed only with friends, served as his religion. When the Elector Palatine offered him a chair at the University of Heidelberg in 1673, he declined because the terms would have inhibited his freedom of conscience. Content with isolation and obscurity, he polished lenses for a living and died, of tuberculosis apparently, at the age of forty-four. He left a number of writings, most of them unpublished: the *Theological-political treatise*, the *Ethics* and his correspondence are of particular interest here. He published the *Treatise* in 1670 to support his friends the De Witt brothers, who were defending religious freedom from Calvinist ministers and Orangist authoritarians. Philosophical liberty does not endanger piety and the public peace, according to the title; on the contrary, piety and the public peace depend on philosophical liberty. To write the *Treatise* Spinoza had suspended his work on the *Ethics*, in which he tried to demonstrate by Euclidian argumentation a metaphysical system developed in earlier writings, especially the *Short treatise*. His Cartesian infatuation with geometry led him to believe that he could adapt this discipline to proof of his metaphysics beyond the suspicion of an egocentric bias.[1] Even his admirers concede that his procedure obscures his thought without tightening his logic, which is less rigorous than he assumes. His liberty with the semantics of Scholasticism further complicates the task of his readers. Faced with malevolent rumours of his alleged atheism, he refrained from publishing the *Ethics*, which nonetheless appeared immediately after his death in 1677.

He trusts reason and suspects experience even more than Descartes, to the point of eliminating all external considerations such as religious doctrine. From

---

1. Descartes had appended 'Raisons qui prouvent l'existence de Dieu et la distinction qui est entre l'esprit et le corps humain disposées d'une façon géométrique' to the 'Réponses aux secondes objections' to his *Méditations*, but this brief text is no more than an experiment to satisfy the curiosity of Mersenne, who had sent him the objections.

Judaism he retains little more than the belief in one supreme God, from whom all other truth must come. Thus rationalism and monotheism blend in a system whose unity and coherence would suffer no exceptions. As in Descartes's metaphysics, the conception of a perfect essence necessarily implies an eternal existence, hence a divine self-cause. Unlike Descartes, however, Spinoza admits no will in God, for will belongs to humanity, and no freedom other than that of determination by his own nature. In reaction to Judeo-Christian anthropomorphism, he denies any similarity between God and men, and even depersonalises God.[2] Belief in a deity that neither Jews nor Christians could tolerate exposed him to slander and persecution, which inspired his advocacy of religious freedom. The *Ethics* describe this deity as God or Nature, but they explicitly define Nature as *natura naturans* and not *natura naturata*,[3] a distinction borrowed from Scholasticism. Despite accusations of pantheism, Spinoza does not necessarily identify God with all things.[4]

But all things exist by virtue of divine logic or causation, which Spinoza conflates. God is a unique substance consisting in an infinite number of attributes, each of them infinite in its own way. They are the different aspects by which substance manifests itself, yet we know only two of them, those of thought and extension (the Cartesian essence of matter). They constitute *natura naturans*, and their modes, *natura naturata*. Each attribute causes and contains an immediate infinite mode (involving essence), which causes and contains a mediate infinite mode (involving existence), which causes and contains an infinite series of finite modes causing and containing each other. 'Of each existing thing there must necessarily be a positive cause through which it exists.'[5] The immediate infinite mode of extension is motion and rest; of thought, the

2. 'Selon Spinoza, *les philosophes qui admettent un Dieu transcendant et personnel sont pris dans une mauvaise dialectique et renvoyés continuellement de l'anthropomorphisme à quelque aveu d'incognoscibilité.*' Gabaude, ii.46.

3. 'I wish here to explain what we should understand by nature viewed as active (*natura naturans*) and nature viewed as passive (*natura naturata*) [...] By nature viewed as active we should understand that which is in itself, and is conceived through itself, or those attributes of substance which express eternal and infinite essence, in other words [...] God, insofar as he is considered a free cause. By nature viewed as passive I understand all that which follows from the necessity of the nature of God, or of any of the attributes of God, that is, all the modes of the attributes of God insofar as they are considered as things which are in God, and which without God cannot exist or be conceived.' *The Chief works of Benedict de Spinoza*, trans. R. H. M. Elwes (New York 1955), ii.68-69. All quotations from the *Ethics* and the *Theological-political treatise* come from this edition.

4. 'Par l'immanence des choses à Dieu est jeté le premier fondement du panthéisme ou, plus exactement, d'une certaine forme de panenthéisme. Ce n'est pas le panthéisme proprement dit, car *tout n'est pas Dieu*. Ainsi les modes *sont en Dieu*, sans cependant être *Dieu* à la rigueur, car postérieurs à la substance, produits par elle et, à ce titre, sans commune mesure avec elle, ils en diffèrent *toto genere*.' Martial Gueroult, *Spinoza* (Paris 1968), i.223.

5. Letter XXXIV to John Hudde (7 Jan. 1666), *The Correspondence of Spinoza*, trans. A. Wolf (New York 1966), p.228. All quotations from Spinoza's correspondence come from this edition.

absolutely infinite intellect. The *Ethics* mentions only one mediate infinite mode: the order of the entire universe. Although Spinoza does not assign it to an attribute, it apparently belongs to extension. This ambiguity does not matter very much, however, because corresponding modes express different aspects of the same thing. Human bodies are finite modes of extension, and human minds, finite modes of thought. The mind is the idea of the body and the body, the object of the mind, even though neither has any causal connection with the other. Since both nonetheless involve the same link in the causal chain and the same degree in the modification of substance, both express the same reality. This attempt to preserve individual personality from division between the attributes and absorption by substance satisfies almost none of the critics. The independence of the attributes precludes the causation of an idea by its object. Every idea derives from another in an infinite series of finite modes in the attribute of thought. Thus 'all ideas are in God' (ii.109).

Spinoza considers the human mind a finite mode consisting in a causal succession of ideas.[6] It derives from another finite mode which in turn derives from another and so on to infinity. The infinite total of these finite modes forms the infinite intellect of God which we recognise as the immediate infinite mode of the attribute thought. Consequently, the human mind is part of the infinite intellect of God' (ii.91).[7] When the mind participates in one of God's thoughts, it may think exactly what he is thinking and, in this case, it has an adequate idea of his thought. But if it thinks more or less than he does, it has only an inadequate idea. When it perceives an extended phenomenon in him, it acquires an adequate idea; when it perceives such a phenomenon by the idea of its own body in sensual contact with others, it acquires an inadequate idea. Spinoza regards adequacy as an intrinsic confirmation of the truth, and inadequacy, as a confirmation limited by external factors. Inadequate ideas supply knowledge of the first kind, and adequate ideas, knowledge of the second and third kinds on a scale of increasing reliability. In the first or least reliable kind, which Spinoza calls imagination or opinion, we recognise knowledge based on sense perception. In acquiring this kind of knowledge, the mind remains passive and submits to external determination. Such knowledge arises from sensations, memory, signs or symbols, hearsay or report and 'vague experience' which Dufour-Kowalska

6. 'The mind is reduced to a flux of ideas determining one another's existence.' David Bidney, *The Psychology and ethics of Spinoza* (New York 1962), p.34. 'Spinoza nie que l'homme "ait" une âme substantielle ou que les pensées particulières soient des modifications d'une substance stable et permanente qui serait l'âme.' Robert Misrahi, *Spinoza* (Paris 1964), p.62.

7. 'L'entendement infini de Dieu, étant un mode, peut, comme tout mode, se diviser en parties, à savoir en entendements finis. Ceux-ci lui sont commensurables et il y a commune mesure entre la science de Dieu et celle de l'homme.' Gueroult, i.407.

describes as perceiving without conceiving.[8] Each of these cases involves the contact of the mind's body with the bodies of other minds, that is the extended objects of other ideas. Knowledge of the first kind suffers the further defects of chance, contingency and impermanence, while knowledge of the second kind is necessarily and eternally true.

Knowledge of the second kind or reason also involves the contact of a mind's body with other bodies, but only insofar as the relationship between them illustrates a rule applying to the whole of nature or a rule applying to human and other bodies. Spinoza calls the universal rules 'notions common to all men',[9] and the general rules 'adequate ideas of the properties of things' (ii.113). In neither case does one learn the rule from experience, but one receives it from God through the attribute and modes of thought. Reason depends on imagination for illustration of the rules it applies and on intuition, the third degree of knowledge, for the derivation of its rules. Reason produces either universal or general truth, and intuition, particular truth. Subject to the eternal necessity of God, both distinguish infallibly between truth and error.[10] Unlike reason, however, intuition operates instantaneously and independently of experience. It discovers the essence of finite modes by locating them in the causal chain and revealing their dependence on an attribute for existence. The mind participates directly in the thought of God, thus sharing the divine perspective. Knowledge of the third kind includes conscience, which Spinoza simplifies by defining it as the idea of an idea. He looks upon mathematics and metaphysics as branches of intuitive science. By his commentary on the following equation, he illustrates all three kinds of knowledge:

Problem: $a/c = b/x$     Solution: $x = bc/a$

One may have learned the solution in school (report, I), arrived at it by experimentation (vague experience, I), proved it by Euclidian demonstration (reason, II) or realised it spontaneously (intuition, III).

Zac observes that the meaning of reason varies with the work. As knowledge

8. 'Le propre de l'expérience commune, de ce que Spinoza appelle "expérience vague", c'est de ne point discerner dans les choses la nécessité de leur nature modale qui est aussi la forme de leur réalité. Et c'est pourquoi la connaissance du premier genre est à la fois passive et fictive, son erreur ne consistant qu'à "percevoir" sans "concevoir", non point à penser faussement mais à ne point penser.' Gabrielle Dufour-Kowalska, *L'Origine; l'essence de l'origine; l'origine selon l'"Ethique' de Spinoza* (Paris 1973), p.191.

9. 'The theory of common notions [...] shows how the human mind can have true ideas insofar as that which is its object is something which is common to the whole of Nature.' G. H. R. Parkinson, *Spinoza's theory of knowledge* (Oxford 1954), p.135.

10. 'Both are immediate knowledge [...] knowledge which is formed by the mind [and] is common to all men. But still there is a difference between them. The common notions are formed by the mind from that which the body has in common with other bodies.' Harry Wolfson, *The Philosophy of Spinoza* (Cambridge 1934), ii.162-63.

of the second kind or of adequate ideas in the *Ethics*, it serves as a synonym of the understanding and designates the essence of man: 'Spinoza n'emploie jamais l'expression "raison divine". Qui dit raison dit raison humaine.'[11] Reason also refers to true science or philosophy, which Spinoza claims as his own. In the *Theological-political treatise* it usually means good sense or the natural light, which he concedes to all men. Defining it as prudence, Zac contrasts it with stupidity and sophistication. But I wonder whether he conforms to Spinoza's intentions when he assumes that reason in the *Ethics* has nothing in common with reason in the *Treatise*.[12] While the two works differ in subject, method and style, Spinoza could hardly have forgotten one while writing the other, and entirely separate semantics seem unlikely in his case.

Might we not therefore legitimately ask which kind or kinds of knowledge he assigns to the natural light? Nowhere does he tell us explicitly. Although the term does not even appear in the *Ethics*,[13] it appears frequently in the *Treatise* and sometimes as an explicit synonym of reason.[14] Clearly it produces knowledge of the second kind and not the first, but does it also produce knowledge of the third kind? A discussion of the natural light early in the first chapter of the *Treatise*, 'Of prophecy', yields the elements of an answer to this question. Having defined prophecy and revelation as sure knowledge revealed to us by God, Spinoza finds that this definition also applies to natural human knowledge. What we learn by the natural light, he continues, depends on our knowledge of God (intuition)[15] and his eternal decrees (common notions). Everyone has natural knowledge because its principles (common notions) are common to all. Yet the vulgar appetite for extraordinary things results in disdain for natural gifts and the exclusion of natural knowledge from the popular conception of prophecy. Yet natural knowledge deserves the adjective divine as much as any other kind, since God's nature (intuition) and laws (common notions), in which we participate, dictate it to us. It differs from the knowledge everyone recognises as divine only in that the latter reaches beyond the former and does not conform

11. Sylvain Zac, *L'Idée de la vie dans la philosophie de Spinoza* (Paris 1963), p.149.
12. 'Loin d'être synonyme de la "connaissance démonstrative", [la raison] est pouvoir de concevoir ce qui est simple et à la portée de tout esprit.' Zac, *Signification et valeur de l'interprétation de l'Ecriture chez Spinoza* (Paris 1965), p.126. This work eclipses Leo Strauss, *Die Religionskritik Spinozas als Grundlage seiner Bibelwissenschaft* (Berlin 1930).
13. The following sentence does appear: 'Even as light displays both itself and darkness, so is truth a standard both of itself and falsity' (ii.115).
14. Elwes's translation of the following passage does not serve our purpose: 'Nec ullus in Vetere Testamento habetur, qui magis secundum rationem de Deo locutus est, quam Salomon, qui lumine naturali omnes sui saeculi superavit; et ideo etiam se supra Legem (nam ea iis tantum tradita est, qui ratione, et naturalis intellectus documentis carent) existimavit.' Spinoza, *Opera* (Hamburg 1924), iii.41.
15. The synonyms in parenthesis come from the *Ethics*.

36

to the laws of human nature (common notions). It is inferior neither in certainty nor in the excellence of its divine source. On the contrary, it includes what Spinoza considers the primary revelation of God, notions explaining natural phenomena and teaching the proper conduct of life (common notions). Our minds receive these notions only because they participate in God's nature (intuition). Indeed the idea of God (intuition) determines everything that we clearly and distinctly understand. The constant association of intuition with the common notions of reason in a text explicitly devoted to the natural light demonstrates that Spinoza assigns both the second and the third kinds of knowledge to the natural light.[16] This conclusion invalidates the distinction by Zac between reason in the *Ethics* and reason in the *Treatise*.[17] Like Descartes, Spinoza disdains the vulgar, acknowledges that they have the natural light (reason and intuition) and doubts their ability to use it effectively without a good method.

In the *Treatise* he submits imagination in the form of Judeo-Christian superstition to a critical analysis by the natural light. While recommending his book to philosophers, he tries in his preface to discourage all other readers. He despairs of extirpating superstition and fear from the minds of the multitude ungoverned by reason and swayed by passions. Masquerading as piety, their prejudices are deeply rooted. So much for the preface. The dialectic between reason and superstition continues in this work itself, as the following examples demonstrate. Prophets distinguish themselves by the power of their imagination rather than the perfection of their thought. Where imagination predominates, reason declines. Faith in rites and stories like those in the Bible comes from sacrificing reason to passion. Contrary to nature, contrary to reason: 'Belief in [miracles]

16. Consider also the following passage: 'Since without God nothing can exist or be conceived, it is evident that all natural phenomena involve and express the conception of God as far as their essence and perfection extend, so that we have greater and more perfect knowledge of God in proportion to our knowledge of natural phenomena: conversely (since the knowledge of an effect through its cause is the same thing as the knowledge of a particular property of a cause) the greater our knowledge of natural phenomena, the more perfect is our knowledge of the essence of God (which is the cause of all things)' (i.59).

17. He also distinguishes between two connotations of the natural light: 'S'il est vrai que le christianisme n'est pas, selon Spinoza, une religion philosophique, que veut-il dire quand il affirme que c'est une religion intellectuelle? C'est que le terme "lumière naturelle" est pris en deux sens différents dans le *Traité théologico-politique*. Est connu par "lumière naturelle", dans un premier sens, tout ce qui s'accorde avec la nature de l'âme, avec les lois de l'esprit capables de former certaines notions expliquant la nature des choses et indiquant le bon usage de la vie. Mais relève aussi de la "lumière naturelle", dans un tout autre sens tout ce qui est conforme au bon sens, et saisissable par l'esprit humain; le "naturel" s'oppose alors au miraculeux, à ce qui est incompréhensible par les moyens naturels de notre intelligence.' Sylvain Zac, 'Le problème du christianisme de Spinoza', *Revue de synthèse* 78 (1957), p.488. I do not find these connotations as distinct as he does and I doubt that Spinoza did either.

would throw doubt on everything and lead to atheism' (i.87).[18] Most of the 'miracles' in Scripture are really natural events unexplained by the text. Events that necessarily contradict the laws of nature occur only in apocryphal insertions. Appealing from the judgement of the natural light to an alleged supernatural light amounts to a tacit admission of exegetic ignorance. There is no external or superior authority in exegesis, so the natural light confers the highest authority on every reader. The allegation of an authority superior to the natural light obscures the truth of Scripture, hence inappropriate mystery, speculation and controversy. Intended to awe the ignorant masses, the attribution of human traits to God drives interpreters unwilling to admit this absurdity to the opposite extreme of metaphorical exegesis. Spinoza protests against blind confidence in the authors of the Bible at the expense of reason, 'a light from on high' (i.192). Reason and theology have no more in common than reason and Scripture. The natural light does not condone the fundamental promise of theology to reward docility by salvation. Spinoza will concede no more than the consolation, by this promise, of the vast majority who ignore reason.

The story of the fall in Genesis, he finds, teaches obedience and Christ, emancipation from this obedience. God condescends to Adam's understanding, according to the *Treatise*. Neither does God behave like an omnipresent and omniscient being, nor does Adam recognise him as such. Appearing in only one place at a time, he asks Adam where he is. He does not even know that Adam has sinned. Adam hides from God and, when discovered, makes an excuse for his sin as if he were speaking to a human master. God walks in the garden calling and speaking to Adam, noting his bewilderment and asking him whether he has eaten the forbidden fruit. God is stooping to imagination, in Spinoza's perspective, so that men will learn to obey him. Another passage in the *Treatise* interprets the fall as a lesson for men who can conceive of God only as a divine prince and lawgiver. God warns Adam of the harm that will come to him if he eats the forbidden fruit. He does not tell him that this harm will be the inevitable result of his act. An anthropomorphic deity, he must enforce his law like any ordinary prince, for it resembles human law in that it has no intrinsic necessity. If Spinoza's God had not wanted Adam to eat the fruit, Adam could not have done it. The Bible appeals to the common people, who cannot understand that God is logical determination, not a lawgiver; that salvation and perdition are logical consequences, not retribution. Thus Spinoza gives a negative answer to the question by which he begins this discussion: 'Whether by the natural light of reason we can conceive of God as a lawgiver or potentate ordaining laws for men' (i.62). Nor does he simply dismiss the story of the fall either, for it

18. Spinoza had an undeserved reputation for atheism, especially after his death.

illustrates what he calls the divine law. God forbids Adam to eat the fruit of the tree of good and evil because he wants him to do good for love of good and not for fear of evil, that is apparently for fear of the consequences. The knowledge and love of good for its own sake allow us to seek it freely, while the fear of evil enslaves us to external authority. In view of this interpretation, Spinoza concludes: '[The] commandment of God to Adam comprehends the whole divine law, and absolutely agrees with the dictates of the light of nature' (i.66). Realising that he may have read his own opinion into the text, he concedes that the author might have intended a different meaning. The uniquely moral nature of the divine law conveyed to us by the natural light nonetheless explains the title he gives his other great work, the *Ethics*.

In this work he advances a hypothesis with the intention of recognising it as false. If men were born free, they would not know the difference between good and evil as long as they remained free. Spinoza describes a free man as one 'led solely by reason', who 'therefore [...] has only adequate ideas', and who 'therefore [...] has no conception of evil or consequently [...] good' (ii.232). Since men are not born free, however, the hypothesis deserves consideration only insofar as we can abstract human nature from the rest of nature and, concurrently, its divine cause from the infinite being. The story of the first man in Genesis, which involves a God uniquely preoccupied with his human creature, implies such an abstraction. He forbids Adam, whom he has made free, to eat a fruit enabling him to distinguish between good and evil. This knowledge will move Adam to fear death rather than desire life. Submitting to the guidance of reason, the free man does not fear death, but desires good for its own sake. Consequently, Spinoza finds that the story of the fall explores the hypothesis he rejects. It illustrates his doctrine that the illusion of absolute freedom condemns men dominated by imagination to slavery. His opposition to the dichotomy between good and evil subverts the traditional foundation of ethics. Identifying slavery with the fear of death implicitly rebukes Christianity.

A proselytic and loquacious Christian named Blyenbergh argued with Spinoza by correspondence in 1665, when the latter put the *Ethics* aside to take up the *Treatise*. Blyenbergh particularly suspected him of implying that God causes the evil in his own creation. But Spinoza objects to the absurdity of God producing anything opposed to himself. Adam's alleged opposition to God reminds him of a square circle. Since nothing can exist without God's leave, sin and evil are necessarily negative in character. Only terms like negation and privation qualify as legitimate synonyms of evil. Adam's disobedience cost him, from the human viewpoint, the privation and, from the divine viewpoint, the negation of a more perfect state. We habitually assign individual things to a class according to their conformity with an ideal definition. Privation characterises a thing that lacks a quality common to the other things in its class. Since God intuits each thing by its essence, however, privation means nothing to him. Negation occurs, on the other hand, when a thing lacks a quality that does not belong to its essence. God knows Adam by Adam's essence, so he finds him lacking in perfection rather than deprived of perfection. Although Adam used to be in a more perfect state, his essence has deteriorated. The difference between privation and negation explains 'why the desire of Adam for earthly things was evil only in relation to our understanding [reason] and not in relation to that of God [intuition]' (p.175). Confining evil to the human mentality suggests that man's preoccupation with it is mere prejudice to the mind of God. So Spinoza intends.

He manifestly accepted neither the Jewish nor the Christian interpretation of the fall. Determinism and, in particular, the determination of the human will precluded any compromise with his background and his friends' religion. Yet familiarity with the myth in Genesis was an experience he had in common with nearly everyone he might wish to influence. It provided him with a valuable medium for the illustration of his philosophy and especially the religious, moral and political ramifications of his philosophy. In the versatile and persuasive *Treatise*, he uses it not only to combat anthropomorphic superstition, but also to promote the freedom of virtue for its own sake, and both by dint of the natural light. In the lofty and austere *Ethics*, he exploits its further potential for arguing that such liberty conditions the will to live. And in the correspondence with Blyenbergh, he invalidates evil as a moral standard. He derives each of these opinions from an analysis of the relations between the three kinds of knowledge as manifested in the story of the fall. This analysis tends to confirm an important theoretical point: the higher the kind, the surer the knowledge.

Spinoza's analysis of the New Testament Christ is less critical. A chapter in the *Short treatise* entitled 'Natura naturata' contains an enigmatic allusion to the Son of God, which it compares with a product or an effect in the world of motion and a product or 'immediate creature' in the understanding. God created the Son 'from all eternity, and [he remains] immutable to all eternity'.[19] Thus young Spinoza substitutes creation for generation of the Son, yet accepts the coeternity of the Son with the Father. In the *Treatise* and his correspondence with Christians he consistently sets Christ above other men, the prophets and even Biblical figures like Moses. Although some critics suspect him of diplomacy or flattery, his biography and writings reveal no urge to please, impress or cultivate his fellow men. Other critics wonder whether he was a covert Christian or even welcome him into the fold, an obvious error. Zac strikes the following

19. Spinoza, *The Short treatise on God, Man and his well-being*, trans. A. Wolf (New York 1963), p.57.

balance: 'L'hypothèse la plus plausible, c'est que bien que Spinoza lui-même ne se rallie pas au christianisme, l'idée du Christ joue cependant un rôle dans l'économie de sa propre philosophie.'[20]

In the *Treatise* he admits the transmission of divine revelation by Christ. The chapter 'Of prophecy' denies that God needs any material intermediation to communicate with us, 'for [...] he communicates [his essence] to our minds' (i.18). Yet one must have a superhuman mind to conceive of ideas foreign to fundamental human knowledge and its derivatives, by which Spinoza apparently means the third and the second kinds of knowledge. He doubts that anyone except Christ has ever had such a mind. God communicated his decision to save mankind directly to Christ without words or vision, while Christ transmitted the message to his disciples orally. His voice was the voice of God that had spoken the ten commandments to Moses. In him divine wisdom assumed human nature and led the way to salvation. After this startling profession of faith Spinoza takes precautions against misinterpretation of his opinion. All of what he has said here is conjecture based on his exegesis of Scripture. He neither confirms nor denies the Christologies of certain churches, 'for I freely confess that I do not understand them' (i.19). What doctrines, which churches? He does not specify here. Nor has he read anywhere in the New Testament that God appeared or spoke to Jesus. He therefore acknowledges a superhuman mind in Christ and the supernatural content of the communication he receives from God, but not a supernatural means of communication between them. This tacit distinction implies that, while he admits the superhuman status of Christ, he denies his divinity.

In an explicit reference to 'Prophecy', 'The Divine Law' confirms this implication when it describes the voice of God as 'a created voice' (i.64). This description likewise recalls the passage about the creation of the Son in 'Natura naturata' of the *Short treatise*. Spinoza could scarcely have thought a creature divine. Then what is the Spinozan Christ? An angel perhaps? Like the angels he acquired intellectual or intuitive knowledge of revelation by the exercise of pure thought (without words or images). Yet Spinoza does not declare Christ an angel. A prophet? Like the prophets he cultivated the imagination of the vulgar. For the benefit of the ignorant and superstitious multitude, he assigned human traits to God and described him as a king or legislator. Yet he surpassed the prophets because they did not receive true and adequate ideas of revelation directly from God as he did. While they imparted knowledge of the first kind to their fellow Jews, he offered knowledge of the second kind to the whole human race. Mere accommodation of the Jewish mentality would not have been enough. His mind had to adjust 'to the opinion and fundamental teaching

20. Zac, 'Le problème', p.490.

common to the whole human race – in other words, to [common notions and true ideas] (i.64). No prophet could have done that. Faithful nonetheless to the Mosaic code, 'he introduced no new laws of his own' (i.71). The Spinozan Christ was hardly a Christian. He did raise the Jewish law from the first to the second kind of knowledge, however, by the substitution of spiritual for physical retribution. To worthy audiences, moreover, he taught no laws, but rather the eternal truths he learned directly from God, thus delivering them from slavery. A sharper image of the Spinozan Christ emerges from this chapter than from the last. Although he shared with the angels the privilege of learning revelation by intuition, he was a man who taught it to other men either by converting it into the common notions of reason or by reducing it to laws or inadequate ideas of report (imagination). A man nonetheless superior to other men.

Spinoza does not accept Christ's miracles or indeed any miracles, because they violate natural laws. He implies in the *Treatise* that the evidence of the resurrection compels no one to believe it. In this case he justifies the plea of ignorance, which Paul condemns in Romans i.20-21.[21] He expresses his opinion more fully and affirmatively in correspondence (1675) with Henry Oldenburg, the inquisitive secretary of the Royal Society. After referring him to 'Miracles' in the *Treatise*, he restates and partially alters his position. He repeats his conviction that we can explain most miracles by natural causes. Rather than dismiss the others as fraud, however, he advises his correspondent, a scientist and a Christian, to suspend his judgement. The evangelists support their accounts of the resurrection appearances by so much detail that we cannot deny their belief in the event. Perhaps unbelievers could have seen the risen Christ too, if they had been in the right places at the right times (an adroit insinuation!). After all the risen Christ appeared neither to Pilate nor to the Roman senate, but only to 'the saints' (p.348), a tactful synonym for followers susceptible to belief in such appearances. How could he ascend to heaven and sit at the right hand of God? God has no right or left, he is everywhere and he 'does not manifest himself outside the world in some imaginary space' (p.348), heaven in other words. Without the pressure of the surrounding air Christ's body would burst. These objections mingle Spinoza's hostility to anthropomorphism with Descartes's plenary physics. Comparing the resurrection appearances to those by God on Mount Sinai, Spinoza infers predictably that such stories appeal to the popular mentality (imagination). How does he then account for the disciples' belief in the resurrection? They had a physical conception of a spiritual event. Paul, to whom the risen Christ also appeared, rejoices in knowing him spiritually

21. 'Ever since God created the world his everlasting power and deity – however invisible – have been there for the mind to see in the things he has made. That is why [men who keep truth imprisoned in their wickedness] are without excuse.'

rather than physically (2 Corinthians v.16). 'I accept Christ's passion, death and burial literally,' Spinoza concludes, 'but his resurrection allegorically' (p.358). As Zac remarks, therefore, he commits the same error that he attributes to Maimonides, an allegorical adaptation of religion to his own philosophy.[22]

In connection with the incarnation he warns Oldenburg against European interpretations of Greek and Hebrew figures of speech. According to the Bible God is a cloud, a tabernacle, a temple. Does Oldenburg think God becomes a cloud, a tabernacle, a temple? Obviously Spinoza does not. Christ made no greater claim for himself than when he said he was the temple of God. Spinoza suggests that Oldenburg interpret this oriental figure spiritually. He identifies the doctrine of 'certain churches' which he pretends not to understand in the *Treatise* as the incarnation: 'God assumed human nature.' It seems no less absurd to him than the proposition 'that a circle assumed the nature of a square' (p.344). It not only violates the laws of nature, but also his monotheism, one of the few Jewish beliefs he never questions. In Christ he nonetheless recognises the greatest manifestation of God's wisdom, which he calls the son of God. He even describes Christ as 'the idea of God' in the *Ethics* (ii.233). While these identifications complicate Christ's relationship with God, they do not substantially contradict the opinion on this subject that Spinoza states more clearly and thoroughly in the *Treatise*. Allegory authorises him to name the man, who has the greatest intuitive access to divine intelligence, the idea, the son or the wisdom of God.

His criticism of miracles also applies to transubstantiation, for which he shares the Protestant scorn. A Protestant recently converted to Catholicism, young Burgh accuses him (1675) of lacking religious faith and exhorts him to follow his example. 'Who has bewitched you,' Spinoza retorts, 'so that you believe [...] you swallow the highest and the eternal, and [...] hold it in your intestines' (p.354-55)? Manifestly the theophagous implications of transubstantiation strike him as particularly blasphemous anthropomorphism. After diagnosing the disease, he prescribes his cure: 'Away with this superstition, acknowledge the reason which God has given you' (p.352). He reminds Burgh of the Huguenot maréchal de Châtillon who fed communion wafers to horses.[23] Although he makes no inferences, he apparently wants Burgh to understand that the impunity of this act refutes the real presence of Christ's body in communion wafers. In the *Treatise* he makes a broader attack on rites that do nothing for beatitude, but merely discipline the masses. He finds that no one has proved the institution of ceremonies like the eucharist by Christ.

22. 'Spinoza [...] n'hésite pas à commettre la faute qu'il reproche à Maimonide et à accommoder l'Ecriture à sa propre philosophie.' *L'Idée*, p.190. 'Il explique allégoriquement les textes et repense le christianisme à la lumière de sa propre philosophie.' *Spinoza*, p.193.
23. At Tirlemont in Belgium (1635).

His interpretation of the holy spirit in Scripture precludes the slightest tolerance of the third person in the Christian Trinity. Nowhere does he however mention the Trinity or the Trinitarian status of the spirit. Instead he studies the etymology of the Old Testament *spirit of God*. First he exhibits the semantic variety of the Hebrew *ruagh* or spirit: breath, breathing or life, courage and strength, virtue and ability, personal feeling, thought, will, passion, the soul, a region (from which the wind blows). Then he enumerates the meanings implied by the Hebrew custom of attributing things to God: a part of nature; something in God's power, dedicated to him or revealed by the prophets (and not by the natural light); a superlative. Finally, he identifies the connotations of the spirit of God in the Old Testament: a dry, violent and deadly wind; great courage, audacity and readiness for any emergency; extraordinary virtue or power; the human soul; human traits assigned to God, such as courage, passion, strength or breath; the Mosaic code; God's virtue or power, strictly speaking, or his law; his goodness and mercy. When manifested by the prophets, moreover, the spirit of God means his thought and judgement. Spinoza comments: 'On our minds also the mind of God and his eternal thoughts are impressed' (i.24). But few men and very few Hebrews appreciate natural knowledge, even though all of them have it in common. Needless to say, therefore, Spinoza's philology ruins the claim of Old Testament support for the Christian version of the holy spirit. He mentions this figure only with respect to two miracles which, along with others, serve as examples of imagination. He does not wonder 'that the holy spirit appeared to those with Christ as a descending dove [and] to the apostles as fiery tongues' (i.25). The first phrase refers to the descent of the holy spirit in the form of a dove on the head of Jesus after he had submitted to baptism by John.[24] The second phrase refers to the Pentecost miracle which, after the ascension, empowered the apostles to continue Christ's mission and extend it to the Gentiles (Acts ii.2-4). Spinoza relegates these visions to fascination with spirits in the vulgar imagination. One could hardly have expected a favourable opinion from the enemy of miracles.

Both his determinism and his monotheism separate him from Christianity. Determinism cannot accommodate the entrapment of the creature by the creator as in the fall, for good would be causing evil. A determinism admitting no exceptions to natural order condemns all miracles. Those of Christ: neither can the living rise from the dead (the resurrection), nor can *natura naturans* become *natura naturata* (the incarnation), nor can bread become flesh (transubstantiation). And those of the holy spirit: neither can flame burn upside down (the Pentecost miracle), nor can *natura naturans* again become *natura naturata* (the

24. Mark i.10; Luke iii.22; Matthew iii.16; John i.32.

44

descent of the holy spirit in the form of a dove). But Spinoza's monotheism is even more incompatible with Christianity than his determinism. Uncompromising in its rigour, it excludes the slightest possibility of a trinitarian divinity or divine persons. Spinoza's hostility to anthropomorphism even eliminates the personality of an only God. He considers Christ a man who enjoyed the unique privilege of receiving the promise of salvation directly from God by intuition.[25] In the third person of the Trinity he sees an illusion that evolved from the Christian and Hebrew imagination. No wonder the slightest echo of his thought provoked Christian outrage!

Unfortunately the destructive potential of his ideas impressed his contemporaries more than his modesty and tolerance. While the Latin text of the *Treatise* limited its readers mostly to scholars, it contains a statement authorising everyone to analyse and evaluate Scripture: 'As the highest power of Scriptural interpretation belongs to every man, the rule for such interpretation should be nothing but the natural light of reason' (i.119). In Latin this passage did not expose the Bible to the masses, but it did invite the scrutiny of libertines at a time when apologetic exegesis by clergymen prevailed. Once the *Ethics* had appeared in the *Opera posthuma*, it aggravated the scandal that the *Treatise* had started seven years earlier. Ignoring the distinction between *natura naturans* and *natura naturata*, Christian polemicists took 'God or Nature' literally. They accused Spinoza of pantheism, and even atheism in view of his God's impersonality. The latter charge seems unfair, for he not only believed in God fervently, but he also had a loftier conception of the divinity than most of his contemporaries.

25. According to Zac, Spinoza attributes to Christ a superhuman means of communication with God: 'La connaissance intuitive de Dieu dont le Christ a le privilège, proche parent de la "science intuitive" du philosophe, est cependant d'un tout autre ordre.' *Spinoza*, p.196. A fourth kind of knowledge? This opinion seems unlikely to me. Spinoza attributes a superior mind to Jesus, but apparently not a superior kind of knowledge.

# Malebranche

SPINOZA'S undeserved reputation for atheism haunted Malebranche because their philosophies vaguely resembled each other. The Jansenist Arnauld and the *philosophe* Dortous de Mairan insisted on this resemblance despite Malebranche's well founded protestations. Both Malebranche and Spinoza attribute matter to a divine cause, but the former's creationism conflicts with the latter's determinism. An Oratorian priest, Malebranche became a philosopher after his exhilarating discovery of Descartes's *L'Homme* in 1664. From Descartes he borrowed some premises and the title of his most famous work, *La Recherche de la vérité* (1674-1675). While continuing to admire Descartes, he henceforth developed an increasingly original philosophy nourished by meditation and stimulated by polemic. He drew inspiration from Augustine too, and disagreement over how to interpret the great Father aggravated his long quarrel with Arnauld. Replies to attacks by Arnauld, which continued even after the latter's death,[1] form an important part of his works. His *Traité de la nature et de la grâce* (1680) particularly angered the Jansenists and their allies. He engaged in other disputes as well, including one with Leibniz.[2] The *Entretiens sur la métaphysique et la religion* (1688) are the most comprehensive description of his mature philosophy, while the frequently revised *Recherche*, which he supplemented by 'Eclaircissements', reveals the evolution of his thought. He had published five editions of this work by 1715 when he and Louis XIV died.[3]

He wanted to provide Christianity with a philosophy that would confound heretics and libertines. His strategy consisted in a rigorous subordination of the creation to the Creator. God not only created the world, but he also conserves it. Unsustained by continuous creation it would cease to exist. Without the constant infusion of divine power it would stop functioning, for God is the only true cause. He makes matter move, he makes spirit think, feel and will according to laws based on divine order. These laws prescribe the appropriate action for

---

1. Two letters by Arnauld dated 22 May and 25 July 1694, the year of his death, appeared in the *Recueil de plusieurs lettres de M. Arnauld* in 1698.
2. Kurt Müller and Gisela Krönert comment on Leibniz's 'Brevis demonstratio erroris memorabilis Cartesii et aliorum circa legem naturae' as follows: 'Diese am 16. Januar 1686 geschriebene Abhandlung is ein Angriff auf Descartes' Dynamik. Leibniz unterscheidet zwischen lebendiger und toter und genetischer und potentieller Kraft. Dies ist der Ausgangspunkt für einen langjährigen Streit mit den Cartesianern Catelan, N. Malebranche und D. Papin, der bis 1691 dauert.' *Leben und Werk von Gottfried Wilhelm Leibniz; eine Chronik* (Frankfurt am Main 1969), p.78-79.
3. Both were also born in 1638.

every occasion in matter and spirit.[4] They reconcile a maximum uniformity and perfection with a minimum economy of means. There are laws for each of the five areas in which occasions arise. They govern relations (1) between bodies, (2) between bodies and finite spirits, (3) finite spirits and God, (4) the angels and inferior beings (Old Testament), (5) Christ and all creatures (New Testament). Let us neglect (4), discuss (1) and (2) immediately, (3) and (5) later. Malebranche considers appearances meaningless: 1. God re-creates a moving body in each successive position along the path it follows. He uses the same procedure to change the speed and direction of bodies in a collision. Bodies carry no energy and exchange none with each other. 2. The union of a body and a mind produces no mutual influence. God moves the body according to the mind's will and modifies the mind by sensations that reflect what happens to the body. In (3), (4) and (5) as well as (1) and (2), God causes the action generally appropriate to the occasion, even when he disapproves of it in a particular situation. He makes exceptions to his laws only when unusual circumstances require them. Unnecessary miracles are beneath his dignity. Divine order, which sets priorities by the degree of perfection, determines necessity. God will retreat from general to particular volition if necessary therefore in order to ensure these priorities.

Even the Creator has to follow divine order. The coexistence of absolute power and immutable order in Malebranche's divinity confirms the allusion to a heterogeneous God by Rome.[5] Malebranche would prefer to describe him as an infinitely infinite being, whose necessary existence he infers from the common notion of infinity. He founds this conception on God's proclamation in Exodus iii.14: 'I am who I am.' An inexhaustible source of being, God creates by giving existence to essence, and his consubstantial Word contains the essences of all possible beings. Whether we realise it or not, we perceive God by 'direct view', but we cannot comprehend him.

This vision of God makes vision in God possible. Our minds are united with the Word, in whom we 'see' the essences or ideas[6] of all that we perceive. The

---

4. 'Dieu même a prévu toutes les suites de toutes les lois possibles qu'il pouvait établir: il a comparé d'une vue éternelle et immuable tous les ouvrages possibles entre eux, et par rapport aux lois dont ils sont des suites: et enfin il s'est arrêté à celles qui ont un plus grand rapport de sagesse, je veux dire de simplicité et de fécondité avec leur ouvrage que toute autre loi, avec tout autre ouvrage.' Nicolas Malebranche, *Réponse aux vraies et fausses idées*, *Œuvres complètes de Malebranche* (Paris 1958-1967), vi.48. All quotations from Malebranche's works come from this edition.

5. 'For Malebranche [...] God must be uncaused and to some extent heterogeneous. The reasons will be that Malebranche guarantees the certainty and universality of necessary truths by depriving them of all connection with creativity or even with activity; and, as a consequence, an *a priori* given, necessary element exists within the Godhead, distinguishable from his will.' Beatrice Rome, *The Philosophy of Malebranche* (Chicago 1963), p.120.

6. 'Pour Malebranche [...] l'idée est une sorte d'être qui existe détaché de notre esprit. Elle n'est

ideas in the Word are universal, infinite, uncreated and coeternal with him. Perception, which depends on the union of spiritual substances, occurs in my mind when one of these ideas unites with my understanding. I perceive a finite portion of an infinite idea which has real and independent existence, whether it refers to a material existence or not. If I saw a golden mountain (one of Malebranche's favourite examples) in my imagination, a dream or a halluci- nation, it would be as real as any mountain in nature. Do mountains really exist in nature? We must rely on revelation for proof of that, for Malebranche combines the empirical contingency of existences in the material world with the rational necessity of essences in the spiritual world. He defines truth as equality of ideas,[7] his favourite example being the equation $2+2$ or $2 \times 2$ equals 4. But he includes equal perfections in the concept as well as equal magnitudes. Magnitude concerns things of the same nature (matter, spirit or divinity), and perfection things of different nature or different modes of things having the same nature. The scale of perfections constitutes divine order. We learn truth by natural revelation on the occasion of natural prayer or attention to the Word,[8] who is divine reason and wisdom. Malebranche identifies us as the occasional cause, and the Word as the true cause of such enlightenment. In his *Méditations chrétiennes et métaphysiques* (1683) Christ tells his devoted follower: 'Comme sagesse éternelle et raison universelle [...] je suis cause véritable de la lumière [...] Tes volontés sont souvent exaucées. Qu'elles le soient même toujours à l'égard de la présence des idées, j'y consens' (x.144).

We perceive the same ideas in divine reason as God does, although we perceive them partially and he entirely.[9] Ideas referring to actual or potential bodies preoccupy Malebranche to the extent that he neglects the others. These ideas are identical, he believes, to the archetypes followed by God in the work of creation. But is there an archetype for every body? Some passages in the first edition of the *Recherche* suggest that there is, while others imply that each

pas précisement l'image de ce qui est, elle est le modèle de ce qui peut être [...] elle est l'objet même auquel l'esprit est immédiatement uni quand il pense.' Léon Ollé-Laprune, *La Philosophie de Malebranche* (Paris 1870), i.145-46.

7. He disagrees with Descartes's opinion that God has created eternal truths.

8. 'La lumière en nous est ce par quoi il nous est *possible* d'être éclairés, l'attention est ce par quoi nous devenons réellement éclairés.' Martial Gueroult in *Malebranche: l'homme et l'œuvre 1638- 1715*, Journées Malebranche, Paris, 1965 (Paris 1967), p.207.

9. 'S'il est vrai que la raison à laquelle tous les hommes participent est universelle; s'il est vrai qu'elle est infinie; s'il est vrai qu'elle est immuable et nécessaire; il est certain qu'elle n'est point différente de celle de Dieu même: car il n'y a que l'être universel et infini qui renferme en soi- même une raison universelle [...] Dieu ne peut agir que selon cette raison [...] Elle est coéternelle et consubstantielle' (iii.131). 'La raison n'est donc pas [...] un pouvoir en nous de distinguer le vrai du faux, fondé sur la véracité du Dieu créateur de toute vérité. Elle est la Raison universelle, dont les normes absolues s'imposent à Dieu comme aux esprits finis.' Geneviève Rodis-Lewis, *Nicolas Malebranche* (Paris 1963), p.84-85.

archetype refers to an element many bodies have in common. Rather than clutter the Word with an endless number of particular ideas, Malebranche began to develop the second alternative in the tenth 'Eclaircissement', where he mentions 'intelligible extension' for the first time.[10] He agrees with Descartes that extension is the essence of matter. Divine reason, he adds, contains an intelligible or ideal extension that corresponds to material extension. He identifies it with the idea of matter, an infinite general essence governing the actual or potential creation of finite particulars. Analogies with matter obscure his descriptions of intelligible extension,[11] thus critical interpretations vary. Though spiritual in nature, it has an infinite number of parts that exclude each other. Each part describes an element of geometry, not by figure but by mathematical relations like those in algebra.[12] According to the *Recherche*: 'Les idées des nombres et de l'étendue [...] sont les règles immuables et les mesures communes de toutes les choses que nous connaissons et que nous pouvons connaître' (ii.374). In the next sentence Malebranche considers the relations between numbers and figures the subject of a universal science yielding knowledge of all the truth naturally accessible to the mind. Comparison of this passage with another one in his *Réponse* to Arnauld's *Vraies et fausses idées* (1683) sheds further light on intelligible extension: 'Je pense à une sphère, quand je considère dans l'étendue intelligible que renferme la Raison une certaine partie intelligible, dont toutes les extrémités sont également éloignées d'une autre qui en est le centre' (vi.99). Since Malebranche excludes figures from intelligible extension, only numbers remain to express the relation or truth described there. While geometry represents material extension, algebra represents intelligible extension,

10. 'Avant les Eclaircissements j'ai toujours dit généralement que nous voyons en Dieu ses créatures *par ce qu'il a en lui qui les représentait*. Mais dans les *Eclaircissements* j'ai été obligé de me servir de ce terme si scandaleux d'*étendue intelligible*, parce que j'ai reconnu par expérience que ma manière d'expliquer trop générale faisait tomber quelques personnes peu attentives dans cette erreur grossière que l'on voyait le soleil, un cheval, un homme par chacune des idées que Dieu en avait lui-même' (vi.243-44). Arnauld and others, whose attacks had forced him to make this change, found the new term scandalous. 'Toute idée finie n'est concevable que sur fond d'infini. Ce premier monde intelligible est conçu à la manière d'un double des existences du présent univers. Il y aurait une idée du cheval, une idée du soleil, etc. Malebranche se défendra plus tard contre Arnauld d'une telle interprétation, mais l'historien ne peut que donner raison à l'adversaire de Malebranche sur ce point.' André Robinet, 'Malebranche', *Histoire de la philosophie* (Paris 1973), ii.513.

11. 'L'étendue intelligible semble [...] recevoir un statut ambigu. Elle est idée, non réalité matérielle, et, d'autre part, elle constitue l'essence de la matière. Elle est la source de toute pensée objective et claire des corps, et, pourtant, elle est souvent présentée comme une sorte de continuum amorphe ne contenant qu'en puissance les idées particulières dont seules nos sensations sembleraient tracer le dessein.' Ferdinand Alquié, *Malebranche et le rationalisme chrétien* (Paris 1977), p.22.

12. In 'Malebranche' Robinet discusses 'deux idées privilégiées. L'idée de nombre exprime dans les *Eléments des mathématiques* (1675) de Prestet l'enseignement que Malebranche donne à l'Oratoire en fonction d'une *Géométrie* cartésienne revue à la lumière des proportions claires d'arithmétique. L'idée de l'étendue fait à elle seule l'essence de toute matière corporelle' (ii.513).

which contains quantitative ideas alone. Malebranche seems to consign quality to spiritual, sentimental and sensual thought. The sun furnishes him with the fond example of a natural sphere that appears smaller on the horizon than at its zenith. He attributes the variation to the perception of a greater or lesser portion of intelligible extension, a naive simplification. While the size of the material sun actually remains constant, that of the intelligible sun conforms to the occasion: 'Le soleil [...] que l'on voit n'est pas celui que l'on regarde' (iii.149).

We look at the sun in the sky, but we see it in a medium of quantitative ideas. When we see intelligible extension, we see God insofar as he represents our world and all possible worlds.[13] We only see an attribute, therefore, and by no means the whole substance. In the *Entretiens*, Théodore tells Ariste, 'lorsque vous contemplez l'étendue intelligible [...] vous voyez alors la substance divine, car il n'y a qu'elle [...] qui puisse éclairer l'esprit. Mais vous ne la voyez pas en elle-même [...] Vous ne la voyez que selon le rapport qu'elle a aux créatures matérielles' (xii.51). He distinguishes between the relative perfection of intelligible extension and the absolute perfection of God himself, between the infinite idea of extension and the infinite infinity of the divine substance. He makes a further distinction between the immensity and the intelligence of this substance. After warning Théotime not to confuse divine immensity with intelligible extension, he explains, 'l'étendue [matérielle] est à l'immensité ce que le temps est à l'éternité' (xii.179). From a human viewpoint, divine immensity is always present in its entirety everywhere, yet without local extension, just as divine reason is always present in all minds. From a divine viewpoint, all bodies are in divine immensity and all minds, in divine reason. Théodore willingly concedes the impossibility of fully understanding this doctrine.

The omnipresence of God nonetheless facilitates our comprehension of his causality in both the material and the spiritual worlds. We can well imagine that causation depends on some kind of contact. The divine cause not only provides the mind with ideas, but also modifies it when appropriate by sensations and feelings that qualify them. Sensations differ from feelings only insofar as they are more acute and hence convey the false impression that they come from outside the mind. Malebranche illustrates this distinction by the difference between heat and a burning pain. Sensations, he insists, never derive from sensual contact with bodies. He regards ideas as objective and sensations as subjective, ideas as clear and sensations as obscure, ideas as the essence of things and sensations as unreliable evidence that they exist. He limits pure

13. 'Malebranche a mis en Dieu l'étendue à titre de réalité incréée, et il l'y a mise formellement. Cela ne revient-il pas à considérer Dieu comme corporel? On peut le craindre, en effet [...] une sorte de divinisation de l'étendue.' Alquié, *Malebranche*, p.213-14.

thought, as in mathematics, to the conception of ideas. According to the tenth 'Eclaircissement'. 'on ne voit par lumière que les nombres, l'étendue et les essences des choses' (iii.142). But perception, as in scientific observation, involves a combination of conception and sensation. One perceives a body when the mind or soul attributes a sensation to the figure of the body specified in intelligible extension, 'car l'âme répand presque toujours sa sensation sur l'idée qui la frappe vivement' (iii.142). The bright colour of sunlight, for instance, makes the circle of the sun visible in the sky.

Before 1695 Malebranche considered that God modified the mind to produce colour and the other sensations in accordance with the laws by which he governed the union of the mind and the body. After that date he held that ideas invested with God's power performed this function. 'La vision de l'idée-objet', Robinet comments, 'cède le pas à la vitalité de l'idée-acte.'[14] He demonstrates that this subtle change in Malebranche's metaphysics has important consequences. Before 1695 Malebranche compared the mind to a mirror in which we see images without noticing the mirror itself.[15] Afterwards he preferred the Augustinian analogy of a seal making an impression on wax. Before, ideas penetrating the mind had no effect on it, a theory inconsistent with experience. Afterwards ideas were effective (*efficaces*), because they affected (*touchaient*) the mind by causing sensations in it. The dichotomy between ideas and sensations therefore diminished and the difference between intellectual and sensual information became relative. Active essences began to participate in the revelation of existences by sensations. Divine laws no longer coordinated separate events in the body and the mind, but rather combined them in a single activity. Ideas that one may either know or feel emerged in Malebranche's *Réponse* [...] *à la troisième lettre de M. Arnauld* in 1699, five years after the Jansenist's death: 'Les perceptions [...] sont [...] des passivetés de l'âme produites en elle par l'efficace des idées divines, qui par là se font ou connaître ou sentir' (ix.961). Since ideas result in sensory perception as well as pure thought and connect the mind with divine power (the Father) as well as divine reason (the Son), we both conceive and perceive in God, as Robinet remarks.[16] Sensory perception recovers some

14. André Robinet, *Système et existence dans l'œuvre de Malebranche* (Paris 1965), p.268.

15. Gueroult refers to 'le plus extraordinaire paradoxe du malebranchisme, à savoir que *l'intelligence ou raison qu'éclaire mon âme* n'a rien à voir avec l'essence de celle-ci, qui m'échappe, mais est constituée, pour le principal, par l'essence de la réalité qui lui est radicalement antagoniste, à savoir *l'essence des corps ou l'étendue intelligible*. Ce paradoxe a sa contrepartie immédiate dans un autre, à savoir que ce qui constitue *l'essence de la matière* en tant que celle-ci a des propriétés excluant radicalement l'esprit, c'est une Idée de l'Intelligence divine, Idée qui à ce titre constitue précisément ce qu'il y a de plus hautement spirituel dans mon esprit, à savoir *la raison et la lumière illuminante* des mathématiques.' *Malebranche* (Paris 1955), i.139.

16. See note 14.

of its lost authority although it continues to rely on intelligible extension. Relegated to the mere preservation of life in the earlier philosophy, experience now reassumes its traditional role in physics and Malebranche redefines dogma as a kind of experience. Yet ideas remain superior to sensations and pure thought continues to surpass thought contaminated by sensory contact. Unlike sensations ideas make a uniform and superficial impression on the mind, and the impression is faint when caused by pure thought. The more general the idea, the fainter the impression.

Before 1695 Malebranche thought the pure understanding was the only source of authentic knowledge. According to the third 'Eclaircissement', we know the essences of bodies 'par *lumière*' and we discern their existence 'par sentiment' (iii.141). The clear idea of a body reveals all the qualities it can possibly have, but an obscure idea or sensation yields no light or evidence at all. We discern the existence of bodies in our presence and of bodies not in our presence by memory or imagination. The reaction to stimulation of the animal spirits in our nerves occasions sensation. Memory awakens when they flow through the marks (*fissures*) on the brain left by the experience of similar events in the past. Vision, memory and imagination present images to the mind, but our perspective distorts the geometry of the bodies they represent. Yet I spontaneously judge the length of the sides on the rear square of a cube to be equal to that of the sides on the front square, the size of the sun to be the same at its zenith as on the horizon and the height of a man walking towards me to remain constant. Although these judgements conflict with the appearances, I rely on them without proof, for which I have no time and of which I may be incapable. How can I do that? God does my geometry for me through natural judgement, an instinct subject to the laws governing the relationship between the body and the mind. This occasional cause eliminates distortion of magnitude, figure and movement by the perspective of my mental images, but it does not correct any errors I happen to make in the perceptions that constitute these figures. God treats all my perceptions as if they were correct: 'Il juge en moi, pour moi et selon moi,' as Alquié remarks (*Malebranche*, p.59). When I sail downstream, the boat seems to remain stationary while the banks of the river seem to pass. In such cases I must rely on free judgement which, contrary to natural judgement, involves my will. God does not determine free judgements, but only natural judgements. All judgements, in Malebranche's opinion, represent relations between things, and all reasonings, relations between relations.

Even after 1695 he denied the accuracy of sensations and he held them responsible for the temptation of the righteous and the seduction of sinners. Before then he thought them useful mostly in providing for natural necessities and warning against danger to life. Although he conceded that they are natural revelations of matter, he advises us to consult Genesis for proof that the material world really exists. His attitude raises some dire questions: Does this world have any meaning for us?[17] Does it serve any useful purpose? If God created it for himself and not for us, as Malebranche argues, he indulged in the kind of vanity epitomised by Louis XIV. In this philosophy matter has more psychological than cosmological value, since it occasions the modifications of the mind.[18] Sensations make the mind aware of itself and this self-consciousness, which Malebranche calls inner feeling, tells it that it exists. Unfortunately, however, inner feeling reveals little more than that, neither the essence of the mind nor the existence of other minds. We can learn the latter only by conjecture. In the *Méditations* the Word refuses to satisfy his follower's curiosity about the mind. Knowing his mind would make him so exuberant and conceited that he would forget his duties and neglect his body, which he should preserve for eventual sacrifice to God. The Word tells him, 'Tu me demandes que je t'apprenne ce que c'est que ta substance, ta pensée, ton désir, ta douleur. Tu ne peux connaître clairement ces choses jusqu'à ce que je te fasse connaître l'idée de ton être en te découvrant ce qui est en moi qui te représente' (x.103). Apparently that will happen only in heaven. Meanwhile the follower must settle for the inner awareness of the modifications in his mind. No less obscure than the other feelings, this awareness will tell him nothing about the nature of the mind. Theoretically, therefore, the beginning of knowledge in Descartes is little more than ignorance in Malebranche. Yet Malebranche himself confirms the mind's immateriality, its immortality, its contingency and the difference between its substance and God's. He distinguishes between the two parts of the mind, the understanding which is passive and the will which is both passive and active. He attributes three faculties to the mind: sense, memory and imagination, pure thought. To account for the influence of divine reason on the understanding and the influence of the divine will on the human will, he invokes the Augustinian principle of the superior acting on the inferior (not a very satisfying explanation). If separated from God, the mind would cease to exist because it could no longer think or will. In the afterlife it will have feelings superior to any in this life. Divine will inclines us to do good, so the only liberty left to our will is that of consent. Consequently, Malebranche professes to know far more about the mind than inner feeling and dogma reveal.

17. 'Sans doute Malebranche déclare-t-il que Dieu nous touche de sensations pour nous signifier ce qui se passe dans le monde des corps; mais ce monde, totalement inefficace et du reste inaccessible, est à la fois, si inutile et si lointain que c'est en vain que la foi oblige à croire à son existence. A cette existence, nous ne saurions, en définitive, conférer aucun sens.' Alquié, *Malebranche*, p.149.
18. Malebranche agrees with Descartes's identification of the mind with the soul.

There are four kinds of knowledge in his opinion. Inner feeling tells him that his mind exists, and direct view, that God exists; neither reveals essence, however. Ideas inform him of the essence of things, but not of their existence, or at least not before 1695. And conjecture indicates the existence of other minds. This inventory reminds us that our ignorance is far greater than our knowledge. Malebranche's pessimism reflects his fervent belief in the dependence of man on God. He would constrain us, if he could, to trust in revelation as much as he does. Descartes's theory of the natural light does not suit him because it allows the human mind too much autonomy. He therefore substitutes, as Gueroult observes, a supernatural light for the natural light,[19] and God becomes the immediate as well as the original source of human intelligence. Malebranche nonetheless adapts Descartes's analogy to his system: 'Les yeux ont besoin de la lumière pour voir [...] l'esprit aussi a besoin d'idées pour concevoir' (ii.247). The light of ideas is pure thought: 'notre lumière, ce sont nos idées, c'est la raison universelle' (vii.64). According to the tenth 'Eclaircissement' the access of men to universal reason distinguishes them from the other creatures: 'Tous [les hommes] sont capables de connaître la vérité' (iii.129). No one doubts that two times two equals four or that a man should prefer his friend to a dog. Indeed the Chinese accept such truths as readily as we do. Since these truths originate in no human mind, they must derive from universal reason[20] and we consult universal reason whenever 'nous rentrons en nous-mêmes' (iii.129). The Word reminds his follower of the latter's conversations with other men, who understand him and approve what he says. When merchants settle their accounts and geometers discuss their theorems, they agree with each other. How could men communicate, if each had his own version of reason? 'Ta raison est universelle, immuable, nécessaire et [...] ton esprit est borné' (x.21). Théodore is certain that men, angels and even God acknowledge the same truths as he does: 'c'est la même lumière qui éclaire tous les esprits' (xii.188). The Chinese philosopher in an *Entretien* of 1708 defines *le Ly* as supreme and eternal truth, wisdom and justice. But the Christian philosopher persuades him that 'le vrai *Ly* [est] une lumière commune à tous les hommes' (xv.1920).

Malebranche not only thinks this light is universal, but also immutable, necessary, eternal and infinite. It must be infinite, he argues, because we cannot exhaust it and it always answers every question we ask it. Such naive arguments inflate his esteem for reason to the point of deifying it. He even declares it

19. See Gueroult, *Malebranche*, i.35-36.
20. 'Si mon propre *esprit* était ma *raison*, ou ma lumière, mon esprit serait la raison de toutes les intelligences; car je suis sûr que ma raison ou la lumière qui m'éclaire est commune a toutes les intelligences' (xi.18).

consubstantial and coeternal with God. The Word says of man, 'je suis sa raison' (x.151). He is God's reason too, for God has reason in common with men. 'Nous [...] concevons [la raison] dans un sens plus indépendante que Dieu même [qui] est obligé de la suivre' (iii.131). Reason unites men with God in a communion of thought and action which Malebranche identifies as the Church. It enables them legitimately to see things from God's viewpoint, an insinuation supporting clerical authority. In short, the Word is infallible: 'Lorsqu'un homme [...] écoute son souverain maître dans le silence de ses sens et de ses passions, il est impossible qu'il tombe dans l'erreur' (i.16).

The teachers and learners in Malebranche's dialogues often 'rentrent en eux-mêmes'. In the *Conversations chrétiennes* (1677) his spokesman Théodore invites young Eraste to arbitrate Théodore's debate with Aristarque. If we can believe Théodore, studies and travels have corrupted Aristarque's mind and burdened it with prejudices. Unspoiled by society, Eraste listens carefully, weighs Aristarque's opinions in his conscience and judges them in the light of reason. 'La nature ou plutôt la raison toute seule parle en lui' (iv.13). Predictably Théodore convinces Aristarque who, at the end of the *Conversations*, follows Eraste's example in converting to Malebranchism. Eraste's uncanny anticipations of Théodore incited public scepticism about his youth,[21] as a notice inserted in the second edition admits. The 'Avertissement' to the *Méditations* concedes the difficulty of trying to imagine what the Word would say in a dialogue with Malebranche himself. Unusually fallible here the author defers to the divine light when the Word corrects his mistakes. The tone is obsequious at times. Even more condescending and pedantic than the Cartesian Christ and the Théodore in the *Conversations*, the Théodore in the *Entretiens* is fastidious as well. His surprising affection for Ariste, an attractive and popular Eraste, results in a course on Malebranchism. No sooner does Théodore meet Ariste in a place that charms the senses than he insists on retreating to the young man's cabinet. Ariste probably enjoys the attention of many admirers in this place, a garden perhaps, a salon or a court, but he willingly closets himself with the austere Théodore. He even offers to make the room completely dark, so that no sensory distractions will hinder Théodore's determination to 'rentrer en lui-même'. Does he nonetheless make this offer facetiously? Théodore does not seem to think so, for he merely asks him to draw the curtains: 'Ce grand jour [...] donnerait trop d'éclats à certains objets' (xi.32). When Ariste asks Théodore to take him up to the enchanted region of philosophy, he apparently intends no irony, but this time Théodore assumes that he does. Though tolerant of Ariste's alleged humour, Théodore denies that his philosophy has anything in common

---

21. Fifteen or twenty according to the 'L'imprimeur au lecteur' of 1677.

with such fantasy. In the ensuing conversation Théodore carries his worship of reason to a ridiculous extreme. Although Ariste submits as tamely as Eraste, he personifies Malebranche's rational ideal more gracefully than the other characters in these dialogues, including the author's projection of himself in the *Méditations*. The Chinese and Christian philosophers in the *Entretien* of 1708, on the other hand, are merely impassible barristers pleading a case which Malebranche biased in favour of Christianity. He personally illustrated his conception of reason more effectively than any of these personae. Contemporaries, who valued the opportunity to converse with him, found him no less subtle and charming than severe.

He persistently seeks to reconcile reason and faith, which Descartes separated. Identifying reason with the Word simplifies such reconciliation, 'car Jésus-Christ ne peut jamais être contraire à lui-même, la vérité incarnée à la vérité intelligible' (xi.71). Thus revelation necessarily conforms to reason, even when we are unable to explain how.[22] Malebranche does not pretend that we can solve the more difficult Christian mysteries such as transubstantiation and the Trinity. All the principal articles of faith are in fact vulnerable to objections that we cannot answer to the satisfaction of finite reason. Malebranche nonetheless defends the right to explain these mysteries insofar as our reason allows, provided our explanation concurs with dogma. He cites the example of the Fathers who elucidated the dogma of the Trinity, men like Augustine, Hilary and Thomas. 'Mais quoi? Sera-t-il permis de raisonner sur la conduite de Dieu? Oui, sans doute' (v.187). We need only limit ourselves to clear ideas that imply no threat to dogma. In the *Méditations* the Word testifies that he often makes revealed truths intelligible to the pure understanding of followers who, 'rentrant en eux-mêmes', pray to him naturally and respectfully.

The Théodore of the *Entretiens* affirms that it takes a 'good' philosopher to understand theology. The better one knows the 'true' principles of metaphysics, the more firmly one believes in the truths of Christianity. Authentic philosophy harmonises with the faith; competent philosophers agree with other Christians. Whether Christ secretly communicates with their minds or teaches them through the public authority of his Church, he never contradicts himself, although contradictions may result from misinterpretation of his message. Truth comes through different channels, but it is always the same. 'Il ne faut donc point opposer la philosophie à la religion' (xii.133). On the contrary, religion enables philosophers to solve otherwise intractable problems. Ariste notes that Théodore extricates himself from philosophical difficulties by resorting to the truths of

22. 'Il est certain que la foi est toujours d'accord avec elle-même, et avec la souveraine raison. Car le Verbe Incarné, l'auteur et le consommateur de notre foi, est cette même Raison souveraine, qui éclaire intérieurement tous les hommes' (xvi.132).

faith: 'Ce n'est pas là philosopher' (xii.204). Théodore dismisses the objection, however, on the grounds that the solution he finds for his problems justifies his source! The necessary truthfulness of God, which Malebranche never doubts, not even as Descartes seems to imply for the sake of method, supports this position. Physicists neither reason against experience, Théodore observes, nor conclude from experience against reason.[23] Though certain of both, they puzzle, he says, over the means of reconciling them with each other. He regards 'les faits de la religion' (xii.339) as experience. Malebranche, who admires Descartes's physics even more than his metaphysics, takes this analogy seriously.

When the facts of religion bring Théodore into conflict with reason, he suspends his judgement. 'Les dogmes de la foi', he believes, 'et les principes de la raison doivent être d'accord dans la vérité' (xii.339). If, despite the frailty of his mind, he resumes his inquiry, he shifts his attention back and forth between ideas and dogmas in a dialectic that often allows him to advance from faith to intelligence. Malebranche expands on this progression in his last work, the *Réflexions sur la prémotion physique* (1715): 'Il arrive souvent que la foi conduit à l'intelligence, et obtient des idées claires de quelques vérités que l'on croyait uniquement par la foi' (xvi.133). In the *Traité de morale* he foresees the eventual superiority of intelligence over faith and even the replacement of faith by intelligence: 'L'intelligence est préférable à la foi. Car la foi passera, mais l'intelligence subsistera éternellement' (xi.34). Although he does not say when faith will pass away, he must have been thinking of the afterlife. He considers faith inferior to reason in another way too. Except for the inconceivable mysteries of Christianity, 'la foi [...] sans lumière, si cela est possible, ne peut rendre solidement vertueux' (xi.34). Blind faith, which thrives on vulgarity and ignorance, is no moral achievement. The more witnesses attesting to a religious fact, the greater the certainty of the fact. The abstract principles of philosophy nonetheless escape most men, hence 'le bon sens veut qu'on se défie de ce qu'en pense la multitude' (xii.331).

Malebranche identifies the light of reason with the grace given all men by the Creator. Attention or natural prayer invokes this grace which, before the fall, assured the freedom of Adam's will, so that he could love God by rational choice. After the fall, however, he needed a supplementary grace to overcome his newly acquired desire for sensory pleasure or concupiscence.[24] Christ

23. Théodore: 'Pour moi, quand un homme a pour principe de ne se rendre qu'à l'évidence et à l'autorité, quand je m'aperçois qu'il ne travaille qu'à chercher de bonnes preuves des dogmes reçus, je ne crains point qu'il puisse s'égarer dangereusement' (xii.353).
24. He was subject to 'la loi de la concupiscence; à cette loi charnelle qui combat sans cesse contre l'esprit, qui lui inspire à tous moments l'amour des biens sensibles, et qui domine sur lui par des passions si fortes et si vives, et en même temps si douces et si agréables qu'il ne peut et qu'il ne veut pas même faire les efforts nécessaires pour rompre les liens qui le captivent' (v.95).

therefore occasions the distribution of a sensory grace that counterbalances concupiscence, thus restoring free will. Malebranche calls it *la grâce de sentiment* or *du Réparateur*. While the divine Word bestows the Creator's grace on all men, the incarnate Word obtains the Saviour's grace only for those he wishes to receive it. These alone are free to love God by rational choice, although some of them prefer not to do so.

Adam's love of God before his fall was all the more worthy, in Malebranche's opinion, because it depended on no sensory incentive. The philosopher, who professes to know this Adam suprisingly well, uses him to illustrate his psychology. Aware that he owed his very being to God, the innocent Adam dedicated himself to the pursuit of the supreme good. In his mind ideas prevailed over sensations, as divine order requires. Although he had the same senses as we do, '[ils] demeuraient dans un silence respectueux et ne troublaient jamais ses idées' (x.145). His sensations, he realised, served no other purpose than to show him how to preserve his health and life. He did not judge the nature of bodies by them, or even the existence of bodies when the sensations corresponded to movements of the animal spirits confined to his body. For he could discriminate between the interior and exterior origins of the impulses making fissures in his brain. He could even stop the flow of animal spirits to the part of his brain where the soul resides and keep them from fissuring his brain. No slave of pleasure and pain, 'il les arrêtait incontinent après qu'ils l'avaient averti, s'il le souhaitait ainsi; et sans doute il le souhaitait toujours à l'égard de la douleur' (i.75). He reduced pain to the level of a sensory warning, such as the prick of a pin point touched by a finger or the warmth of a fire on an extended hand. He could moderate sensory pleasure too and discover by taste, for instance, that a fruit is edible without enjoying its flavour. Unlike pain, however, pleasure lingers in the memory. God did not want Adam to neglect him 'pour examiner la nature de quelque fruit, afin de s'en nourrir' (i.75). Since the capacity of his soul was finite, he could not explore the infinitely complex structure and movement of matter. His control of the animal spirits in his body resulted from God's supension of the law governing the communication of movement. God honoured his innocence by this miraculous privilege and the further privilege of living in an ideal environment. The contemplation of God's perfections brought Adam a cerebral joy that eclipsed all sensory pleasure. The complete submission of his understanding and will to God harmonised with the latter's intentions in creating him.

Indeed his innocence seems impregnable: 'Comment le premier homme a-t-il pu s'éloigner de Dieu?' (iv.95) wonders Eraste. Puzzled by the same question, Gueroult explores all possible answers only to find none of them compatible with Malebranche's thought.[25] Alquié in turn stresses the difficulty of reconciling Adam's liberty with the necessity of his sin. Malebranche, 'qui veut scruter tous les mystères',[26] tries to prove the impossible by subtle argument. Although human will is God's will in man, he submits, all men including Adam are free to give, suspend or refuse their consent to sensory incentives, whether they tend to good or evil. As God continually creates men, he instils in them the desire for happiness, so that they will seek the joy of loving him. Though legitimate in itself, Adam's pursuit of happiness deviated from this joy and turned to the illusory pleasures of sense gratification.

As for the exact temptation to which he succumbed, Malebranche entertains several possibilities. Was it the beauty and sweetness of the forbidden fruit, a presumptuous vanity inspired by his natural perfections or his excessive infatuation with Eve and fear of hurting her? 'Apparemment tout cela a contribué à sa désobéissance' (i.75). The *Conversations* draw the traditional parallel between Adam's love for Eve, and Christ the second Adam's love for his Church. Typically Malebranche denies that the necessity of Adam's love impaired his free will. He holds Adam responsible for the fall rather than Eve. God does not punish innocent people. Eve neither lost control of her senses when she partook of the fruit nor blushed over her nudity as she offered it to Adam. Her body belonged to Adam, so they remained innocent until he partook of the fruit himself. Only then did their senses revolt and God punished Adam's sin, not Eve's. When the devil disguised as a serpent told Eve that the fruit would make her resemble God, she must have understood that her union with God would sanctify her. For how could a woman resemble God more closely than that? God's irony in Genesis iii.22 reveals that Adam took the devil's promise seriously: 'See, the man has become like one of us!' Adam seized a false opportunity to deify himself because, fascinated by sensible objects, he had forgotten God. Rather than union with God, he yearned for usurpation of his dignity. Thus the devil exploited the creation of man in the image of God and perverted his natural wish to resemble his Creator. Adam's sin, moreover, initiated the proliferation of paganism, by which the devil sought to ruin the cult of the one true God.

What does Malebranche nonetheless regard as Adam's principal motive, his vain presumption or his sensual appetite? Rodis-Lewis cites his presumption,

---

25. 'On ne voit plus comment il pourra jamais décider à pécher' (iii.231).

26. 'Le péché fait partie du dessein de Dieu. Mais pour s'insérer dans le cours de son exécution, il doit, d'une part, être librement commis, et, d'autre part, résulter d'une sorte de nécessité. Malebranche, qui veut scruter tous les mystères, est donc conduit à présenter une psychologie d'Adam garantissant sa liberté et expliquant cependant sa faute.' Alquié, *Le Cartésianisme de Malebranche* (Paris 1974), p.460.

and Alquié, after others, his appetite,[27] an opinion better supported by the texts. From the start Malebranche suggests, the union of the soul with the body condemned Adam to seduction by sensual pleasure. Before 1695 he thought the light of reason has no emotional impact on the soul. Before and after he thought that pleasure does make such an impact and that reason authorises pleasure as a natural aid for the support and protection of life. Though unmoved by pleasure himself, God causes it, thus implying that he approves of it. To what extent, however? Adam's guilt depends on his ability to know when pleasure stops helping to sustain life and starts subverting his will.[28] At this point of no return he yielded to the temptation of pleasure and failed to arrest the flow of animal spirits to the brain, so that sensations began to flood his soul. As pleasure occupied the limited capacity of his understanding, it forced duty out. His attention (natural prayer) decreased and hence the enlightenment of his soul by reason (the Creator's grace) as well. Thus pleasure exploited the tolerance of reason until it dominated the understanding. Once it had usurped the control of the will from reason, the will in its pursuit of happiness began to confuse sensual pleasure with spiritual joy. Distracted, it neglected God. Though indeliberate, this neglect was intentional since the will consented to it. Yet Malebranche's ingenious psychology does not absolve his God of letting the disaster happen.

In the fall, the human will rebelled against the divine, of which it nonetheless remains a finite though alienated mode. The enormity of Adam's crime does not consist in eating a forbidden fruit, but rather in disobeying God. The disproportion between God and man magnifies an otherwise trivial sin. Malebranche conceives of this sin and concupiscence, its result, as negative in character. Since Adam failed to obey him, God withdrew the privilege of control over the animal spirits. This lack of control is concupiscence, which immediately upset the subordination of the body to the soul, so that the master became a

27. 'Vouloir être comme Dieu, c'est la tentation originelle' (Rodis-Lewis, p.234). 'Dans le VIIIe *Eclaircissement* [...] apparaît [...] cette tentation éthique, profonde, de se prendre soi-même comme objet de sa propre perfection, ce qui n'a rien à voir avec le plaisir sensible.' Rodis-Lewis, 'La connaissance par idée chez Malebranche', *Malebranche: l'homme et l'œuvre*, p.174. 'Adam [...] goûtait [...] les plaisirs que le corps occasionne. Et la lumière ne mouvant pas son âme plus qu'elle ne meut la nôtre, ces plaisirs étaient en fait ses seuls plaisirs, et donc, en réalité, les seuls mobiles de son action.' Alquié, *Malebranche*, p.53.

28. Before the fall Adam 'savait [...] que [...] Dieu [...] était la cause [du plaisir]; on concevra qu'Adam pouvait penser qu'en goûtant le plaisir sensible, il louait Dieu. Tout cela expliquerait qu'il eût laissé le plaisir sensible partager son esprit, se disant: "cela m'est permis." Dans ces conditions, pour qu'il ne péchât point, il lui aurait fallu connaître très exactement à partir de quel moment le plaisir avait terminé son rôle d'avertisseur.' Ginette Dreyfus, 'Le problème de la liberté de l'homme dans la philosophie de Malebranche', *Malebranche: l'homme et l'œuvre*, p.172-73. At the root of Adam's sin 'se trouve un relâchement de l'attention qui est sans motif. En un sens, on pourrait dire qu'il n'y a pas ici décision véritable, mais plutôt abandon indélibéré.' Dreyfus in *Malebranche: l'homme et l'œuvre*, p.248.

slave. Adam could no longer stop the flow of animal spirits, the opening of fissures in his brain[29] and the modification of his soul by sensation. In reverting from a privileged to a natural state, however, his psychology remained otherwise intact. Attention continued to elicit ideas, and the flow of animal spirits through the fissures in his brain, to effect the modification of the soul by sensations. Yet the occasioned interaction of the spirits, the fissures and the sensations resulted in mutual reinforcement, thus accelerating the spirits, deepening the fissures and intensifying the sensations. A vicious circle. Relentlessly sensation, passion and imagination harassed the soul, distracted its attention and impeded the reception of ideas.

Confusing sensations with ideas, the understanding accredited the misrepresentation of the material world by sensation. Ephemeral pleasures obstructed the will's quest for lasting joy, while natural judgements encroached on the jurisdiction of free judgement. Unable to suppress pain or distinguish between sensations originating inside and outside the body, the soul suffered and succumbed to the illusions of dreams and hallucinations. Ignorant of its dependence on God, the soul loved itself more than him and preferred sensible things to him. Instead of annihilating the soul, God subjected it to concupiscence, which is worse. The curse continues according to Malebranche, who attributes the disorientation of fever and insanity to Adam's sin. Unlike Malebranche's contemporaries, the innocent Adam had no need for a doctor and a director of conscience. The shame first experienced by Adam and Eve persists: 'La honte [...] d'un homme nu n'est qu'un sentiment confus qui le porte à se cacher parce qu'en cet état il ne peut lier de société raisonnable' (xvii.1.540). Shameful since the fall, certain parts of human bodies particularly escape control. Malebranche distinguishes, moreover, between sensual and intellectual shame, the latter being the plight of one whose dress does not sustain his rank, an impoverished nobleman in shabby clothes for instance. Concupiscence substituted force for reason so that men, 'quoique naturellement tous égaux' (xi.243), stratified themselves in classes. God and reason accept these classes for lack of a better order. Since Adam's sin abolished the law of reason, we need a written law to govern our society. The disorder he introduced into the world explains why the wicked enjoy this life, while the virtuous yearn for a better one. The loss of control over the animal spirits exposed the soul to the fury of demons. Even the beasts that prey on us respected Adam's innocence. Concupiscence plagues almost every aspect of human life.

In Malebranche's theology concupiscence differs but slightly from original

29. Or remove the fissures: 'Apres son péché, il perdit tout d'un coup le pouvoir qu'il avait sur son corps. De sorte que ne pouvant plus arrêter les mouvements, ni effacer les traces que les objets sensibles produisaient dans la partie principale de son cerveau [...] [etc.]' (v.95).

sin. He defines concupiscence as an effort and original sin as the success of this effort in children: 'La concupiscence n'est que l'effort naturel que les traces du cerveau font sur l'esprit pour l'attacher aux choses sensibles [...] le péché originel n'est autre chose [...] que ces efforts [...] comme maîtres de l'esprit et du cœur de l'enfant' (i.248). The reign or triumph of concupiscence, he adds, appears to be the same thing as original sin in children and actual sin in adults. He concedes that the Fathers who preceded Augustine do not discuss the transmission of original sin as such. They did not need to provide half-hearted Christians with believable explanations of the holy mysteries. 'Leur siècle n'était pas si incrédule, ni si malin que le nôtre' (iv.106). Comparing original sin with hereditary infirmity, Augustine cites parents with the gout who have children vulnerable to this disease and sick trees whose rotten seeds produce stunted saplings. Apparently impressed by these examples, Théodore (*Conversations*) reasons that, since souls do not reproduce, only bodies could transmit original sin. The body subjects the soul to an accumulation of sin inherited from ancestors whose numbers double with each successive generation.[30] Descartes's work persuaded Malebranche that a foetus receives both the inherited and the original thoughts of its mother by means of the physiological communication between their brains. Presumably animal spirits from the mother's brain open fissures similar to its own in the brain of the child in her womb. The fibres of the prenatal brain are so tender that it fissures deeply and hence permanently. These fissures are even deeper than those in the mother's brain. The child will never be able to eliminate them as he will eliminate some of the more shallow ones acquired from experience after birth. On the contrary, sensory experience will deepen them as it did in the case of Adam and Eve as well as that of the greatest saints. Each generation therefore reinforces its genetic inheritance and concupiscence along with the rest. Thus we inherit a fatal legacy: 'dès que nous sommes formés dans le ventre de nos mères, nous sommes [...] infectés de la corruption de nos parents' (i.247).

In support of his theory Malebranche argues that the bodies of the pregnant mother and her child are really one body with the same blood and the same animal spirits. Strong emotion in the pregnant mother occasions fissures in the foetus's brain that will in turn occasion the same emotion even more strongly under similar circumstances in the child after birth, even though he will be experiencing them for the first time. A man may faint at the sight of a snake because of fissures that opened in his brain before he was born when a snake frightened his mother. Mary Queen of Scots witnessed the murder of her Italian

30. 'L'homme ne peut échapper au péché parce qu'il ne peut se soustraire à son corps, et à tous les corps qui, dans l'histoire, ont abouti au sien.' Alquié, *Malebranche*, p.476.

secretary when she was pregnant with the future James I of England, who therefore had a phobia against naked swords. Although Malebranche joins Descartes in relegating animals to the status of machines, he accredits the belief that some young pointers 'arrêtent naturellement à cause seulement de l'instruction qu'ils ont reçue de leur mère qui a souvent chassé étant pleine' (iii.112). Eraste suspects that there may be a human exception to this rule of inheritance: How could pious women who love God give birth to wicked children? Théodore reminds him that love for God is spiritual and not sensual. If a pregnant woman who loves God thinks of him as a venerable old man, her child will love old men. Since concupiscence infects all children from the womb, they love sensible things instead of God, who wastes no pity on them before baptism.

Malebranche considers original sin a social as well as a genetic contagion. Society exposes people to strong emotions and those who share such an emotion have similar fissures in their brains. Thus the proliferation of vice reinforces concupiscence. In the *Conversations* Théodore identifies Aristarque as one of 'ces honnêtes gens du monde' (iv.108) who like material things too much and never consult their consciences. Vivacity and imagination convince and excite them, and they befriend each other hastily. '[Ils] ont un double péché originel, celui qu'ils ont reçu de leur mère [...] et celui qu'ils ont reçu par le commerce du monde' (iv.109).

But how does God, the ultimate cause, escape responsibility for the double sin of his creature? Malebranche gives this problem the attention it deserves. The condemnation of infants who die without baptism particularly challenges his ingenuity. Since they do not choose to sin, he observes, God punishes them less severely than those who abuse their liberty. Conceived in iniquity, they immediately fall to concupiscence. They therefore love sensible things instead of God who hates them.[31] Since they live in disorder, divine justice forbids the extension of Adam's original privilege to them, so that they cannot suppress concupiscence. Nor do guilty parents deserve innocent children. Eraste objects: 'n'est-ce pas Dieu qui met dans l'enfant ce que vous appelez désordre' (iv.101)? For God made the laws that assure the corruption of the entire human race. As Théodore explains elsewhere, however, these laws are just, because they conform to divine order and 'Dieu a fait l'homme libre' (iv.44). Man was free to resist temptation and he yielded to it, a fact. 'Maintenant tout est dans le désordre: mais c'est une suite du péché qui a tout corrompu par la nécessité même de l'ordre. Car l'ordre même veut le désordre pour punir le pécheur'

---

31. 'Un enfant qui vient au monde avec un amour habituel, naturel et nécessaire qui le dérègle et qui le dispose a préférer à Dieu les objets sensibles est fils de colère. Dieu le hait' (x.182).

(x.39). Although God foresaw that Adam would sin, he allowed him to do it. If he had inclined Adam's will to resist the temptation, Adam would have lost his freedom and resistance by him would have no merit. To save Adam from the consequence of his sin, God would have had to resort to a particular will like the one by which he had privileged his innocence to begin with. But God acts by general will unless divine order indicates otherwise: why should he stoop to a particular will for fear of losing a profane cult? 'Le rapport du fini à l'infini est nul' (ix.1099). If by virtue of his general laws a physical object had started to drop on Adam's head before the fall, God would have stopped it by a particular will. Divine justice would have required the protection of an innocent creature. God could have prevented Adam's sin too: 'Oui. Mais il ne le devait pas',[32] for doing nothing preserved his dignity. Divine order obliges him, moreover, to calculate the best result he can obtain by the simplest means according to general laws and he does not waste his efforts on ends unworthy of them. This economic necessity prevents him from creating a perfect world, hence the existence of evil and original sin. He would have preferred for Adam to remain innocent but, by letting him sin, he accepted the least possible evil commensurate with divine order and his grand design.

Malebranche predicates this design on the assumption that God derives more glory from a reformed creation than the original one: 'la réparation de son ouvrage doit l'honorer davantage que sa première construction' (iv.124). Other-wise, he argues, God would not have allowed Adam to spoil his work. The end justifies the means, as Gueroult notes.[33] Malebranche nonetheless defends a father's right to keep his switches ready for the punishment of a child likely to disobey him. Should not the father even show the child these switches to remind him of his duty? Adam has only himself to blame for the fall. Knowing that he would sin, God let him do it, so that the ensuing corruption of the entire race would necessitate a second Adam.

God used Adam's sin to accommodate the incarnation, but he could have achieved this purpose in a thousand other ways. He chose the simplest one that conformed with his general will. Although he could have annihilated Adam's soul, he continued to sustain it in preparation for Christ's advent. Rather than the death of the soul, therefore, Adam brought only the death of the body on his race. If he had not sinned, the Word might have become an angel, instead of a man, to unite with the creation. Yet the incarnation has an advantage over this method: 'En se faisant homme, [le Verbe] s'unit en même temps aux deux substances, esprit et corps, dont l'univers est composé et [...] sanctifie [ainsi]

32. To Leibniz, 14 Dec. 1711, xix.813.
33. 'Le bien devient la fin et le mal le moyen' (ii.109).

toute la nature' (xii.204-205). He becomes a man for the sake of God and not man. He only acts in God's interest and God, only in his own. God's deceptive reprieve of Adam's soul from oblivion 'engraisse la victime pour le sacrifice' (iv.42) of judgement day. Christ saves us in order to judge us and sacrifice us to God. He set the eternal fires of hell and saved the souls condemned to suffer there. Malebranche does not subscribe to the sentimental and benign figure of Christ in the usual tradition. He subordinates the relationship between the fall and the redemption to the one between the creation and the incarnation. As Théodore tells Eraste, 'le premier dessein de Dieu a été l'incarnation de son fils. C'est pour lui que nous sommes faits, quoiqu'il soit incarné pour nous. Nous sommes faits à son image; car il est homme dans le dessein de Dieu, avant qu'il y eût des hommes' (iv.120). The creation of the type precedes the incarnation of the prototype. God condescended to create this world so that, once it had proved unworthy of him, his Son might elevate it. He assigned Christ the mission of sanctifying his creatures' worship of him. The fall and redemption are merely steps in this direction.

Malebranche borrows the doctrine of satisfaction from Anselm, who calculated the degree to which Adam had offended God's honour by a feudal method. The greater the harm, the greater the offence, but also, the greater the inferiority of the offender to the offended, the greater the offence. The disproportion between the finite Adam and the infinite deity aggravated his crime so much that only God himself could atone for it. Since a person cannot atone for an offence against himself, however, the Son atoned for an offence against the Father. The union of the Son's human and divine natures excludes the Father and the Holy Spirit. The Son alone was born of Mary, suffered death and rose from the dead, 'non dans sa nature divine, mais dans son humanité sainte' (xii.136). Distinct therefore from the Father, the Son particularly qualified as a redeemer because he had served as God's agent in the creation and united with humanity in the incarnation: 'Une personne divine unie à la nature criminelle peut [...] satisfaire pour elle' (v.182). Although his human nature suffered finitely on the cross, his divine nature multiplied the value of his sacrifice by infinity. Men owe him a debt they cannot repay, so he has the right to do with them as he wishes. By his self-sacrifice, therefore, the Son achieved the honour and the power his Father had intended.

How Jesus's soul decided to sacrifice itself is the subject of a narrative in the *Deux lettres* against Arnauld published by Malebranche in 1687. As soon as God creates this soul, it discovers that the creation needs reform and sanctification. Seeing that divine justice requires satisfaction, it learns from the Word that God wants it to sacrifice itself. Not that divine law compels it to die for sinners: God does not punish the innocent for the sins of the guilty. It nonetheless perceives that Jewish sacrifice does not please God. Its self-sacrifice would honour God and sanctify men. Its death would be worthy of the divine attributes and appropriate for the corruption of the world by the contagion of sin. 'Elle s'offre donc volontairement et librement, non par instinct, mais par raison' (viii.839). That is, by an irresistible desire to obey God's law inspired by love for him. Thus Jesus's soul dies with the satisfaction of knowing that its will concurs entirely with divine law. We can only wonder how Malebranche obtained these intimate details.

The Christ in his *Méditations* reminds us that he sacrificed himself by submitting to a most cruel and infamous death. He cried out to his Father as one abandoned by him. They treated him 'comme un ver' (x.83), as an outcast, as an object of vulgar contempt and hatred. Covered with wounds, drained of blood and spirits, deeply humiliated, nailed to a wooden cross and exposed to the insults of an ungrateful populace, he was the model of a Christian. His followers will deserve eternal bliss only after suffering all the evils of this life patiently like him. Malebranche cites another example of his patience in the *Recherche*. Slapped by an officer of the high priest in Jerusalem, he did not lose his temper or take the revenge available to him as the Son of God. Instead he forgave his offender, unlike Cato, the target of Malebranche's polemic here.

Malebranche assures us that nature and the Bible are full of figures referring to Christ, his humiliation and his exaltation. Ariste draws a parallel between Christ and worms, which crawl on the ground and live a sad and humiliating life. 'Mais ils se font un tombeau d'ou ils sortent glorieux' (xii.272). Thus the Creator figures the life, death and resurrection of his Son and all Christians as well. While Théodore accepts this parallel, he worries about exposing Christ to the ridicule of comparing the great with the small. Ariste is thinking of silk worms in particular, for he raised them when he was a child. He enjoyed watching them make cocoons and bury themselves alive 'pour ressusciter quelque temps après' (xii.258). Although Malebranche takes such evidence more seriously than Théodore cares to admit, he does not rely on it for proof of miracles like the resurrection.

Founding Christianity on right reason, Théodore affirms that Jesus irrefutably established the authenticity of his mission and his qualities. 'Sa résurrection glorieuse est tellement attestée qu'il faut renoncer au sens commun pour la revoquer en doute' (xii.336-37). Though sceptical of latter-day miracles, Malebranche accredits those reported by the New Testament as historical facts. He recommends the mediation of the second person between the two natures, the finite human and the infinite divine. Mediation enables the incarnate Son to distribute sensual grace as the occasionalist agent of the Father. The source of all grace, the Father has made him the sole distributor of grace. The Father, in fact, does not want us to reach or please him without mediation by the Son. He wants us, in other words, to depend on Christ entirely for salvation. Divine nepotism. Malebranche carries this doctrine to the extreme of admitting our right to reproduce only on the condition of mediation by the Son: 'Sans [...] notre médiateur, ce serait un crime épouvantable de communiquer à une femme cette misérable fécondité, d'engendrer un ennemi de Dieu, de damner une âme pour jamais, de travailler à la gloire de Satan et à l'établissement de la Babylone infernale' (xi.230). Michel Adam who edited the *Traité de morale*, the source of this outburst, notes that, five years before the publication of the work, Rome had condemned marriages motivated by sensual desire.[34] Perhaps this decision encouraged Malebranche to exaggerate the traditional intrusion of the celibate priesthood in family life.

His occasionalist mediator completes the general will of the Father by acts of particular will. He does not reproduce this general will, Gouhier remarks, but rather spares God the necessity for resorting to a particular will.[35] Though free to act as he wishes, he applies divine law to particular cases. Might one then describe his freedom as particular and not general? Perhaps we should interpret the following statement in this way: 'Son âme sainte forme ses désirs *d'elle-même* [...] quoiqu'elle soit determinée par la lumière du Verbe' (viii.826). Malebranche uses the limitations of this soul to explain the irregular distribution of sensual grace. In the *Méditations* the author asks Christ why he does not apportion grace to each of us according to need. Does he not know our weaknesses and the use we will make of any grace we receive? He died for us all and yet he does not save us all. Why does he allow so many nations to embrace perdition? Why does he give some of the righteous a grace they do not need? Christ replies that, as a man and occasionalist cause of grace, he does not necessarily have actual knowledge of future will. Only God can inspect hearts and ascertain the necessary and contingent inclinations of the future. The finite capacity of Christ's human soul could not hold the infinite amount of information potentially available to it through the Word. While hypostatically joined with the Word, this soul does not emanate from the Word. It would be completely ignorant of the future, if God did not reveal future events to it on request, and it should not abuse this privilege. It should restrict its curiosity to information useful for its mission. Other works give additional reasons. Since the human nature of Christ is not divine, it should not pretend to be. Neither can the distributor of grace inspect hearts nor can the inspector of hearts distribute grace without self-conflict. Generosity and justice are incompatible.

34. See xi.295, n.71.
35. See Henri Gouhier, *La Philosophie de Malebranche et son expérience religieuse* (Paris 1926), p.138.

If the omniscience of the efficient cause determined the occasionalist cause, the latter would lose its liberty and hence its merit. This argumentation accounts for the injustice of predestination without refuting it.

Malebranche illustrates the distinction between Jesus's actual and potential knowledge by his ignorance of the time when last judgement (the kingdom of heaven) would occur. Asked by the disciples, he replied that only the Father knew and not the Son.[36] But Malebranche insists that Jesus could have known if he had wanted to. Perhaps he did not want to at the moment, because telling the disciples would have been inappropriate. While his soul cannot accommodate an actual knowledge of all things, it can avoid, by charity, propriety or economy (convenience), an actual knowledge of things it prefers not to know. Why did Jesus not tell the disciples his motive for withholding the information? Malebranche is implying that he deceived them. In the *Méditations*, on the other hand, the risen Christ does not deny that he knows how the will of God creates and conserves all other beings. Instead he refuses to reveal this mystery to the author: 'Lorsque tu m'as interrogé sur la conduite de Dieu, ne t'ai-je pas répondu à proportion que je te trouvais capable de si grandes vérités' (x.96). Otherwise the author should be content with the wisdom available to his soul from universal reason. The Word illuminates, penetrates and perfects our souls, but they are not hypostatically united with him like Christ's soul. His union with the Word gives him unlimited access to the infinite knowledge of God. He has a right to know all ideas, essences and means; all past, present and future events and the infinitely infinite relations between all things. Although his soul, like ours, does not have an infinite capacity he has the power to suspend his judgement, so that he may choose his knowledge wisely. His soul is therefore superior to ours by its unlimited potential knowledge and its selection of actual knowledge.

In the *Méditations* his person does not always say which of his natures is speaking and, even when it does, some of the ambiguity remains.[37] 'Je suis consubstantiel à mon père' (x.221), declares the divine nature in article XIII of meditation XIX for instance. 'J'aime ma propre raison, le Verbe éternel dans lequel je subsiste' (x.223), professes the human nature in article XV of the same meditation. Malebranche deserves praise for giving Christ a voice in his dialogue, but the difficulty of uniting the two natures in one persona would daunt even

36. Mark xiii.32; Matthew xxiv.36.

37. 'La distinction entre "Verbe éternel" et "Verbe incarné" devient le moteur unique des pensées de Malebranche relatives aux mystères. Architecte de la création, le Verbe éternel n'est pas seulement le réceptacle des mondes possibles et des voies, mais aussi le véritable motif de l'acte transcendant. Quant au Verbe incarné, il gouverne le règne de la grâce, sans que cette spécialisation soit plus remarquable que celle par laquelle le Verbe éternel gouverne et motive la création.' Robinet, *Système*, p.126.

more skilful writers. While his philosophy accommodates the role in which he casts him, his theology obstructs it. He tries to avoid another problem by a modest estimate of his ability to reproduce Christ's thought accurately: 'Si le Verbe, auquel je suis uni comme le reste des intelligences, me parle clairement dans le plus secret de ma raison, j'ai un corps insolent et rebelle que je ne puis faire taire, et qui parle souvent plus haut que Dieu même' (x.7). He invites his readers to attribute the errors in the *Méditations* to him and the truth to the Word. He is fortifying them against his opponents who may dispute the testimony he assigns to Christ or even his right to assign it. This tactic did not deter his critics, however. Jurieu imagines the surprise of Scholastics who discover that 'le Verbe est devenu cartésien sur ses vieux jours'.[38] If we make a philosophy teacher of him and put our own words in his mouth, he may seem like a fool or liar. The Huguenot minister would limit his testimony to his New Testament sayings. Arnauld also objects to Malebranche's use of Christ as a spokesman, a device he finds wrong and ridiculous. Malebranche exploits their common respect for Augustine in his reply. Divine wisdom, in Augustine's opinion, communicates with human mediators in the secret of their reason. Thus Malebranche feels obliged to acknowledge the divine source of what ungrateful men pretend to draw from their own souls. In reality God gives them their ideas according to the general laws governing the union of the soul with universal reason. Among them are the ancient philosophers, whom the Word of the *Méditations*, acting as a divine judge, treated harshly. He exposed them, he says, to shameful passions that drove them to disorder and he let them perish (sentenced them to hell?). They deserved this fate for abusing his generosity, using him to further their ambitions and bathing in his light to dazzle other men. Thus the traditional Christian rivalry with pagan philosophy impassions even Malebranche.

Since reason, in his anthropology, could no longer save men after the fall, it appealed to them through the senses by the incarnation. 'Le Fils de Dieu [...] s'est rendu sensible pour se faire connaître aux hommes charnels et grossiers. Il les a voulu instruire par ce qui les aveuglait' (ii.175). Consequently the most fervent believers are not always the most intelligent men. While Christ's human nature teaches us through sensation, his divine nature, which has lost none of its power in the incarnation, continues to enlighten our understanding.[39] During the four thousand years before the incarnation, however, reason did not influence men very much, for they rarely bothered to consult their consciences. Thus Christ adapted his gospel to their stupidity: 'Il a rendu la vérité sensible par ses

38. Pierre Jurieu, *L'Esprit de M. Arnauld* (1684), i.78-79.
39. In the *Méditations* he says, 'Je ne parle aux hommes qu'en deux manières, ou bien je parle à leur esprit immédiatement et par moi-même, ou bien je parle à leur esprit par leurs sens' (x.27).

paroles, l'ordre aimable par ses exemples, la lumière visible par un corps qui l'accommode à notre faiblesse' (iii.147). Men are so thoughtless, even in matters of vital concern to them, that they rarely take his message seriously. Yet Christ's intention remains to bring them to reason by means of faith. His human nature guides them towards a possible reunion with his divine nature, a reunion that will surpass their present connection with it.

The human Christ has three titles: mediator between God and man, head of the mystic church and architect of the temple in Ephesians ii.20-22: 'You are part of a building that has the apostles and the prophets for its foundations and Christ Jesus himself for its main cornerstone [...] one holy temple [...] where God lives.' Malebranche transfigures him from cornerstone to architect, conflates the temple with Augustine's mystic body of true believers and stresses the distinction between this architect and the head of the mystic body. The members of the body are the stones in the temple which houses the church: 'nous en serons les pierres vivantes, élues avant la création du monde en Jésus-Christ, prédestiné avant tous' (xvi.129). The architect describes his project in the *Méditations*. When he walked the earth, he had already made the plan he is following in heaven now. He prepared his disciples for their mission by word and example, then gave them their orders after the resurrection. Ascending to heaven, he became the high priest in the order of Melchizedek and sat at the Father's right hand. After sending the Holy Spirit, he began to distribute grace to the souls he had chosen for his heavenly church. When all the nations of the earth had yielded to his authority, he encouraged the apostles, by his revelations and miracles, to evangelise the Gentiles. He intervened in person to convert a zealous defender of the synagogue (Paul) into an apostle. Thus the work proceeds. As Rodis-Lewis remarks, 'le principe ordonnateur demeure: les hommes pour Jésus-Christ et non l'inverse' (*Nicolas Malebranche*, p.294). The architect's plan fits neatly into the grand design of God, since the sanctification of his creatures' cult enhances his glory. Could he achieve this purpose without the incarnation? No, because there would be no irrefutable proof of his Son's divinity.

To the relations between the persons in the Trinity, the relation between the Word and the human soul bears a distinct resemblance, diminished by the fall. The Father engenders the Son by consulting his own wisdom and creates a soul by willing the existence of his Word's essence.[40] God loves himself, so the Son as well as the Father loves the divine substance, which the Father

40. 'Comme Dieu est à lui-même sa lumière, la perception nécessaire qu'il a de sa propre substance est la génération de son Verbe; et la perception nécessaire de cette même substance, en tant que diversement et imparfaitement imitable par toutes les créatures possibles, est l'idée ou le modèle éternel de ces mêmes créatures' (ix.968).

communicates to the Son in its entirety. The Holy Spirit, who also shares the entire substance, proceeds from this love.[41] As the Christ of the *Méditations* tells the author, 'chaque personne divine t'a imprimé son propre caractère' (xi.151). The Father sustains him by his power, the Son enlightens him by his intelligence and the Spirit inspires him by his love. Though equal in dignity, each person has the right to delegate the next by virtue of his priority in the process of generation. Thus the Father sends the Son to us, and the Son, the Spirit. God's ultimate motive in all that he does is glory, but a person can neither honour himself nor give satisfaction for an offence against his own honour. Exclusive of the Father and the Spirit, the union of the Son with human nature enables him to honour the divine substance by sanctifying the creation and to atone for the infinite offence of a finite creature (Adam) by sacrificing this nature. The necessity for honouring and satisfying God confirms, in Malebranche's opinion, the plurality of divine persons stipulated by dogma.

Thus reason, which comes from God, justifies belief in a mystery it cannot explain. Indeed this very mystery provides reason with a further argument in support of its own authenticity. How could a truth 'aussi opposée à la raison humaine' have spread all over the world and triumphed everywhere the apostles preached unless they knew of it? 'Un peu de bon sens' (xii.334) would persuade us that they learned it from Jesus himself. Besides, the more it shocks human reason, the less it could have convinced so many people in so many distant lands by natural means. The miracle of widespread belief in such a mystery proves its divine origin. In the *Recherche*, however, Malebranche doubts that one can persuade men disinclined to believe it. He even admits that the arguments advanced for this purpose will convince only those who are ready to accept the Trinity without examination. Later attempts by him to accredit the dogma do not necessarily show that he changed his mind.

He embraced the traditional doctrine that Christ, by his crucifixion, initiated a continuing process of sacrifice. As victim and priest, Christ eternally offers himself and all the members of his mystic body. At the right hand of the Father, he does openly what he does under the cover of sensory appearances by the ministry of a priest standing before the altar. In the *Méditations* he describes the eucharist as an extraordinary source of grace and hence a sacrament superior to the others which merely transmit grace. Whether we realise it or not, we commune on reason constantly by his presence in our souls and abundantly by our presence at his table.[42] Distracted by our senses, however, we are seldom aware of his presence, so he instituted the sacrament of his body and blood to

---

41. Or from the divine will, as Malebranche sometimes says.

42. 'La substance spirituelle de ton être ne peut se nourrir que de la substance intelligible de la raison' (x.190).

nourish our souls by means of our bodies: 'Je me suis servi de la foi qui parle à l'esprit par les sens' (x.192). While we break bread into pieces for the nourishment of our bodies, he offers himself in his entirety to every soul. The better we digest him, the more reasonable we are. Communion not only unites us with him, but also with God and all other Christians. Adam did not need the eucharist before the fall, because he ate the fruit of immortality in paradise. Nor did this fruit have the sensual allure that spoils our appetite for spiritual food. The Hebrews who ate manna in the desert are dead, but Christians who partake of Christ's living substance will have eternal life. At the heavenly table they will eat the same sacrificial victim and sacramental substance as God himself. The sacrament is 'un gage qu'un jour notre foi se changera en intelligence' (x.45). Yet only the pure of heart should commune often (an allusion to the quarrel over frequent communion). Those who are sick with sin will run the risk of death if they commune too often. They should purge their conscience by penitence before approaching the altar. The eucharist will poison those who have a corrupt heart.

The *Recherche* censures 'les rois et même les reines d'Angleterre' (i.334) for banning the worship of Christ in the eucharist. They require communicants to kneel, according to the ancient tradition, as if they were worshipping the eucharist. Such contradictions result from political intrusion in the affairs of the Church. Does the eucharist, on the other hand, contain the body and blood of Christ or merely the figure of his body and blood, as Calvin maintains? Théodore undertakes to settle this score in the *Entretiens*. Everyone agrees, he submits, that the apostles knew the answer. They taught what we must believe in all of the churches they founded. The councils decided such issues by hearing testimony from thousands of witnesses, who reported the faith of the many countries they represented. The bishops, in particular, knew whether their diocesans professed the presence of Christ's body and blood in the eucharist. Asked for their opinion, they declared their belief in the conversion of the bread into Christ's body and of the wine into his blood. They also proclaimed an anathema against those who disagreed. The bishops who did not attend the council either approved its decision or implied their approval by their silence. Otherwise they would have objected, 'car les Grecs n'épargn[aient] pas trop les Latins' (xii.328). This naive echo of an ancient resentment exposes Malebranche's ignorance of how the real presence evolved. Neither councils nor disputes between the East and the West had much to do with it. The idealistic apology of the way councils solved dogmatic problems omits the sordid politics of the ancient and medieval Church.

Even if Christ had abandoned his Church, Théodore continues, 'il faut avoir renoncé au sens commun pour préférer l'opinion de Calvin ou de Zwingle à celle de tous ces témoins qui attestent un fait qu'il n'est pas possible qu'ils ignorent' (xii.328). Here we encounter the apologetic technique of establishing historical 'facts' by the alleged testimony of innumerable unidentified witnesses. Assuming that they explicitly knew the letter of the current dogma, the apologist overcomes scant documentation by an elaborate argumentation. Malebranche makes matters worse by treating the real presence as if it had been enacted by the ancient and not the medieval Church. He rejects as practically impossible the hypothesis that all the churches founded by the apostles agreed on an error. He rejects as absolutely impossible the further hypothesis that they agreed on the error of which the Calvinists accuse the Catholics. For the Church decided that a man's body is in an infinite number of places at the same time, that it occupies the same space as a communion wafer and that, when the celebrant recites the consecration, the bread of the eucharist becomes the body of Christ, and the wine, his blood. Could the bishops have imagined a more extravagant doctrine? Would they have dared to proclaim it? Only a madman would consent. If Christ had abandoned his Church, the ancient Christians would, on the contrary, have committed Calvin's error, 'parce qu'effectivement cette erreur ne choque ni la raison ni les sens' (xii.329). Only the successors of the apostles can tell us what Jesus meant when he said, 'This is my body.' The Calvinists would have us believe that the early Christians understood them figuratively and not literally. Did Calvin know the tradition better than the ancient bishops? No ancient authors warn against the literal interpretation of Jesus's saying. None object to the natural meaning of the words despite the incredible implications.

Théodore concedes the figurative interpretation of a few Fathers, but only with regard to the sacrificial parallel between the mass and the cross. They accept the figurative meaning without denying the literal one. They even fear that the real presence will jeopardise our faith. They therefore reassure us by invoking Jesus's authority and God's power. Typically Malebranche makes no attempt to document these wishful assumptions. All of them founder on the evidence that the eucharist was not much of an issue before the tenth century and received little attention from theologians before the second half of the fourth. Ancient Christians were satisfied with a vague understanding of Christ's eucharistic presence, so vague in fact that Protestants and Catholics have always quoted from them in contradicting each other. Oblivious of such considerations, however, Théodore presses his attack on the absent Calvinists: '[Plus] la décision du concile [de Trente] paraît choquer la raison et le bon sens, plus [...] elle est conforme a la vérité' (xii.330). No idea frightens the imagination like the presence of Christ's body in heaven and on the altar at the same time. Yet all the Christian churches founded by the apostles endorsed this mystery. The best of all witnesses, the bishops themselves attest this fact. Thus a superior and infallible authority guaranteed by Christ himself certifies it.

Despite Théodore's peremptory tone, this attack on the Calvinists seems academic in comparison to an earlier polemic with the Jesuit Louis Le Valois. A few subtle paragraphs in the *Recherche* that support the Cartesian theory of transubstantiation gave the Scholastic Le Valois a pretext to accuse a Cartesian philosopher and theologian of Calvinism. The other Cartesians defending the theory had no reputation for theology, so the Jesuit could not easily hold them responsible for the latent heresy he saw in it. Under the pseudonym of de La Ville he ignored Malebranche's later deviation from Cartesianism in his *Sentiments de M. Descartes […] conformes aux erreurs de Calvin sur le sujet de l'eucharistie* (1680). It is ironical that the *Recherche* censures the Calvinist criticism of transubstantiation explicitly and defends the Cartesian theory implicitly. In the authr's opinion, the Calvinist objection to the simultaneous presence of Christ's body on the altar and in heaven convicts these heretics of presuming to know the limits of God's power. Although the analysis of sacred mysteries should not go too far, the study of matter would help us to understand transubstantiation without threatening dogma. The Fathers, who regarded this mystery as incomprehensible, were content to advance vague analogies that indoctrinate us more than they instruct us. Tradition therefore favours believers who submit to faith and refrain from curiosity. We should not expect philosophers to explain how Jesus's body comes to be present in the eucharist. Obscure explanations would compromise their philosophy, and clear explanations, their theology. New theories of transubstantiation would only provoke controversy. While these insinuations could scarcely have pleased enemies of the Cartesian theory, they by no means challenge them to reply.

In the *Sentiments*, however, Le Valois slandered Malebranche in a way he dared not ignore. As a priest the Oratorian had to defend his othodoxy, so he answered the Jesuit by pamphlets, anonymously at first and then openly. His basic defence was to expose the hypocrisy of attacking a rival philosophy on theological grounds in hopes of persuading the Church to condemn it. The *Sentiments* refer to a Strasbourg edition of the decrees enacted by the Council of Trent denying that the essence of Jesus's body is extension and that it retains its extension in the eucharist. On the contrary, La Ville argues, the parts of his body collapse into each other and form a geometrical or unextended point, yet the real existence of the body subsists. This is the Scholastic explanation of transubstantiation and it prevailed when the Council met. Faithful to conciliar tradition, however, the bishops avoided such philosophical considerations in their decrees for fear of committing the Church to a trend. Nor does the Scholastic explanation appear in the more reputable editions of these decrees, as Malebranche points out. The language of the decree on transubstantiation, he observes, does not exclude Descartes's theory, which the Church had never formally condemned. Despite their hostility to transubstantiation, the Calvinists tend to prefer Cartesianism to Scholasticism, hence the opportunity of Descartes's theory.

La Ville insists that transubstantiation reduces Jesus's body to a geometrical rather than a physical point, as the Cartesians affirm. Such a reduction would not only eliminate biological organisation, but also imply an immaterial body and hence a figurative presence. Might the Cartesians not retort the accusation of Calvinism against La Ville? If they made a heresy of a philosophical opinion by inferring unintended consequences from it, they would be treating him as unfairly as he treats them. Malebranche defies him to find a Church Father who states that a man's body can be reduced to a geometrical point without losing its organisation. Five objections to the Cartesian transubstantiation, which he has borrowed from the Strasbourg edition,[43] appear nowhere in Bossuet's *Exposition de la doctrine catholique* (1671) approved by the pope. Malebranche contradicts La Ville's denial that Augustine considered extension the essence (actually an essential property) of matter.[44] He ridicules the Scholastic rebuke of Luther's protest that transubstantiation implies the eventual destruction of the entire creation. In the Scholastic context it would indeed. Only Scholastics would dare pretend that the world would survive the total loss of extension. 'La raison et la tradition sont donc pour [les] cartésiens' (xvii.1.489). The Scholastics themselves are betraying Catholicism to the Calvinists.

Both reason and experience convince the Cartesians that the reduction of Christ's body to an imperceptible physical point leaves its inner extension, the organisation of its parts, intact.[45] Reason, because it confirms the infinite divisibility of matter, and experience, because microscopes reveal organised

---

43. '(1) [...] Le corps de Jésus-Christ dans l'eucharistie perd beaucoup de son étendue sans rien perdre de sa substance. (2) [...] Les parties du corps de Jésus-Christ sont toutes pénétrées les unes dans les autres sous les espèces du pain et du vin. (3) [...] Le corps de Jésus-Christ est sans étendue dans le saint Sacrement de l'autel et [...] par conséquent l'essence du corps ne consiste pas de l'étendue. (4) [...] [Les] Pères du Concile [...] conçoivent le corps de Jésus-Christ dans l'eucharistie, sans y concevoir l'étendue propre du corps de Jésus-Christ, et par conséquent l'idée du corps selon [eux] n'est pas la même que l'idée de son étendue. (5) [...] Le corps de Jésus-Christ qu'ils conçoivent sans son étendue dans l'eucharistie est un véritable corps: et ainsi [...] quand ils le conçoivent de la sorte, ils conçoivent quelque chose de réel' (xvii.1.487).

44. 'Malebranche rappelait que saint Augustin avait toujours considéré l'étendue comme une propriété essentielle de la matière' (Gouhier, p.178).

45. Does this point contain a tiny replica of Christ's entire body or one of his 'essential' body which Malebranche identifies as the part of the brain where the soul resides? The latter may also be much smaller than a grain of sand. According to Trent Christ's body is not naturally present in the eucharist. Reproduced under the appearances of bread, the part of the brain housing the soul would include his divinity, his soul and his body as it was born of the virgin and ascended to heaven. How the essence of a body can be the entire body remains to be seen! Malebranche seems to have preferred the less contradictory alternative.

bodies a thousand times smaller than a grain of sand. Neither the scale nor the material determines the nature of a body, but rather the organisation. Transubstantiation reorganises bread and wine into flesh and blood. Once a priest has consecrated the bread and wine, the same body of Christ is present as the one in heaven and the one he had in the cradle. The identity of a body depends on God's will that it exist. It will exist continuously or in as many places and at as many times as he wills. However numerous these places and times may be, it will have only one essence and, if it is a human body, only one soul. In transubstantiation God wills the existence of God's divinity, soul and body in every crumb of bread and every drop of wine consecrated by a priest. Yet this divinity, soul and body keep their unity and identity. After exposing this theory in the 'Démonstration de la possibilité de la présence réelle' (1680-1681), Malebranche concludes, 'c'est la raison seule qui nous a conduits' (xvii.1.504).

Identifying reason with the Catholic Christ entitles him to this conclusion as well as the others he draws concerning the eucharist, original sin, the Trinity and Christology. Emasculated by this conflation, reason can no more question Catholic dogma than the Catholic Christ himself. Merging the natural light with the Son of God therefore liquidates the embarrassing traditional conflict between reason and faith. No one has founded a more coherent philosophical and theological system on the natural light than Malebranche.[46] A remarkable achievement despite its flaws, the theory of intelligible extension attempts to explain just how God shares his intelligence with his creatures. The bond of religion and reason might have made a decisive impact on a Christianity beleaguered by rational doubt, if devoted followers of Malebranche had success-fully popularised his elegant, subtle and complex thought. Unfortunately for him and Christianity, his most influential 'disciples' were the atheist Meslier and eventually the theist Voltaire.[47] Why did no enlightened and courageous Catholics defend his memory and teach his metaphysics? The Church sorely needed renovation, reform, rebirth in the age of reason. Why did no saint rise to the occasion and the opportunity? Critics cite the inertia of a massive institution, the conservative fear of change, a fondness for prerogative and a habit of corruption. Certainly none of this would have favoured a Malebranchist renewal. To this general reason, however, might one not add a particular one?

46. 'Il insiste en effet sur l'identité du Verbe éternel, raison universelle qui éclaire tous les esprits, et de Jésus-Christ, verbe incarné et chef de l'Eglise. Puisque c'est une même sagesse qui nous parle dans l'évidence rationnelle et dans la révélation de l'Ecriture, il y a une sorte d'homogénéité entre les vérités de la science et celles de la révélation. L'intelligence peut ainsi pénétrer la foi, et la remplacera un jour.' Alquié, *Malebranche*, p.17.

47. See Jean Meslier, *Mémoires des pensées et des sentiments de Jean Meslier* (posthumous) and Voltaire, *Tout en dieu* (1769).

Malebranche met with fierce Catholic and Protestant opposition, not all of which stemmed from the usual rivalry and hostility. His writings convinced most of his opponents that his metaphysics really threatened Christianity. Why was this? Compromise requires sacrifice and his conflation of reason and faith sacrifices more than most of his Christian contemporaries could accept. In his thought Christ's human nature tends to abstraction at the expense of the gospel Jesus whom he neglects. Yet the power of Christianity has always radiated from this Jesus, who has little in common with reason, Malebranchist or otherwise. This deficiency aggravates the flaws in his system which, when subject to critical analysis, demonstrates how reason can try and fail to solve the great problems of Christianity and Catholicism. Despite his powers and efforts, he hardly convinces the modern reader that reason must accept the two natures and the Trinity, acquit God of Adam's sin and convict all of Adam's ancestors, approve the multipresence of Christ's one whole body and its intact existence in a microscopic point. He even tries to prove transubstantiation by its very defiance of reason, a manoeuvre reminiscent of Pascal, but scarcely convincing in Malebranche's context. Little wonder that he persuaded too few of his contemporaries to exploit the potential of his metaphysics. The failure of so resourceful a thinker to accredit the Christian and Catholic mysteries by rational demonstration can only raise the question of whether such accreditation is possible.

# Leibniz

MALEBRANCHE'S correspondent and opponent Wilhelm Gottfried Leibniz was a philosopher and lay theologian from Leipzig. He cultivated a scholarly public by his letters and by his articles in Bayle's *Nouvelles de la République des lettres* as well as the *Acta eruditorum* which he had helped to found. After decisive years in Paris (1672-1676), he accepted the Duke of Brunswick's patronage and resided in Hanover until his death in 1716, except for a voyage to Southern Germany, Italy and Austria (1687-1690). His curiosity resulted in enormous learning, and his imagination in many discoveries despite his respect for tradition. Competent in fields as diverse as jurisprudence and mining, he gave much of his attention to philosophical proselytism and religious syncretism. Malebranche adopted his differential calculus but not his philosophy, which Arnauld and Bayle subjected to Cartesian criticism, while Locke refused to correspond with him. Disappointed, Leibniz resorted to an imaginary dialogue with the Englishman in the *Nouveaux Essais sur l'entendement humain* (1765), which follow the same order as Locke's *Essay concerning human understanding* (1690). Although Newton's disciple Samuel Clarke was a willing correspondent, on the other hand, he would not abandon Newton for Leibniz. Since Descartes had died before Leibniz could write to him, the great correspondent settled for De Volder, who contested his deviations from the new orthodoxy. Another correspondent, the Jesuit Des Bosses, kept distorting Leibniz's philosophy by his attempts to adapt it to the Scholasticism of his order. These critics nonetheless obliged him to develop it more thoroughly than he might have if he had only listened to his numerous admirers. The worst of these, Wolff did lasting damage to his posthumous reputation by a systematic but unwitting caricature of his philosophy.

Leibniz wrote many letters in an attempt to reunite the Catholic, Lutheran, Anglican and Calvinist churches. This project inspired his correspondence with Bossuet in particular. The destruction caused by the religious wars, especially in Germany, the persecution of the Huguenots and the threat of continuing conflict dramatised the need for ecumenical reunification. Dedicated to this cause, Leibniz sought avenues of reconciliation in discussions between willing Lutherans and representatives of other churches, but in vain. The divisions in Christianity served the interests of religious and political authorities too well for so generous a design, with a few exceptions like Duke Johann Friedrich who had brought Leibniz to Hanover. Yet Leibniz's knowledge of theology and his ability to reconcile conflicts in doctrine established his superiority as a mediator in such negotiations, a superiority enhanced by his peculiar faith. A Lutheran by education, he refrained from practising this religion and, for a while, Catholicised the doctrine to the limits of its possibilities. His attitude exposed him to attempts by Catholics to convert him and accusations of indifference by Protestants, but neither of these understood his ecumenical vocation. The *Théodicée* (1710), the only book he published, defends the Christian God from insinuations of responsibility for evil by Bayle. In addition to his books, articles and letters, the enormous quantity of papers he left complicates study of his philosophy and religion. Despite the persistent labour of devoted scholars, publication of his works remains partial and fragmentary.

Still, they have revealed a more coherent Leibniz than once assumed. His gift for ratiocination apparently inspired his belief in a rational God imposing the order of the divine mind on the creation. 'It sanctifies philosophy,' he tells us, 'to make its streams arise from the fount of God's attributes'.[1] In fact his ontology derives from his logic so directly that Gurwitsch calls it 'Panlogismus',[2] a simplification. Yet an understanding of his system depends on logical principles he stresses himself. He defines truth as possible existence. One may prove contingent truth by the experience of actual existence, and necessary truth by the implication of a contradiction in the converse of the proposition. Analysis reduces necessary truths to an explicit identity, and contingent truths to an implicit identity, for further analysis in this case results in an infinite regression. Thus the subject of every true proposition contains all possible predicates. And there has to be a reason why the proposition is true, one that sufficiently explains it, 'a sufficient reason'. The predicate-in-subject principle and the law of sufficient reason prove far more useful to Leibniz than one might expect. His confidence in logic encouraged him to use and recommend syllogisms at a time when the limitations of this device were evident. Tempted like Descartes by the illusory promise of mathematics, he dreamed of a 'universal characteristic', an algebra of ideas. In pursuing this project, he sought to reduce ideas to their common denominators, substitute symbols for these and arrange them in an order susceptible to calculation. Needless to say, he never completed the project.[3]

His God, who preferred a creation to nothingness, made the world by a reflexive act of the divine mind. Not just any world, but the best one possible

1. Leroy Loemker, trans., *Philosophical papers and letters* (Dordrecht 1970), p.353.
2. Aron Gurwitsch, *Philosophie des Panlogismus* (Berlin 1974), p.3. 'Gemäß dem Prinzip der logico-ontologischen Äquivalenz, läßt sich jede logische Struktur ins Ontologische und umgekehrt jede ontologische ins Logische übersetzen' (Gurwitsch, p.3-4).
3. It may seem more feasible today.

short of the perfection reserved to him. His aesthetics required a full and contiguous creation with no vacuum in matter and no gaps in the chain of being. Nor did his creativity permit the identity of any two things, hence the absolute diversity of this world. In keeping with his ethics, he coordinated all the parts to achieve a harmony of the whole. Leibniz identifies the basic components of the creation as substances: 'The ideas of God are the substances [...] of things' (Loemker, p.118). He rebukes Locke for his irony over the existence of substances and Descartes for his definition of material substance as extension. All substances, in his opinion, consist of force or, as we would say, energy, for energy depends on a sustaining power. 'A being which subsists in itself has a principle of action within it' (Loemker, p.115). As a subject each substance contains all of its past, present and future predicates. Every substance is a self-developing programme that results in a continuous series of states, each of which evolves from the previous one. Though autonomous, they limit each other by the exclusive degree of perfection each attains. When some approach perfection, others retrograde equivalently, but relations between them are purely circumstantial and phenomenal. Despite the independence of each, all emanate from God and all participate in his pre-established harmony. Each is intelligible only in terms of the whole system. This theory of substance has the merit, as Leibniz saw it, of eliminating the Cartesian dichotomy between matter and spirit.

Once he had adopted the theory, he made more refinements than changes. The decision to call substances monads, which came late in his career, was a refinement rather than a change. He defines monads as ultimately simple, indivisible, immaterial existences occupying no position in space. Each consists of active and passive energy that oppose each other. The ratio between them varies within a monad and from monad to monad. The higher the monad on the monadic scale, the greater the ratio of active to passive energy and vice versa. Thus the energy of the divine source at the top is wholly active. 'Les autres substances dépendent de Dieu comme les pensées émanent de notre substance.'[4] Only in this case does Leibniz admit a continuous creation, for he rejects occasionalism. His God has created every monad so that it will operate independently of him and all other monads unless and until he destroys it. He coordinated them once and for all when he made them, hence a universal and eternal harmony (pre-established harmony). Each monad is an absolute unity 'perceiving' or representing an infinite plurality, the metaphorical centre of a circle serving as the focus of innumerable radii. Each constantly represents the

4. C. I. Gerhardt (ed.), *Die philosophischen Schriften von Gottfried Wilhelm Leibniz* (Berlin 1875-1890), iv.457.

contents of all the other monads and the divinity, but each from its own viewpoint.[5] He describes them as separate and abbreviated worlds. Within a monad, each representation derives from the previous one and generates the next one in a process which he calls appetition. The ratio between positive and negative energy in a monad determines the relative proportion of distinctness to confusion in its representations. Its viewpoint, which distinguishes it from other monads, depends on this relation. Distinctness increases, for instance, as positive energy increases and negative energy decreases. Unlimited by any viewpoint, God perceives the entire creation by a perfectly distinct intuition. Through him alone do monads have any communication with each other, because appetition is the unique source of representation in them.

The phenomena simultaneously represented by all of them constitute the material world, which has no greater reality than this collective representation. Loath to abandon empirical reality, however, Leibniz regards these phenomena as 'well-founded', unlike illusions, dreams and hallucinations. Every monad perceives them from its own viewpoint depending on the peculiar mixture of distinctness and confusion in its representation. Although monads occupy no position in space, the ratios of active to passive energy in them determine the geometrical relations between the phenomena they represent. In his correspondence with Clarke, Leibniz denies the absolute existence of space and time defended by Newton. According to Leibniz, space consists in the relations between coexisting phenomena, and time, in the relations between successive phenomena. Thus space and time are well-founded phenomena; likewise the qualities of physical objects. Leibniz designates confusion or negative energy in monads as 'primary matter', which corresponds to 'secondary' or ordinary matter in the world of appearances. He attributes physical qualities such as extension, solidity and inertia to the resistance of passive energy in monads.[6] Physical force and movement come from metaphysical or 'primary' energy. Even efficient causes amount to well-founded phenomena, for cause-and-effect analysis results

5. 'Das Psychische, das Leibniz allerdings nicht in dem korrekten modernen Sinne als Bewußt-seinsprozesse überhaupt auffaßt, besteht für ihn in irgend einer Art von Vorstellungen des Universums.' Gerd Fabian, *Beitrag zur Geschichte des Leib-Seele-Problems* (1925; rpt. Hildesheim 1974), p.24. 'What is disturbing about the monads is not so much their unimaginability as the circularity in describing each of them. Each one depends on all of them, so where does the description get started?' Marguerita Levin, 'Leibniz' concept of point of view', *Studia leibnitiana* 12 (1980), p.221-28.
6. 'Passive derivative force, as repeated or diffused through an aggregation of monads, is that by which one body resists the action of other bodies. It is also that which is extended, has magnitude and figure. As such it constitutes extended mass or secondary matter. Active derivative force, on the other hand, as attributed to aggregates of monads, and measured by mass and velocity ($mv^2$), is *vis viva*. It is the cause of motion.' Robert McRae, *Leibniz: perception, apperception and thought* (Toronto 1976), p.136.

in an infinite regression ultimately grounded in final causation. Pre-established harmony assures the concurrence of efficient and final causation.[7] How does Leibniz therefore justify the dependence of physics on metaphysics dictated by his Christianity? He deems unity essential to elementary being, but he finds no such unity in matter which he considers infinitely divisible. He concludes that unity exists only in the metaphysical sphere.

Yet matter requires an explanation, so he ascribes it to accidents supported by substances. Every monad represents its own piece of secondary matter more distinctly than other monads do, however small this piece may be. An object composed of secondary matter is the particularly distinct representation of monads belonging to an aggregate. When one monad in an aggregate dominates the others[8] by a distinct representation of the changes taking place in them, the aggregate qualifies as an organism, the metaphysical equivalent of a living creature. Made by God, organisms can neither be generated nor destroyed by natural means. Birth and death have no greater metaphysical significance than a sudden increase or decrease in secondary matter.[9] Although subordinate monads enter and leave the organism, the dominant monad remains forever.[10] More aggregates are organisms than one might suspect for, not only do organisms consist of ever smaller organisms, but also many escape our detection: 'Every body [...] is [...] like a cheese filled with worms' (Loemker, p.521).[11]

Organisms include plants, animals, men, genii and angels. The dominant monad in an animal organism is an unselfconscious soul, with an empirical memory and power of attention, which makes sensory associations. The spirits or rational souls in higher organisms have even greater advantages over ordinary monads. With apperception complementing perception, a spirit can know that it perceives as well as what it perceives. Once aware of what it does and who it

7. 'The notion of cause [...] A may be said to act on B if A expresses God more distinctly than B does.' G. H. R. Parkinson, Preface, *The Leibniz-Arnauld correspondence* (Manchester 1969), p.xxiv.

8. 'Aggregates can become genuinely individuated things, "real unities", only by virtue of the presence of a dominant monad (or *entelechy*), a monad of the system which, because of its hierarchic structuring, can perceive with a high degree of clarity all the other monads of the system.' Nicholas Rescher, *Leibniz: an introduction to his philosophy* (Oxford 1979), p.114.

9. 'Pourquoi l'âme ne pourrait-elle pas toujours garder un corps subtil, organisé à sa manière, qui pourra même reprendre un jour ce qu'il faut de son corps visible dans la résurrection' (Gerhardt, vi.533).

10. 'Je n'admets donc point qu'il y a des âmes entièrement séparées naturellement, ni qu'il y a des esprits créés entièrement détachés de tout corps' (Gerhardt, vi.545).

11. 'Als er anläßlich eines Besuches in Holland bei Leeuwenhoek mit dem Mikroskop bekannt wurde und in einem Wassertropfen – an dem mit bloßem Auge nichts Sonderliches zu sehen war – Millionen von Mikroorganismen wimmeln sah, übte dieses Erlebnis einen tiefen Eindruck auf ihn aus.' Anna Simonovits, 'Die dialektische Einheit von Einheit und Mannigfaltigkeit in Leibniz' Philosophie', *Studia leibnitiana supplementa*, Akten des Internationale Leibniz-Kongresses 1966 (Wiesbaden 1969), i.82-83.

is, it achieves independence and responsibility. Self-consciousness enables it to learn from past experience and seek or avoid future contingencies. Reflection leads to the discovery within itself of necessary truths which introduce it to mathematics and logic. It need only distinguish, abstract and analyse its own contents. Inductive and deductive reasoning reveal God and the Aristotelian categories, such as substance and causation. Thus apperception educates the rational soul: 'Tout doit lui naître de son propre fonds, par une parfaite *spontanéité* à l'égard d'elle-même, et pourtant avec une parfaite *conformité* aux choses de dehors' (Gerhardt, iv.484). Unlike inorganic or bare monads, however, spirits perceive God even more distinctly than the universe. While representing the infinite finitely, they consider alternatives and pursue the one that seems best to them. Evidently these 'petits dieux [ont] en eux quelque rayon des lumières de la divinité' (Gerhardt, iv.479). As members of an exclusive society they converse with the divine leader. Did he create them in the beginning along with the other monads? Or does he create them at the conception or birth of the organism they will dominate? Though undecided, Leibniz prefers an intermediate solution, the miraculous conversion of animal to rational souls as needed. Despite the differences between spirits, animal souls and bare monads, he admits neither missing nor multiple links in the chain of monads. 'Il n'y a pas de point de vue inoccupé', as Belaval comments.[12] The perfection of divine creativity excludes the possibility of such flaws.

This ideal inspired a doubt that troubled him towards the end of his career. How could he reconcile the continuity of the creation with the isolation of its basic elements, the monads?[13] He illustrated the conflict between universal and monadic unity by the impossibility, as he saw it, of making a line out of points.[14] The coherence of organisms and the foundation of phenomena in his system seemed inadequate to him. As a solution for the problem, therefore, he considered the introduction of a substantial bond that would unite the monads of an organism with its soul in a composite substance. Since every organism consists of smaller organisms, the organic union includes the component organisms, the components of these components and so on, except for their souls. As Leibniz reassures Des Bosses, the substantial bond of a human spirit does not embrace

---

12. Yvon Belaval, *Pour connaître la pensée de Leibniz* (Paris 1952), p.207.

13. 'Leibniz grants that there would be trouble if both the indivisible constituent and the continuum to which it belongs could both at once be real, but this, he holds, cannot happen and thus the collision between indivisible and continuum is prevented' (Rescher, p.104).

14. One of the two kinds of questions about infinity that preoccupied Leibniz was: '*ob das Unendliche als ein Ganzes zu betrachten sei*, als ein Etwas, das sich nicht aus endlichen Teilen zusammensetzt, für das Endliche nicht etwa einen Teil, sondern nur eine Modifikation bedeutet. Oder man müßte sich das Unendliche als eine Reihe endlicher Größen vorstellen, die einander ad infinitum folgen, also *als Summe endlicher Größen*' (Simonovits, i.98).

the soul of a worm in its intestines, but only the organisms constituting this parasite without their souls. When God unites an organism by a substantial bond, this bond concentrates and materialises the active and passive energy in all the monads of the organism. 'It corresponds accurately [...] to the [...] perceptions and appetites' (Loemker, p.608) of these monads and therefore reifies the phenomena of the organism.[15] While the monads are eternal, the bond is temporal[16] and changes constantly according to the influence they exert on it. God may insert other organisms, separate the bond from its own organism, transfer it to another or destroy it. When an organism loses its bond, the monads keep the unity of mutually distinct perceptions under the dominance of the soul, but the organism's material reality reverts to phenomena. The theory of the substantial bond, which Leibniz develops in his correspondence with Des Bosses (1706-1716), conflicts with his earlier philosophy in several ways and especially by the influence of substances (monads) without any exterior relations.[17] Apparently he did not have enough time before his death in 1716 to solve all the problems raised by the theory and he may never even have intended to adopt it. Did he in fact entertain it merely to allay Des Bosses's Jesuit fears that his monadology threatened transubstantiation?[18] No, he seems to have taken it more seriously than that.

With or without a substantial bond, the dominant monad in the human organism represents far more than it ever realises. We are certainly not aware of perceiving the entire universe. Leibniz has an ingenious reply to this objection:

15. 'A substantial chain superadded to the monads is in my opinion something absolute, such that although it corresponds accurately, in the course of nature, to the affections of the monads, that is, to their perceptions and appetites, and can therefore be taken to be within the monad in whose body its body is, it can nevertheless be independent of the monads in a supernatural sense and can be removed and adopted to other monads while its former monads remain' (Loemker, p.608).

16. 'Leibniz is afterwards led by Des Bosses to admit that this substantial bond must, if it is to be theologically serviceable, be imperishable like the individual soul.' Bertrand Russell, *A critical exposition of the philosophy of Leibniz* (London 1949), p.152. Leibniz admitted the eternity of substantial bonds in 1716.

17. 'These chains will have what reality they possess in the modification of each monad and in the harmony or agreement of the monads with each other' (Loemker, p.609).

18. Yes, according to Broad: 'Leibniz was anxious to show that the theory of monads could be reconciled with the Roman Catholic doctrine of transubstantiation. It is in this connexion that Leibniz puts forward the theory of the *Vinculum Substantiale*. So far as I can see, he never says that he himself holds this theory [...] It appears to me that Leibniz himself holds that the theory that ostensibly material things are *phenomena bene fundata* gives all that the Roman Catholics *ought* to demand.' C. D. Broad, *Leibniz: an introduction* (Cambridge 1975), p.124-25. No, according to Mathieu: '*Vinculum substantiale* [...] Si tratta [...] di ben altro che di una formula escogitata per compiacere all'impostazione data dal corrispondente a un problema teologico: si tratta di un problema centrale della filosofia di Leibniz' (p.55). Vittorio Mathieu, *Leibniz e Des Bosses (1706-1716)* (Torino 1960).

'Il y a [...] une infinité de perceptions en nous [...] dont nous ne nous apercevons pas, parce [qu'elles] sont trop petites et en trop grand nombre ou trop unies.'[19] We have minute perceptions of aggregates so small and numerous that we cannot tell them apart. We have confused perceptions of aggregates so numerous and similar to each other that we cannot distinguish them from each other. In both cases, Leibniz concludes, we can only perceive each of them unconsciously. Thus apperception accompanies neither minute nor confused perception. The roar of the surf on the beach consists of many splashes, none of which can be heard alone or distinguished from the others. The perception of each splash is unconscious. A confused conscious perception often emerges from a mass of unconscious perceptions by a wakeful mind. Hearing many splashes we listen to the surf. Unconscious perceptions account for heedless decisions and behaviour. Confused conscious perceptions never emerge from the unconscious percep-tions of an unconscious mind. Yet unconscious perceptions not only continue during dreamless sleep, fainting spells, etc., but also occur before conception and after death, thus persisting from creation to eternity. Leibniz expands on Descartes's theory that the human mind never stops thinking by the inclusion of unconscious thought and the extension of the privilege to animal minds.

He also opposes unconscious perception to Locke's attack on innate ideas in the *Essay concerning human understanding*. The massive refutation of innate ideas in book I of this work leaves the potential of unconscious perception and the derivation of truth from this source unscathed. But Leibniz seems to confuse unconscious perception with the unknown knowledge we can infer from known knowledge. 'Je suis pour les lumières innées', he wrote to Thomas Burnet: 'Il n'y a pas seulement dans notre esprit une faculté, mais encore une disposition à la connaissance dont les connaissances innées peuvent être tirées. Car toutes les vérités nécessaires[20] tirent leur preuve de cette lumière innée' (Gerhardt, iii.291) He compares the acquisition of this knowledge to the work of a sculptor carving a statue of Hercules from a block of marble in which the veins form the embedded figure of the god. The apperceptive mind, he neglects to comment, resembles both the sculptor and the stone. Even Locke admits that 'les idées qui n'ont point leur origine de la sensation viennent de la réflexion' (*N.E.*, p.36), but only in book II after condemning innate ideas in book I. Reflection amounts to apperception. Leibniz's spokesman Théophile finds in the *Nouveaux Essais* that apperception reveals pure or intellectual ideas, which qualify as innate.

Robinet has gleaned the following examples from the text: existence, God, being, unity, equality, possibility, power, substance, duration, change, activity,

---

19. Leibniz, *Nouveaux essais sur l'entendement humain* (Paris 1966), p.38. Henceforth: *N.E.*
20. And some contingent truths as well.

perception, effort and appetite. He adds others that Théophile abstracts from sense perception: whole, part, extension, number and time. Finally, he cites situation in Leibnizian space and time.[21] All of these concepts and perhaps some of the thousand others Leibniz says he has omitted figure in his metaphysics. Although each has its own priority on his scale, he does not disclose the entire scale. Intellectual ideas combine with each other to form truths of reason (necessary truths), which Théophile separates from truths of fact (contingent truths). He also distinguishes between original and derivative truths of both kinds. The original truths of reason include the basic principles of geometry, arithmetic, logic, metaphysics and even mechanics, as Leibniz states elsewhere. He furnishes the examples of the identity principle, the equality of equals from which equals are subtracted and the horizontal stability of weights balanced on a scale.[22] He regards the truths immediately derived from original truths of reason as innate too: 'toute l'arithmétique et toute la geométrie sont innées et sont en nous d'une manière virtuelle' (*N.E.*, p.62). Like intellectual ideas, original ideas of feeling, many of which involve the ego, enjoy the same status. They constitute original truths of fact, which differ from other such truths in that they do not come from sense experience. Leibniz divides them into psychological truths like the *cogito*, which depend on the natural light alone, and moral truths, which depend on instinct as well. The truths immediately derived from these are likewise innate.

This proliferation of innate ideas and truths alarms Philalèthe, a disciple of Locke who debates with Théophile. Yet Théophile persistently denies that any of Locke's criticism applies. When Philalèthe invokes Locke's objections to proof of innateness by universal consent, Théophile replies that such consent is merely an indication or a confirmation of a doctrine substantiated by other arguments. Philalèthe protests against encouraging people who, convinced of their own good sense, assume it to be innate. Théophile retorts, 'les vérités innées prises pour la lumière naturelle de la raison [...] sont enveloppées dans les principes immédiats que vous reconnaissez vous-même pour incontestables' (*N.E.*, p.80). Philalèthe dares not dispute the simplest elements to which analysis can reduce these truths, because réflexion identifies them as innate ideas put in the mind by the Creator.

The natural light is the portion of his infinite intelligence that he replicates in the human mind. Leibniz gives an account of it in the *Discours de métaphysique* (1686), where he declares, 'Dieu est le soleil et la lumière des âmes' (Gerhardt, iv.453). How ancient a pedigree it has, he exclaims, for men like Plato and

21. André Robinet, 'Grundprobleme der *Nouveaux essais*', *Studia leibnitiana supplementa*, Akten des Internationalen Leibniz-Kongresses 1963 (Wiesbaden 1969), iii.21.
22. See 'Sur ce qui passe les sens et la matière' (1702), Gerhardt, vi.495.

Guillaume de Saint-Amour promote it! Determined to establish that no other influence affects our minds, he denies that they have any doors or windows. They have ideas of all things only because of God's influence on them. Just as the effect expresses its cause, 'l'essence de notre âme est une certaine expression ou imitation ou image de l'essence, pensée et volonté divines et de toutes les idées qui y sont comprises' (Gerhardt, iv.453). We do not see all things in God, but rather by him. We see the sun and the stars, because he has given us ideas of them and maintains them in the mind. Does the continuous influence of the natural light not conflict with pre-established harmony? No. In animating the mind, God follows the laws he has established. He produces and conserves our being in such a way that our thoughts come to us freely and spontaneously in the order prescribed by the complete notion of our substance. We can learn nothing of which we do not already have an idea in the mind, ideas being the raw material of all thought. Consequently, 'notre âme exprime Dieu et l'univers, et toutes les essences aussi bien que les existences' (Gerhardt, iv.451). Thus its reach seems to exceed its grasp.

Leibniz exploits the metaphorical possibilities of the concept in an essay entitled 'Aurora seu initia scientiae generalis a divina luce', which he wrote in 1693 or later. Here he draws a parallel between progress in the use of heat and light, on one hand, and the cultivation of the mind, on the other. While primitive men use friction to kindle a fire, learned men focus the rays of the sun, an allusion to contemporary research in optics.[23] A comparison follows the parallel: these methods differ by the degree to which they improve the mind. And then a transition: though subservient still to the senses, we undergo a sacred agitation that produces heat and light in our mind, thus 'demum coelestis lux affulget' (Gerhardt, vii.55). Leibniz suggests that physical and mental activity both consist in a continual exchange of movement, heat and light. Either we reverse divine thought by proceeding from effect to cause, from experience to reason, from confused to distinct notions 'et velut cum Moyse terga Dei' (Gerhardt, vii.55). Or beginning, on the contrary, with the simplest ideas, that is the divine attributes, we continually draw eternal truths from the fountain of essence. The rhetoric obscures a simple contrast between *a posteriori* and *a priori* logic. Leibniz evidently prefers to contemplate God from the front, however, for he immediately ascribes the glory of eliminating ignorance to *a priori* logic. He concedes that we know most sensible things, though not without confusion, 'miro providentiae instituto' (Gerhardt, iv.55). Yet the Creator sowed the seed of the highest doctrines in our minds. Thus the natural light not only

---

23. The most important recent work was that of Newton between 1665 and 1675 on refraction and the reflecting telescope, but Leibniz refers to the earlier efforts of Fermat, Descartes and Snell.

demonstrates the truths of mathematics, but also those of a general science far superior to geometry and algebra. The natural light also combats prejudice, illusions, obstination, rash judgements, hidden vanity, the sectarian severity of an arrogant piety and internecine hatred: 'haec monstra regni tenebrarum non nisi luce illata dispelluntur' (Gerhardt,iv. 56). The moral competence of the natural light inspires this use of the clerical vocabulary.

Since truths derive from ideas, the natural light attains the universal and eternal truths in the mind of God. This proposition appears in 'Ce qui passe les sens et la matière' (1702) and Leibniz's correspondence with the Electress Sophie Charlotte from the same period. 'Née avec nous' (Gerhardt, vi.490, 496), the natural light, he says, brings to our attention all the necessary truths we are aware of. We can even elicit them from a child by asking him Socratic questions. The senses merely indicate what exists, while the natural light reveals what is necessary, must be and could not be otherwise. Leibniz defines it as 'la force des conséquences du raisonnement' (Gerhardt, vi.489, 494). It enables us to know God's order and impose this order on everything under our control, so that we bear a modest resemblance to him. It also procures us the right of citizenship in the state under his rule, together with genies and angels.

A few years later, Leibniz discussed it again in a letter to Lady Masham (30 June 1704), in whose manor Locke resided. Hoping to draw the author of the *Essay concerning human understanding* into the discussion, he affirmed that 'notre entendement vient de Dieu' (Gerhardt, iii.353) and he described it as a ray from this sun. When we proceed by order, as the nature of the understanding requires, we find that what conforms best to the understanding also conforms to divine wisdom. Events never contradict judgements dictated by the natural light, a claim Locke may have thought vulnerable. But he died a few months later and Leibniz abandoned the publication of the *Nouveaux essais*, the kind of dialogue he would have like to pursue with the reluctant Englishman. He had no illusions about Locke's resistance to his philosophy, however, for Philalèthe snaps back into his orbit many times before Théophile succeeds in jerking him out of it. Even so, how could a disciple of Locke accept Théophile's assertion that 'toutes les pensées et actions de notre âme viennent de son propre fonds, sans pouvoir lui être données par les sens' (*N.E.*, p.59)? Locke may have realised that the inevitable collision between them over this basic point would have disrupted any discussion they started. A few pages later, Théophile argues that very often (always?) we learn the nature of things by observing the nature of the mind and its innate ideas which form the natural light: 'on n'a point besoin de chercher au-dehors' (*N.E.*, p.69). We may discover innate moral truths either by instinct or the natural light, but the natural light alone gives us a distinct idea of them.

The natural light only differs from divine intelligence, according to the *Théodicée*, 'comme une goutte d'eau diffère de l'océan'.[24] The finite portion of reason that God has given us is homogeneous with the infinite whole. Leibniz therefore disagrees with Bayle who assigns a superior reason to God. He considers the light of reason no less a gift of God than the revelation. This innate light, which consists of simple ideas and compound notions, can be proved by Scripture and reason. Scripture attests that God inscribed his law in our hearts, while reason demonstrates that necessary truths can only come from 'principes implantés dans l'esprit' (*Th.*, p.443). Induction from the senses never yields any necessary truth, because God does not communicate with us directly through them. With access to the natural light the understanding is the 'région des vérités éternelles ou des idées dont elles dépendent' (Gerhardt, vi.614), as we learn in the 'Monadologie' (1714). These eternal truths coexist with God, for he did not create them, despite Descartes's opinion to the contrary. Since God follows them just as we do, we imitate him in our 'département' (Gerhardt, vi.605). Our mind functions in our little world just as his does in the big world, an allusion to the natural light in the 'Principes de la nature et de la grâce' (1714).

The natural light eclipses sense experience in Leibniz's philosophy, but he maintains that the mind cannot think without this experience. The intervention of the senses, he writes Sophie Charlotte, enables him to reason and compose 'cette lettre' (Gerhardt, vi.514). Thought requires apperception which in turn requires perception, the metaphysical equivalent of sense experience. Pre-established harmony assures an exact parallel between spiritual and material activity: 'il n'y a jamais pensée abstraite qui ne soit accompagnée de quelques images ou traces matérielles' (Gerhardt, vi.533). Leibniz implicitly agrees with Descartes that, whenever a thought occurs to the mind, a mark appears on the brain. He also believes sense experience, in contrast with the natural light, to be passive, confused and erratic: an echo of the contempt for the alleged source of evil by theologians like Augustine? Not according to Leibniz: 'On n'a pas [...] besoin de chercher l'origine du mal dans la matière' (*Th.*, p.341). The relegation, in fact, of matter to the status of well founded phenomena never really satisfied him and especially towards the end of his life, when he exper-imented with compound substances united by substantial bonds.

In his opinion, notions (concepts) produced by a particular sense are clear because they allow us to recognise the object perceived. They are not distinct, however, because analysing them results in an infinite regression. Such analysis in other words yields a continuous series of causes each becoming in turn an

---

24. Leibniz, *Essais de Théodicée* (Paris 1969), p.85. Henceforth: *Th.*

effect that requires further analysis: 'il faut que la raison suffisante ou dernière soit hors de la suite [...] des contingences' (Gerhardt, vi.613). This sufficient reason can only be a final cause, the will of God. Thus the truths of fact we acquire from sense experience are no less analytic than other truths of fact and the truths of reason, even though the completion of the analysis surpasses our ability. Truths being a kind of notion, Leibniz distinguishes between notions derived from a particular sense and those from the common sense, which combines perceptions by several senses.[25] The former, which he identifies as sensible notions, may represent, for instance, the colour and softness of flowers, the latter, which he identifies as sensible and intelligible, their shape and number. The imagination can produce or reproduce both of these, but not a third, intelligible notions. While only the second and third qualify as distinct, all three are necessarily innate: 'tout ce qui arrive a l'âme [...] est une suite de sa notion, donc [...] toutes ses [...] perceptions lui doivent naître (*sponte*) de sa propre nature' (Gerhardt, iv.458). The notion of the mind contains all of its past, present and future perceptions. Nothing can enter it from the outside,[26] not even sense experience itself. Then how does Leibniz explain this experience? As Robinet comments, knowledge from the 'bottom' of the mind contrasts with that from the 'surface' rather than the exterior.[27] Truths of reason come from the bottom and truths of fact from the surface, which consists in 'la liaison des phénomènes, c'est-à-dire la connexion de ce qui se passe en différents lieux et temps, et dans l'expérience de différents hommes, qui sont eux-mêmes les uns aux autres des phénomènes' (*N.E.*, p.329). Leibniz does not guarantee this '*criterion*' for, while it practically excludes dreams, a logical and durable dream does not seem impossible to him. Still, such a dream would resemble a self-printing work of fiction. Just as geometry confirms optics, truths of reason confirm truths of fact.

Since Leibniz attributes necessary truths to reason, his conception of reason itself deserves special attention. The relationship between reason and the natural light provides us with a convenient approach. 'La raison ici est l'enchaînement des vérités que nous connaissons par la lumière naturelle' (*Th.*, p.87). The internal and divine light of ideas, he tells Sophie Charlotte, constitutes right reason and the inferences made by reasoning are part of the natural light. In a letter to Thomas Burnet he defines reasoning as the analysis of ideas or notions

25. 'Leibniz can allow a relative [...] validity to Locke's distinction between primary and secondary qualities. The primary qualities are what we become acquainted with by the common sense' (Broad, p.141).
26. 'Dans la rigueur de la vérité métaphysique, il n'y a point de cause externe qui agisse sur nous excepté Dieu seul' (Gerhardt, iv.453).
27. Robinet, 'Grundprobleme', iii.27.

which he treats as synonyms. According to a note he added to a letter from Foucher, 'reason is the sum of requisites' (Loemker, p.161), each of which connects two things that cannot be understood without it.[28] Théophile identifies reason as 'la vérité connue dont la liaison avec une autre moins connue fait donner notre assentiment a la dernière' (*N.E.*, p.421). It especially qualifies as reason when it not only causes us to make this judgement, but also produces the other truth. Indeed this is how Théophile describes *a priori* reason. Causes are to effects as reasons, to truths, so *reason* even serves as a synonym of *cause*. Théophile also accepts Philalèthe's use of reason to designate 'la faculté qui s'aperçoit de cette liaison des vérités, ou la faculté de raisonner' (*N.E.*, p.422). Despite the overlapping semantics of the terms, the preceding statements imply two propositions: (1) right or *a priori* reason, reasoning and the natural light are similar; (2) 'la droite raison est un enchaînement de vérités' (*Th.*, p.86). Although passions and prejudices may contaminate reason, we can discriminate between right and corrupt reason by orderly procedure as well as the rejection of all undemonstrated opinions and all demonstrations that do not conform to the basic rules of logic.

Leibniz endorses Descartes's opinion that 'le bon sens est donné en partage a tous' (*Th.*, p.86), but his good sense does not necessarily consist of intuition as well as demonstration. The chain of truths results in an intuition only when an exhaustive analysis of the concept occurs instantaneously, an unusual event outside God's mind: 'Quand mon esprit comprend à la fois et distinctement tous les ingrédients primitifs d'une notion, il en a une connaissance intuitive qui est bien rare' (Gerhardt, iv.449-450) Good sense implies a minimum ability to connect truths of reason and fact[29] in a logical sequence tending to intuition as a possible but unlikely result. Théophile believes that, when well applied, good sense can accomplish all the mental tasks that do not necessitate quickness of execution. If, as we read in the *Théodicée*, a man with an ordinary mind carefully follows the rules of common logic, he can refute the most compelling objections to the truth if they masquerade as demonstrations founded on reason. The overall coherence of any demonstration compensates for uncertain truths in the sequence, for successive requisites accumulate probability. As Robinet observes, 'la raison signifie la totalité des déterminations y compris les confuses

28. 'Le passage du moins connu au plus connu résulte de l'effort de l'esprit logique pour enfermer dans une chaîne de probabilité montante un certain nombre de phénomènes. La Raison est cette liaison même, non l'un des termes de ce mouvement, mais le moyen terme, qui rend possible, logiquement, l'enjambement de l'esprit.' Robinet, *Leibniz*, p.40.

29. 'La raison, consistant dans l'enchaînement des vérités, a droit de lier encore celles que l'expérience lui a fournies, pour en tirer des conclusions mixtes; mais la raison pure et nue, distinguée de l'expérience, n'a affaire qu'à des vérités indépendantes des sens' (*Th.*, p.50).

et les affectives'.[30] The tighter the logic of the requisites, the greater the probability of the demonstration. The accumulation of efforts or possibilities tending to reality produces physical movement or mental progress from ignorance to knowledge of increasing probability. Memory ensures a similar, but inferior kind of sequence which we share with the animals. When the first of two consecutive events which occurred in the past recurs, the animal anticipates the recurrence of the second as well. If you shake a stick at a once-beaten dog, he will howl and run away. The reflexive mind enables us to rise above this instinct and approach God by reason and learning. God reasons for animals, as Belaval remarks, and we reason for ourselves.[31]

Théophile does not object when Philalèthe describes our reason as a natural revelation by God. Since he gave us the light of reason as well as that of revelation, a conflict between them would set 'Dieu contre Dieu' (*Th.*, p.74). Neither can reason discredit a truth accredited by revelation nor can revelation accredit a truth discredited by reason. Yet the impossibility of such a contradiction does not preclude authentic mysteries like those of Christianity. The defence of these mysteries raises three problems, as Leibniz wrote to Basnage de Beauval: (1) elimination of obscurity, (2) proof by natural reasons and (3) rebuttal of objections. We cannot always solve the first and 'encore moins' (Gerhardt, iii.144) the second, but we can always solve the third. There is no valid argument against the truth. The Christian mysteries would violate reason, he tells Jaquelot, if we could not refute all objections to them. They are above reason, however, because we cannot explain them. To illustrate the traditional distinction between truths against and above reason, Leibniz offers Burnet a political analogy. A great prince, known for his wisdom, may not exploit a great opportunity or avoid a great danger. Foolish people will accuse him of committing an error, but others will attribute his decision to unknown superior reasons. The prince's reputation would persuade these people that he has such reasons.[32]

Truths of reason confirm truths of fact above reason without explaining them, for analysis results in infinite regression here too. No truths ever contradict each other: 'la vérité ne saurait être double, ni contraire à elle-même'.[33] The mysterious truths surpass reason because they do not fit into the logical sequences of reason, even though they contradict none of the truths in these sequences. From our incomprehension of these mysteries Bayle concludes that

30. André Robinet, *Leibniz et la racine de l'existence* (Paris 1962), p.67.
31. See Belaval, p.213.
32. Leibniz was the Aulic Councillor of the duke of Brunswick-Luneburg. Such an office would seem to require respect for the wisdom of the prince.
33. *Textes inédits d'après les manuscrits de la bibliothèque provinciale de Hanovre*, ed. Gaston Grua (Paris 1948), p.68.

our reason is not the same as God's. Leibniz disagrees. He ascribes this opinion to the misunderstanding of right reason and the confusion of right reason with lesser, corrupt or false reason. When he insists that the sacred truths of fact are not contrary to reason, but above it, he means right reason. From consideration of revealed truth, however, he does not exclude lesser reason, which mingles truths of fact with truths of reason. Faith depends on the experience of the witnesses who attest the miracles of revelation and 'dans la suite des temps on en connaîtra davantage par l'expérience' (Gerhardt, vi.508). Faith in fact requires intelligence, which will replace faith when Christianity reaches its fulfilment. In Bayle's diction-ary, nonetheless, 'la religion et la raison paraissent en combattantes' (*Th.*, p.39). Leibniz wrote the 'Discours de la conformité de la raison avec la foi', which serves as an introduction to the *Théodicée*, in order to answer this challenge to one of his most profound convictions. His God would never do anything unreasonable. Friedman calls him 'le plus grand philosophe du sens commun chrétien'.[34]

Do we really know, however, what kind of Christian he was? Born and raised a Lutheran, he ostensibly remained one until his death, yet he rarely practised this religion. Although for a while he professed a faith closer to Catholicism than Lutheranism, he resisted all attempts by Catholics to convert him. He intended the anonymous *Theological system* (written *ca*.1684) as a neutral expo-sition of Christian doctrine which might facilitate the return of the major Protestant churches to the Catholic fold. A Catholic translator (de Broglie) wonders why, 'arrivé à ce point, [il] s'y soit arrêté'.[35] The reason must have been pride, for he certainly thought deciding between Lutheranism and Catholi-cism less important than reintegrating the Lutheran, the Anglican and the Calvinist churches in the Catholic Church. A conservative, as Hoffmann stresses,[36] he wanted to restore the doctrinal unity of the ancient Church and probably for the good of society as well as that of salvation. In ravaging his homeland, the Thirty Years War had done great harm to both. To remedy such ills, he sought to reunite the churches rather than the sects and reconcile the orthodoxies rather than the heresies. With the Socinians, for instance, he had no patience. For the purpose of reintegration and others as well perhaps, he gave doctrine a higher priority than ritual. Despite the energy, imagination and persistence with which he pursued this goal, he achieved no significant success.[37]

34. Georges Friedman, *Leibniz et Spinoza* (Paris 1946), p.206.
35. Albert de Broglie, trans., *Système religieux de Leibniz* (Paris 1846), p.xxvi-xxvii.
36. 'Leibnizens tiefste Tendenz ist auf völlige Rationalisierung des Christentums gerichtet, aber sein konservativer Character läßt es zu keinem konsequenten Auswirken derselben kommen.' Heinrich Hoffman, *Die Leibniz'sche Religionsphilosophie in ihrer geschichtlichen Stellung* (Tübingen 1903), p.91.
37. 'Tous les essais d'union des églises eurent quelque chose d'artificiel et de sénile. Il faut

One might even wonder whether he valued Christianity less than the unity of Christendom. In the *Théodicée*, Hoffmann finds, he supports revealed theology little more than insofar as it resembles natural theology.[38] While this natural theology withstands the test of reason, on which he founds it, the rest of revealed theology obviously does not.

He sometimes portrays Christ as the great prophet of reason, but he presents the traditional figure of Christian apology in 'Jesus am Kreuze', a poem written for his half-brother in 1684. Although Jesus has departed from this life, we read, his death enables us to follow him to another life. The blood that cleanses us flows from a wound in his side, through which he reveals his loving and suffering heart. He spreads his arms on the cross as if to embrace anyone who accepts his love. His head hangs down to kiss the poet. Blessed is the man who offers his love until the moment of death. May our feeble soul, unable to rekindle his stone-cold heart, enjoy the sweetness of his love. The poet makes no mistakes in versification, but his ingenuity hardly overcomes the lack of inspiration.[39] The poem tells us less about the sincerity of his faith than the wisdom of not writing much poetry.

He presents the prophet of reason in the preface of the *Théodicée*, where he describes him as the divine founder of the purest and most enlightened religion. Finishing what Moses had begun, 'Jésus-Christ [...] acheva de faire passer la religion naturelle en loi, et de lui donner l'autorité d'un dogme public' (*Th.*, p.27). According to the *Discours de métaphysique* (1686), he expressed divinely what the ancient philosophers suspected vaguely, the gospel kingdom of heaven or Augustine's city of God which Leibniz identifies with his own republic of spirits. In this context, however, Jesus resembles the philosophers more than God. Study of Leibniz's religion convinced critics like Hoffmann, Baruzi, and

n'avoir tenté de vivre successivement la vie protestante et la vie catholique pour croire que de telles unions, à peu près réductibles à des anéantissements, se peuvent réaliser [...] Tous les constructeurs de projets ont négligé, en les diverses formes chrétiennes, l'évident souci qu'elles avaient de rester elles-mêmes.' Jean Baruzi, *Leibniz et l'organisation religieuse de la terre* (Paris 1907), p.265.

38. 'Da das bestehende Christentum der Vernunftreligion recht wenig ähnlich sieht, so wird Jesus für die natürliche Religion in Anspruch genommen und die kirchliche Entwicklung mit ihrem Wertlegen auf Ceremonien und Glaubensformeln als ein Abfall [...] So sehr diese Gleichsetzung von Christentum und Vernunftreligion in der Konsequenz Leibniz'scher Gedanken liegt, so wagt er doch nicht, sie rein durchzuführen. Das deistische Schema wird durchbrochen, indem das Christentum zwar im wesentlichen mit der natürlichen Religion identisch sein, daneben aber noch Mysterien enthalten soll' (Hoffmann, p.88).

39. Here for example is the first stanza of the poem: 'Jesu, dessen Tod und Leiden / Unsere Freud und Leben ist, / Der Du abgeschieden bist, / Auf daß wir nicht von Dir scheiden, / Sondern durch des Todes Thür / Zu dem Leben folgen Dir.' Leibniz, *Sämtliche Schriften und Briefe*, Preussische Akademie der Wissenschaften (Berlin, Darmstadt 1923- ), i.IV.667. Henceforth *S.S.* Note that *Tür* and *Dir*, which rhyme here, were pronounced like *Tier* in certain parts of Germany in Leibniz's time.

Robinet that his writings prove no profound belief in the divinity of Christ. While Pichler bases his contrary opinion on explicit statements by the philosopher,[40] Leibniz seems to have made them rather to facilitate the reunification of Christendom than to profess his own faith.

Most of these statements concern the two natures, a dogma that invited the abstract speculation at which he excelled. He was only twenty-three when he answered the *Objections to the Trinity and the Incarnation* (1665) by Fausto Sozzini's grandson Andreas Wiszowaty. In his 'Response' he converts the Socinian's arguments into syllogisms and refutes them one by one. I will follow his order but not his procedure. If the supreme God is, as Wiszowaty learns from Paul, 'Pater ille ex quo omnia' (Gerhardt, iv.119),[41] did he not also create the Son? No, replies Leibniz, because the Son himself created all things, as the Socinian concedes. By *all things* Paul means all created things. Nor does his language conflict with the Trinity, for all things come from the Father and through the Son according to 1 Corinthians viii.6; all things are from, through and in the Father according to Romans xi.36. Since all things come through Christ from God, Christ can be God. In 1 Corinthians viii.6 Paul refers to Christ's divine nature and in Acts ii.36 Peter refers to his human nature: 'God has made this Jesus.' Wiszowaty denies that the being through whom the supreme God creates all things can himself be the supreme God. Leibniz disagrees on the grounds that God the Father can create all things through the Son. In Wiszowaty's opinion Jesus's ignorance of the day when the kingdom of God would come[42] disproves his divinity. Predictably Leibniz replies that Christ's human nature does not know what his divine nature knows. He typically accuses the Socinian of twisting the meaning of Scripture to suit his polemic, but the latter might legitimately have hurled this charge back at him.

We can regard something made of iron and wood, Leibniz continues, as either body or soul. Why then cannot Christ be both man and God 'pro diversis partibus' (Gerhardt, iv.121)? Ignorance of God's design suits the human part of Christ during the state of humility before its exaltation. At other times, however, his divine nature completes his human knowledge by the production

40. 'Jesus kommt nicht in Betracht als Inkarnation der Gottheit' (Hoffmann, p.87). 'Il se trouve dépourvu de toute place privilégiée par rapport aux autres grands réformateurs de l'humanité.' Robinet, *Leibniz*, p.75. Baruzi add little. On the other hand: 'Der leibnizsche Christus ist der historische, überweltliche und persönliche, wie die Propheten ihn vorher verkündigt und die Evangelisten nach seinem Leben und Wirken schildern. Er hat stets an dieser gläubigen Überzeugung festgehalten, und es findet sich auch nicht die geringste Spur eines Zweifels zu irgend einer Zeit.' Aloys Pichler, *Die Theologie des Leibniz* (München 1869), i.348.
41. 'Quoniam ex ipso, et per ipsum, et in ipso sunt omnia.' Romans xi.36, *La Sainte Bible polyglotte*, ed. Fulcran Vigouroux (Paris 1898-1909).
42. Mark ix.1; Luke ix.27.

of new accidents, if not by the communication of divine qualities. In further replies to Wiszowaty Leibniz affirms that the creation of the world by Christ does not involve his human nature, that the entire Trinity, and not his divine nature alone, begot his human nature. The final syllogism in the 'Response', which he borrows from Wiszowaty himself, distinguishes between the incarnated and unincarnated divinities, thus implying polytheism. He parries this thrust by assigning incarnation to the Son's divine person and denying it of the divine substance in this person!

'On the incarnation or [*seu*] the hypostatic union', which he apparently wrote at about the same time, treats the second subject in this title more obviously than the first. Hypostatic bonds, he states, unite (1) God and a mind, (2) a mind and a body or (3) two bodies depending on the same mind. Was he thinking of the real multipresence in (3)? Probably, for the idea conforms to his eucharistic theory. (1) and (2) evidently apply to the two natures, but does (1) also apply to the Trinity? No, two minds cannot be united hypostatically, Leibniz stipulates, unless one is perfect and the other imperfect, because an imperfect mind can act outside of itself only through its own body. Although he considers neither a hypostatic union of perfect minds nor the Trinity here, he may have thought of this hypostatic bond as one uniting God with three perfect minds. In (2), he explains, the hypostatic bond does not unite the inferior mind with the corpuscles of animal spirit transpiring from the brain, but rather with the centre of the brain itself which produces them. Not even death separates this subtly mobile substance from the centre. Leibniz faces the same dilemma as Descartes in trying to unite the illocal with the local. How can the mind *inhere* in the brain? He borrows this term from the Scholastics who conveniently define it as achieving this very union. It enables him no more than it enabled them to avoid the expedient of describing the mind as if it were somewhere in the brain.

As if in anticipation of Spinoza, he denies the possibility of a hypostatic union between God and bodies or the world. Aside from creation and destruction, God induces motion in matter by recreating it along the path of movement. Since this motion does not last – Leibniz would change his mind about that – God does not act on matter continuously,[43] thus no hypostatic bond unites him with it. A hypostatic bond does unite him with minds in which he is the principle of action, while minds with their own principle of action are free. Elsewhere, as we have seen, Leibniz identifies the minds dependent on God (or instinct) with those of the subhuman animals, and the minds independent of him with those of men and the superhuman creatures (genii and angels). God does not usually act in minds with their own principle of action, except the one with

43. According to his monadic philosophy, substantial energy results in constant bodily motion.

which he is hypostatically united (Christ's). In a hypostatic union one thing must perpetually act in another, which is its immediate instrument of action. God acts on a body by creating it continuously and the mind acts on its body by making it move. 'Deo vero instrumentum est mens, Deo unita qua Deus agit in corpora aliter quam creando' (*S.S.*, i.ii.534). The hypostatic union of Christ's two natures consists in the action of the divine in his human mind and hence on his human body.

A hypostatic bond cannot unite one thing with another unless one is the immediate instrument of the other and has in itself its own principle of action. Leibniz defines the hypostatic union itself as the action of this principle. Such a union requires: (1) a thing subsisting in itself or having in itself its own principle of action; (2) another thing united with it; (3) the action of subsisting through unity or the united instrument of subsistence; (4) the immediacy of this action, which does not belong to the union. The future advocate of monads apparently added number (4) to preserve the independence of related things from each other, relations being in his opinion mere coordinates of independent things. Needless to say the action in one thing of another hardly seems compatible with this conception, which reflects the distant influence of Scholastic nominalism. In an algebraic formulation of hypostasis Leibniz replaces (1) by A, (3) and (4) by B, (2) by C. Thus A acts through B on C, but only through B. To this schema he anticipates an objection containing the only explicit allusion to Christ in the text. If the divinity acts on Christ's body through his mind alone, how can his human nature be immediately united with his divine nature? 'A hic non est Deitas tantum,' replies Leibniz, 'sed Deitas cum omni quod ei unitum est' (*S.S.*, i.ii.534). A hypostatic bond unites the hypostatic union of God and Christ's mind with his body, hence a double hypostasis. The immediacy of the action (4) belongs to the divinity, even though the action itself (3), or Christ's mind in this context, is the immediate instrument of the divinity in its union with his body. Leibniz concludes that the union of the two natures is absolute and perfect. In a paper related to the *System*, he speaks of three natures, for he has divided the human nature between Christ's mind and his body. This triple distinction elucidates the double hypostasis in 'The incarnation or the hypostatic union', since the union of the first two natures (divinity and mind) is itself united with the third (body).

The *System* tells us how the divine nature came to assume the human. By a decree of the Trinity[44] one of the divine persons assumed a created nature 'pour gouverner la cité de Dieu, c'est-à-dire la république des intelligences [...]

---

44. 'Comme il avait été décrété dans le secret éternel du conseil divin qu'une des personnes de la divinité' (*Système*, p.29).

et pour la soumettre comme son roi' (*Système*, p.29). Why Leibniz saw no conflict between the republic of minds and the monarchy of Christ I cannot explain. Since the Son contains all essences and hence all existences, the author continues, incarnation suited him in particular. The Son assumed human nature because it represents all the other natures superior and inferior to it. This representation enables him to redeem them, the purpose of the Trinitarian decree. Except for sin he embraced human nature in both its spiritual and its physical entirety, before glorifying it by his patience and suffering. He exceeded it only by his miracles. Leibniz approves the Patristic analogy between the union of the two natures and that of the mind with the body. As the mind and the body form one man, the two natures form one person, but without any human imperfections.

The *Théodicée* recommends that we acknowledge the closest possible union between the two natures and leave it at that. According to the *System*, which goes further, Christ's human nature acquires the perfections of the divine, with which it shares none of its imperfections. Having said this, however, Leibniz regrets that the Church opened 'the communication of idioms' to discussion in the fourth century. Few such objections appear in the *System*. Whether and to what extent we must attribute the properties of one nature to the other seems superfluous to the author and liable perhaps to cause mischief. We need only attribute the properties of both to Christ himself, he submits. We can say that God suffered in Christ, that human knowledge and power are unlimited in him. But we can no more attribute divine power, immensity and eternity to his human nature than human birth and passion to his divine nature. His human nature received as much perfection, science and power as it could have. It kept these assets during the worst of his humiliation on earth, when his glory shone as the sun through the clouds. In negotiating later for the reunion of the Protestant churches in Germany, Leibniz went still further. Christ's divine nature communicates attributes that do not involve God's immensity to his human nature, but not those that do. Omnipotence, omnipresence and omniscience belong to the first category; lifegiving force and unlimited power to the second. The Lutherans and the Calvinists agreed that the human nature has omnipotence in the same way as it has divinity, through its union with the divine nature in the person of Christ.

The English antitrinitarian Stephen Nye had attacked the two natures in his *Considerations on the explanations of the doctrine of the Trinity* (1693-1694). When Leibniz's nephew Friedrich Simon Loeffler proposed to refute this anonymous work by a mathematical method, the philosopher advised him on how to do it. While this geometrical argumentation does not interest us here, several of the arguments Leibniz makes by way of demonstration deserve our attention. Since the creation of all things continues, he reasons, one creature such as the Arian Christ could not be God's agent in creating the others. God would create him at the same time as he creates them. Thus Christ, to whom Scripture attributes the properties of the supreme God, must be more than a creature. The Son of God in the strictest sense, a hypostasis of the divinity generated before time hardly resembles a creature. Leibniz cites the first chapter of John as proof. Both Scripture and the ancient Church prescribe the worship of Christ as if he were God, indeed they confer the supreme divinity on him. Consequently, 'Christus non est angelus'[45] as the Neo-Arian Englishman claims. Angels, who have none of the divine attributes, are mere creatures. All of these arguments, Leibniz notes, apply to the Spirit as well as the Son.

He accuses the Neo-Arian Whiston of worshipping a creature in a letter to Thomas Burnet (1714). The only antitrinitarian to refrain from this error, which he compares to paganism, is Fausto Sozzini's opponent Francis Daviditz. He also dismisses the disputes involving Nestorius and Eutychius as wars of words. Rather than condemn the title Mother of God, Nestorius only objected that it implied a material and not a logical truth. In the *System* Leibniz censures most of the Christological heresies, ancient and modern. The Council of Nicaea (325), he asserts, merely confirmed an established doctrine. In Christ Hellenistic Fathers like Origen had already seen two kinds of Son, the coeternal Word and the first creature of God. Leibniz condemns the Arians for abandoning the first kind, the Photinians and Socinians for abandoning both and worshipping a figure they considered a mere creature.

In his opinion the council at Constantinople in 680 against the Monothelites had burdened Christianity with a troublesome addition to dogma. He tried to pry an acknowledgement of this innovation out of Bossuet, who insisted that the dogma had never changed. If the great defender of Catholicism admitted such a precedent, he thought, further exceptions and these in favour of reunification with the Protestants might be possible. Although Leibniz was trying to milk a stone, his arguments are persuasive. Even contemporary Catholics, he finds, cannot understand the distinction between the two wills in Christ when they hear of it. No wonder 'les plus habiles gens de ce temps-là ne demeuraient point d'accord!'[46] Christ had a human soul, Bossuet argues, so two natures imply two wills. Since the person of Christ is the subject of his two natures, Leibniz replies, one will might as well inhere in it as one in each of the two natures. If the council had not condemned them, the Scholastics would probably have disagreed over the number of wills in Christ too. Several of them affirmed

---

45. *Theologiae cursus completus*, J. P. and V. S. Migne (ed.), viii (Paris 1839), col. 762.
46. *Œuvres de Leibniz*, ed. Louis Foucher de Careil (1859-1875; rpt. Hildesheim, New York 1969), i.434. Henceforth: Foucher.

that neither matter nor form acts, because 'l'action appartient au composé' (Foucher, i.391). They applied this principle to the union of the soul and the body: what would have kept them from extending it to the union of the two natures? Bossuet ignored most of these arguments.

Discussions of the two natures often overlap with those of the Trinity in Leibniz's writings. Among others the 'Response' to Wiszowaty defends both doctrines. One can abstract trilinearity immediately from a three-lined figure, the Pole reasons, but not from a triangle, even though a triangle also happens to be a three-lined figure. Linearity differs entirely from triangularity since parallel lines never form an angle no matter how far they extend: 'Ergo triangulum non est trilineum, quod est absurdum.' Thus Wiszowaty implies the absurdity of a Trinity that does not consist of three Gods. Yet Leibniz easily refutes the syllogism by the fact that everything trilinear has trilinearity, so 'triangulum est trilineum' (Gerhardt, iv.120). Instead of three Gods, there are the 'intelligens, intellectum et intellectio' of one God, by which he can 'posse, scire et velle' (Gerhardt, iv.123). Leibniz rejects Wiszowaty's inference of three foundations, which suggest composition and hence the imperfection of God. He maintains the three powers resembling the three faculties of the human mind. 'Judicium, idea et intellectio' (Gerhardt, iv.123) multiply the mind no more than size, shape and weight triple a stone. Unseparated from each other the Trinitarian persons prevent the corruption of any one. Can God generate God, Wiszowaty demands? Yes, replies Leibniz, provided one divine person generates another. But if this event does not continue even now, it had to begin and end? Yes, it began and ended before time: 'simul enim generari incepit et desiit' (Gerhardt, iv.124)! Thus young Leibniz avoids absurdity by embracing mystery, a tactic inconsistent with the later 'Discours de la conformité de la raison avec la foi'. Does the entire Trinity submit to the incarnation? No. Then the incarnation either divides it or it already consists of parts, so that God is separated from himself. On the contrary, God himself remains indivisible, while the divine persons differ from each other and one separates from the other two in the incarnation: 'divisi a se seu differentes sunt illi qui sunt Deus' (Gerhardt, iv.124).

We have already examined one of four papers on the Trinity that foreshadow the *System*. It compares the three persons and one nature of the Trinity with the one person and three natures of Christ. According to another, Justin, Athanasius and Augustine authorise the following parallel: 'Quemadmodum mysterium Trinitatis optime illustratur similitudine mentis in se reflexae, ita mysterium incarnationis optime illustratur unione mentis et corporis' (Grua, p.180). The analogy between reflexive thought in the human mind and in the Trinity reappears in the other two papers. In 'De Deo Trino' Leibniz prefers to define and illustrate this mystery rather than try to demonstrate it, an impossibility he says. Nothing illustrates the diversity of the persons within the unity of the substance better than the mind knowing itself. The difference between understanding and being understood implies the existence of both a perceiving and a revealing power, which nonetheless constitute the same mind. These correlatives cannot always be identical with each other. The Father diversifies the divinity by understanding and loving himself, hence the generation of the Son and the proceeding of the Spirit. Yet all three persons participate in divine knowledge and love. Such a separation of mental functions from each other implies disunity rather than unity, and weakness rather than strength. This simplistic exercise in abstraction bodes ill for the Leibnizian Trinity.

In 'De scriptura ecclesia trinitate', the fourth paper, he credits traditional apologetic errors. Here he suggests 'ut [...] Trinitatem possimus satis evincere ex scripturis, traditione non adhibita' (Grua, p.177). Scripture manifestly agrees with tradition, which founds its authority. Thus Scripture supports the Trinity far more than the antitrinitarians admit, for they take liberties with the text. The Holy Spirit communicates the truth about the divinity by his inspiration of both Scripture and tradition. The Council of Trent confirms the unanimous opinion of the Fathers ('unanimem consensum Patrum', Grua, p.177) and, as Augustine says, to dispute the authority of the entire Church is most insolent madness. Rejection of the Trinity therefore runs the risk of damnation. 'Si natus essem in Ecclesia Romana,' Leibniz testifies, 'profecto ab ea non recederem etsi omnia crederem, quae nunc credo' (Grua, p.178). Yet his definition of person deviates from Catholic dogma. He defines it as a unique uncreated self-sustaining substance that nonetheless involves an essential relation. If he had published this paper, theologians would not have questioned the essential relations between persons, but rather the equivalence of substance and person.

God is a perfect and powerful mind. This conviction inspired further illustration of the divinity by analogy with the human mind. According to an undated paper, God thinks what no senses perceive, like the mind of a dead human body. Thinking produces 'verbum et amorem' (Grua, p.559) in God, intellect and will in man. God resembles the human mind in that he knows he exists because he is aware of himself thinking, a divine *cogito*. He differs from the human mind only by his infinite powers. The *System* reapplies the analogy to the Trinity. The author identifies power, science and will as the three principal faculties of the mind, which cannot function without the participation of all three. Christian antiquity assigns power to the Father, the source of the divinity; wisdom to the Son, the Word of the divine mind, and will or love to the Holy Spirit: 'De la puissance de l'Etre divin [...] émanent les idées des choses, vérités sublimes que la sagesse embrasse, et qui deviennent ensuite les objets de la volonté' (*Système*, p.29). This sequence, in Leibniz's opinion, establishes the order in which we should name the divine persons, but he does not pretend that the triple analogy with the mind explains the Trinity. On the contrary, the existence of three persons in one God 'dépasse toutes les conceptions de la raison' (*Système*, p.25), which merely informs us that God is unique. The author attributes the titles Father, Son and Holy Spirit to the necessity for making them somehow accessible to human comprehension. Though plausible, this remark implies untraditional intentions behind the development of the Trinity in the fourth century. Unfortunately Leibniz does not elaborate, but merely describes the Son as born of the Father, and the Spirit as proceeding from them both according to the Romans and from the Father through the Son according to the Greeks. Excluding tritheism, he stresses unity. Let the antitrinitarians object to what they see as a contradiction, an abuse of the number three, a denial of the fact that three divine beings are three Gods and not one! None of these arguments moves Leibniz, who maintains that multiplying the divine persons does not multiply God, an absolute substance consisting of three relative substances.[47] While this distinction improves on the formulation in 'De scriptura', it remains heretical. As de Broglie perceives, 'de tous les dogmes chrétiens [...] il n'en est aucun [...] qui ait plus embarrassé sa philosophie' (*Système*, p.321). This difficulty went largely unseen, for otherwise it would have undermined his influence as a mediator between the churches.

His ecumenical attitude conditions the 'Remarques sur le livre d'un antitrinitaire anglais' (1693), in which he again discusses Nye's anonymous *Considerations*. From the outset he emphasises the importance of worshipping only one God by the highest cult. He invokes the first commandment against a tritheism of three absolute substances and subordinationism which reminds him of paganism. Sabellianism or modalism, which features three aspects of God, does no less violence to Scripture, he contends, than Socinianism. He admits that nature, insofar as we know it, furnishes no example of anything like the Trinity. He insists, however, that we can do without such an example as long as we avoid contradiction and absurdity. For the modal distinctions between the understanding and the understood in the human mind, we must imagine the substitution of absolute distinctions incomprehensible to us. Thus Leibniz's attack on modalism brings an adjustment in his own theory of the Trinity. Reversing the tendency in the *System*, he states, 'ce qui est contradiction dans les termes l'est partout'.[48] He accordingly condemns the semantic double standard he detects in the pages of certain Scholastics. He also introduces a

---

47. 'Sunt [...] substantiae singulares intelligentes essentialiter relativae per relationes paternitatis, generationis et processus.' Migne viii, col. 763 (letter to Loeffler cited above).
48. Migne viii, col. 767.

change in the generation of the second two persons, which he now describes as '[une] production éternelle' (col. 767). The three persons participate in all external action except the incarnation of the Son and sanctification by the Spirit, an addition. For the first time, apparently, Leibniz regrets that the Church elaborated on the basic doctrine of the Trinity in its attempts to silence adversaries. While explanations depend on definitions, he notes, neither Scripture nor tradition define the terms they use adequately. Like astronomy, theology resorts to hypotheses, yet Christian mysteries do not require explanation: '*le meilleur serait de s'en tenir précisément aux termes révélés*' (col. 768). This wish seems naive, since Scriptural language had already proved inadequate for the defence of the Trinity in the fourth century, as the 'Nicene' Creed demonstrates.[49] Leibniz's satisfaction with the vague trinity in the Bible scarcely harmonises with his rigour elsewhere.

In the 'Discours de la conformité de la foi avec la raison', he denies that the propositions 'le Père est Dieu [...] le Fils est Dieu et [...] le Saint Esprit est Dieu' contradict the further proposition 'il n'y a qu'un Dieu' (*Th.*, p.65). The logic of A=B and C=B, so A=C does not hold, because *Dieu* means divine person in the first three propositions and divine substance in the last. A warning follows never to abandon necessary truths in order to support Christian mysteries. Otherwise the enemies of religion will use this pretext to decry both mystery and religion. Yet his own support of the Trinity does not always respect the kind of logic he assigns to these truths.[50]

Leibniz's apology of the two natures and the Trinity reveals more determination than conviction. He supports the two natures more effectively than the Trinity which, as his translator de Broglie discovered, frustrates his considerable efforts. The same in both cases, his strategy consists in setting the mystery above reason by rational argumentation. His confidence in his ability to accomplish this exploit exceeds the value of the results. He discusses the Trinity, moreover, less rigorously and consistently than the two natures. In both cases, the rationalist's inappropriate faith in a partial and hence arbitrary revelation raises suspicion of his motives.

Nor does he convincingly absolve God of responsibility for evil, another daring enterprise he undertook. The urgency, as he saw it, of solving this problem fired his enthusiasm as much as the difficulty. Any rational justification of God necessitates a limitation of his power, however the apologist may choose to do it. Probably Leibniz would not have confessed to limiting God, yet he

49. See my *Christ and his 'associates' in Voltairian polemic* (Saratoga 1982), p.76-77.

50. 'Dans une perspective monadologique, la triplicité des personnes en Dieu peut paraître singulièrement embarrassante.' Pierre Burgelin, 'Théologie naturelle et théologie révélée chez Leibniz', *Studia leibnitiana supplementa*, Akten des Internationalen Leibniz-Kongresses 1966 (Wiesbaden 1969), iv.16.

deprived him of the power to determine necessary truth which Descartes had given him. The Leibnizian deity must accept truth of which the contrary implies a contradiction, even though Leibniz camouflages this contradiction by assigning all such truths to the divine mind. Since God has the necessary truths in his mind, they may not seem to limit his thought, but obviously they do. This sleight of hand absolves him of responsibility for all that is necessary, or so Leibniz would have us believe. Once he establishes this principle, he faces many further, but lesser difficulties. He eventually eliminates them by demonstrating, in one way or another, that they depend on necessary truth.

He defines metaphysical perfection as absolute existence, so his God exists necessarily. There is no other perfect being because it would be God too, a theological impossibility, and the two perfect beings would be identical, a metaphysical impossibility. Except for God all monads are necessarily imperfect and their imperfection (the amount of primary matter they contain) varies according to the position of each in the infinite chain of being. Metaphysical evil, the source of all other evil, consists of imperfection, thus God escapes responsibility for the necessity of evil in his creation. Metaphysical evil causes moral evil (human misbehaviour) and physical evil (natural adversity), but all three are negative in character because Leibniz conceives of evil as a deficiency. The mind of God contains an infinite number of consubstantial and coeternal essences that he did not make and cannot change. Although each has the potential to form an existence, every one of these possible existences can coexist only with a finite number of others, those with which it is compatible or compossible. God has the liberty to choose any combination of essences capable of forming a coherent world and the power to create this world. Yet he can neither create more than one nor create one combining incompossible existences.[51] Here again, Leibniz is limiting God. His deity can decide whether to create a world and which world to create, if he chooses one from an infinite number of possible worlds, but he must create one of these. As Des Bosses wrote to Leibniz, 'God cannot have created any one of these monads which now exist without having constituted all the rest' (Loemker, p.611). Although God cannot make perfect creatures, his own perfection moves him to make the best he can and hence to choose the best possible world for creation.[52] His standard of excellence qualifies as a necessary truth, so we share it with him:

51. 'Each substance within a possible world carries within itself an ineradicable imprint of all the rest [...] None of its substances can be abstracted from that world and none adjoined to it without undoing the intricately woven fabric of compossibility relationships' (Rescher, p.59).

52. 'There are not, as with Descartes, partial imperfections compensated for by the perfection of the whole. Each part of the world aids in the maximization of perfection by contributing the maximum of perfection that is, under the circumstances, possible for it' (Rescher, p.40).

'Cette vérité que tout ce que Dieu fait est raisonnable et ne saurait être mieux fait frappe d'abord tout homme de bon sens, et extorque, pour ainsi dire, son approbation' (*Th.*, p.316) Since perfection consists of existence, a creation is better than no creation. And the best one maximises, as Rescher observes (p.29), '*the variety of its contents*' and '*the simplicity of its laws*'. After considering all possible worlds, therefore, God chose the one that combines the greatest possible variety with the greatest possible simplicity.[53] Nowhere does Leibniz however pretend, as Voltaire insinuates, that this world is a delight.[54]

The choice of this world resulted in the creation of the first man described in Genesis and all his posterity. If God had not chosen the best possible world, the first man would have been someone else. Thus Leibniz speaks of possible Adams, a plural that troubled Arnauld, accustomed as he was to the traditional uniqueness of the Adam in Genesis. A merely semantic disagreement? No, because Arnauld did not admit the possibility of other first men, not even in Leibniz's peculiar context. The best of all Leibnizian worlds includes an Adam who disobeys God. All the Adams who obey God would be compossible only with inferior worlds. Since every subject contains all of its own predicates, the complete notion of a possible Adam not only includes those of all his posterity, but also everything that would ever happen to him or any of them if God created this Adam. It even reflects the entire world with which this Adam would harmonise, 'each individual substance being an expression of the whole universe'.[55] Consequently, God cannot adapt the best possible Adam to the best possible world. He can only choose the best possible world and accept the Adam compossible with it. In choosing ours, he has in effect chosen the one in Genesis. The contrary opinion seems so impossible, absurd and impious to Leibniz that he tells the Landgrave of Hessen-Rheinfels, 'all men are fundamentally of the same opinion' (Mason, p.16).

Accused by Arnauld of restricting God's liberty, he denies the charge on the grounds that God has a choice. God does not forfeit his liberty by making this choice in advance of consequences which he foresees. Nor does necessity force him to choose the best, but rather his freedom allows him to make this choice

53. 'Il résulte du principe de raison suffisante que, Dieu choisissant le meilleur et l'être étant préférable au non-être, il n'y a pas de vide dans la création: d'où le principe de continuité. Le meilleur réclame le maximum d'effet avec le minimum de dépense: d'où le principe de moindre action ou des voies les plus courtes' (Belaval, p.258).

54. 'Un monde avec le mal pouvait être meilleur qu'un monde sans mal: mais on est encore allé plus avant dans l'ouvrage, et l'on a même montré que cet univers doit être effectivement meilleur que tout autre univers possible' (*Th.* p.364). Pangloss in Voltaire's *Candide* (1759) proclaims: 'Ceux qui ont avancé que tout est bien ont dit une sottise: il fallait dire que tout est au mieux.' *Romans et contes* (Paris 1966), p.180.

55. *The Leibniz-Arnauld correspondence*, ed. H. T. Mason (Manchester 1967), p.57.

which he desires: 'Dieu est toujours porté infailliblement au meilleur' (Gerhardt, iii.402).[56] Leibniz preserves divine liberty by a distinction between inclination and necessity, human liberty by a distinction between motivation and necessity. Both are vulnerable to the charge of sophistry. How can the choice of a world determine Adam to sin without necessitating this sin? No more than a subtle difference between Leibnizian definitions of the terms absolves the Creator of the responsibility for it. Yet Leibniz stresses the reality of all logic, however subtle. His conception of liberty seems more ancient than modern: 'It is the highest freedom to be impelled to the best by a right reason. Whoever desires any other freedom is a fool' (Loemker, p.146-47). The self-determination of the programmed monad in a pre-established harmony with the rest of the universe satisfies his standards. He even militates against the possibility of absolute freedom, 'une chimère qui choque le bon sens [...] [car] c'est un des plus grands principes du bon sens que rien n'arrive jamais sans cause' (Gerhardt, iii.401). An unmotivated choice between equally attractive alternatives would be an effect without a cause and therefore impossible. Equidistant from equal quantities of hay on one side and oats on the other, Buridan's ass would have starved to death.

The *Théodicée* warns against confusing liberty with indifference or a lack of motivation. This confusion results in the error of denying that a predictable event can happen freely. Though determined and certain, an event may not be constrained and necessary. This distinction evidently applies to human beings, but less evidently to an omniscient and omnipotent being. Can God suspend his power to do while exercising his power to know? Yes, says Leibniz, apparently on the evidence of his juridical studies.[57] God foresees Adam's sin and allows him to commit it without compelling him in any way: 'Adam a péché librement, et [...] Dieu l'a vu péchant dans l'état d'Adam possible, qui est devenu actuel, suivant le décret de la permission divine' (*Th.*, p.335). The psychology of the Adam in the best possible world, which God decided to create, determines his sin. Yet this psychology does not force him to commit it, so God has no responsibility for it. Since human liberty inclines Adam to do good, he is responsible for his sin and we cannot blame it on God. Adam therefore deserves

56. 'As for moral necessity, this [...] does not derogate from liberty. For when a wise being, and especially God, who has supreme wisdom, chooses what is best, he is not the less free upon that account: on the contrary, it is the most perfect liberty not to be hindered from acting in the best manner.' *The Leibniz-Clarke correspondence*, ed. H. G. Alexander (New York 1956), p.56.

57. 'Lorsqu'on a prévu le mal, qu'on ne l'a point empêché, quoiqu'il paraisse qu'on ait pu le faire aisément, et qu'on a même fait des choses qui l'ont facilité, il ne s'ensuit point pour cela *nécessairement* qu'on en soit le complice; ce n'est qu'une présomption très forte [...] on appelle *présomption* chez les jurisconsultes ce qui doit passer pour vérité par provision, en cas que le contraire ne se prouve point' (*Th.* p.70-71).

the punishment he receives. Might God not have intervened by a miracle, however, to keep him from sinning? Leibniz wrote Malebranche that God could not reasonably disrupt the work of creation to prevent the fall: 'Cette complaisance pour une seule espèce de créatures, quelque excellente qu'elle soit, aurait été trop grande' (Gerhardt, i.360). Although God allows Adam to sin, he neither wants him to nor derives any satisfaction from his fall. On the contrary, he wants his creatures to do only good. Sometimes they sin in spite of him and this evil eventually results in good. Punishment and satisfaction may correct the evil or even produce a greater good than before the sin. While God does not wish such evil, he permits it and, in fact, supports it to the extent of maintaining the laws of nature by which it occurs. 'Il en sait tirer un plus grand bien' (Gerhardt, iv.432).

Leibniz effectively endorses the traditional opinion that original sin necessitated the advent of Christ. His description of the doctrine in the *System* nonetheless deviates from tradition. The first man succumbed to concupiscence, 'le péché animal' (*Système*, p.11), so that through him original sin spread to the entire human race. All men contract a vice that slows their benevolence and quickens their malevolence, obscures their intelligence, subjects them to their senses. The contagion spreads from parent to child, not from soul to soul, but rather from body to body. 'Ce ne peut être [...] que par ses rapports avec les objets extérieurs que [...] la disposition à pécher prend naissance dans l'âme' (*Système*, p.10). Here is an innovation that Leibniz would discard later. The contagion, we read, enslaves all men to sin and they would dash to their ruin if the hand of God did not hold them back. Published only a few years later, the *Discours* adds that, even before original sin cost us our innocence, an original imperfection exposed Adam to the temptation of sin. 'La racine du mal', explains Leibniz, 'est dans le néant, c'est-à-dire dans la [...] limitation des créatures' (Gerhardt, iv.454). Already in 1686, therefore, he sought to acquit God of any responsibility for the fall. The very thought that evil might implicate the Creator seems to have haunted him during most of his career. In his correspondence with Des Bosses, he describes original sin as a defect in the soul that corresponds to a defect in the body. In another letter, he considers it ignorance, a vice, an obstacle to active virtue, 'virtutis agendi impedimentum' (Gerhardt, ii.317). It differs from ordinary vice no more than an innate from an acquired condition. The obstacle causes a reaction more healthy than the state of indifference preceding it. Five years later Leibniz wrote Des Bosses that original sin consists in a predetermined, but not a compelling urge to sin. Adam had no such tendency before the fall, either to good or to evil. Seven months later, however, Leibniz had changed his mind: the urge to do good prevailed in Adam before the fall, even though the seeds of future evil lay dormant in his soul.

The fall and original sin receive more attention in the *Théodicée* than anywhere else in Leibniz's works. Bayle's ambivalent analysis of the Creator's apparent responsibility for evil had troubled him deeply. He therefore wrote the *Théodicée* to answer the threat he saw in Bayle's insinuations. After emphasising the necessary imperfection of Adam, he argues that his disobedience naturally produced unfortunate consequences. Despite God's righteous irritation, he did not punish Adam by corrupting his body and soul. Nor did he make any arbitrary decree against him as Bayle implies. Leibniz joins the infralapsarians in their opposition to the supralapsarians, who think God decided to punish Adam even before he knew Adam would sin. He disagrees with Augustine and others who believe that original sin irrevocably condemns an arbitrary majority of Adam's offspring: 'il est étrange que le péché d'autrui doive condamner quelqu'un' (*Th.*, p.36). The idea of a divine tyrant with no justice or benevolence, using his absolute power for the creation of millions condemned to suffer eternally, revolts him. Widespread belief in such a travesty, he warns, would turn men against each other and against the true deity. It would do as much evil as the serpent who persuaded Eve that God had not prohibited the forbidden fruit for her own good. While God created a man capable of sin, Adam sinned of his own accord and God re-created him after the fall. 'La même raison qui lui a fait créer l'homme innocent, mais prêt à tomber, lui fait recréer l'homme lorsqu'il tombe, puisque sa science fait que le futur lui est comme le présent, et qu'il ne saurait rétracter les résolutions prises. (*Th.*, p.120). The last point is not entirely clear, but Leibniz seems to have meant that the maintenance of the creation continues according to the same divine laws. God made man free, man abused his liberty and fell from grace, yet he remains free. Satan, who seduced him, holds him in bondage only because man 's'y plaît […] il est esclave volontaire par sa mauvaise concupiscence' (*Th.*, p.283). Regeneration is nonetheless within his reach.

Many of these tenets reappear in the *Cause de Dieu plaidée par sa justice*, a condensation of the *Théodicée* published by Leibniz in 1710. The author rejects Bayle's contention that God infused a sinful nature in Adam and his posterity as punishment for his transgression. This sinful nature evolved rather from the first sin 'comme par une connexion physique'. *Comme* means *as if* here, for 'les âmes des descendants se sont trouvées infectées en Adam même' (*Th.*, p.440). On the strength of contemporary research in biology, Leibniz endorses the infinitely successive encapsulation of human germs in Adam. Each germ consists of a rudimentary minute body that will eventually develop into a man or woman. Each body already has a sensible soul which the creator, naturally or supernaturally ('je n'en décide pas', *Th.*, p.440), will convert into a rational soul at conception. This event would otherwise be insignificant, since Leibniz accepted the recent scientific opinion that men alone transmit the germ and the soul, while women merely provide a womb for the incubation of the foetus. When Adam sinned, therefore, the contagion immediately spread to all the encapsulated germs of the human race because of their physical contact with each other. The infection of each also contaminated its soul. But how could an as yet irrational and hence amoral soul undergo such contamination? Leibniz neither asks nor answers this question.

He opposes the damnation of infants and infidels who die unbaptised. Since infants dying before their parents can baptise them have committed no sin, how can a just God condemn them? 'Personne ne peut être malheureux sans sa faute' (*Système*, p.12). A deleted sentence follows in which Leibniz notes the opinion of several pious and learned men: God does not refuse the light necessary for salvation to anyone who sincerely seeks the truth, and not even in countries ignorant of Christ's name and gospel. Leibniz probably deleted this sentence because he was referring to Lutheran theologians, whose testimony would compromise the ecumenical neutrality of the *System*. In the *Théodicée* he observes that Lutheran theologians trust in divine justice and clemency for the salvation of infants who die without baptism. He expects a similar Catholic opinion eventually to prevail over the severity of Augustinians like Nicole. They would have God withhold his grace from unbaptised infants and grant it to others who do not deserve it. Furthermore, pagan virtues are not false, as they claim, and pagan deeds are not all sins. Augustine's scorn for what he calls '*splendida peccata* [...] choque la raison' (*Th.*, p.271).

Evidently Leibniz does not admit the direct consequences of original sin advocated by Augustine and his followers. A radical alteration in human nature would, as Pichler remarks, violate his law of continuity.[58] He sees no divine punishment in original sin, but rather a natural effect. It does not enslave us, for we willingly submit to it by the same abuse of human liberty as Adam did. It neither incites us to further sin nor condemns us to death, which does not consist in the traditional isolation of the soul from matter. Leibniz even exempts the mind from hereditary guilt by promoting the rational transcreation of the sensible soul at conception. The Council of Trent, he complains, overreacted to Protestantism when it adopted a severe version of original sin.

The eucharist held his attention more than original sin or any other aspect of Christianity. For motives ranging from the illustration of his philosophy to the reunification of the Christian churches, he comments on private mass, the

---

58. 'Für eine so buchstäbliche Auffassung des mosaischen Erzählung ist im System des Leibniz schlechterdings kein Platz, sie widerspricht direkt seinen Gesetz der Bewegung und Continuität; denn dieß wäre wahrhaftig ein *salto mortale*, wie es nach ihm in der Natur keinen gibt' (Pichler, i.320).

lay cup, sacrifice, the real presence and especially transubstantiation. Yet he rarely communed himself. In 1687 he told the Landgrave of Hessen-Rheinfels that he had not taken the Lutheran communion for many years. His secretary Eccard testifies that he communed only once in the last nineteen years of his life.[59] Catholics like the Landgrave, who hoped to convert him, and Protestants as well interpreted his abstention as a symptom of papist affinity. Although this interpretation surprised him, he preferred not to clarify his position. In his comments on Ernst's letter, he denies the charge of indifference and insinuates that he abstained from Lutheran communion because he disagrees with some of the doctrine. Indeed he probably questioned the tenets that hindered reunification with the Calvinists and the Catholics. Certainly in his opinion reunification deserved a higher priority than purity of faith, whatever that faith may be. In the *System*, however, he concedes more to Catholicism than to Protestantism and this inequity implies a willingness to appease the most powerful and least yielding church. His steadfast profession of the Lutheran faith seems to have served more as a negotiating position than an expression of deep convictions. Born a Catholic, he admits, he would have believed all that he believed as a Lutheran.

He found transubstantiation consistent with his faith at the beginning of his career and inconsistent at the end. His early 'Refutation of Thomas White's Hypothesis' (1668?) defends the dogma from this English Catholic. White's theory, he objects, implies that the substance of Christ's body increases by generation and decreases by corruption as communion wafers are consecrated or digested: 'Nam Thomas Anglus est in ea haeresi' (*S.S.*, vi.1.505). Anxious no doubt to make a name for himself, the youthful theologian subjects White's text[60] to a scathing analysis (of no interest here) that hardly resembles the diplomacy of later years. Written at the same time, apparently, 'On transubstantiation' attempts to prove the dogma by means of Scholastic concepts 'tantum clare expositis conficiemus' (*S.S.*, vi.1.508). More clearly than the Scholastics? So it seems. The demonstration that follows adapts the theory of substance in 'The incarnation and the hypostatic union' to transubstantiation. Substance consists in the union of a body with a concurrent mind. Everything virtually or really separate from a mind is an accident. Human substances unite our bodies

59. 'Das Abendmahl [...] hätte Leibniz doch fleißiger empfangen sollen. Denn sein Secretär Eccard versichert, daß Leibniz die neunzehn Jahre (1697-1716), wo er ihn kannte, seines Wissens niemals dieß gethan habe, ausgenommen ein einziges Mal während seines Aufenthaltes in Wien, als dort die Pest grassirte, wo er in der lutherischen Kirche dasselbe empfing [...] Das Zeugniß des Landgrafen Ernst, der in seinem Empfehlungsschreiben von 27. November 1687, daß er Leibniz auf die Reise mitgab, ausdrücklich sagte, es habe dieser ihm gestanden, daß er seit langen Jahren nicht zur lutherischen Communion gegangen sei' (Pichler, ii.435-36).

60. A preface to Kenelm Digby's *Demonstratio immortalitatis animae rationalis* (Paris 1655).

with our minds, while substances lacking reason unite their bodies with God's mind. Changing the concurrent mind transubstantiates the body. The substitution of Christ's human mind for the divine mind in the substances of bread and wine converts them into those of his body and blood. Thus consecrated bread and wine are substantially identical with the body that suffered for us. Their appearances or accidents subsist because changing the concurrent mind does not affect them. 'For mind is compatible with all accidents which do not receive or lose essence through it, but only action' (Loemker, p.116). Although a mind has no position in space, it acts upon a body which does, thus a mind can act in more than one place at a time. Christ's mind acts on his body under the appearances of bread and wine wherever and whenever they are consecrated. His body not only exists in heaven, therefore, but likewise in all these places at all these times.

In his first extant letter to Arnauld (Nov. 1671) he disclosed that he no longer believed the essence of matter to be extension, as Descartes had said. Convinced that this opinion ruins the real multipresence, he substituted energy for extension. The fear of imperilling the dogma therefore determined the most fundamental and original principle in his philosophy. He was 'clearly very sensitive to any philosophical threat to Christian doctrine', as Barber notes.[61] Transubstantiation and the real multipresence, Leibniz tells Arnauld, are really the same thing and they even contain each other. Crediting himself with this discovery, he infers that the Augsburg Confession unwittingly concurs with the Council of Trent on this point.[62] 'De ipsa igitur mysterii ratione ac modo, si durationem adimas, sentiunt nescientes' (Gerhardt, i.76). Lutherans and Catholics only disagree on whether to limit the real presence to the moment of reception or extend it from consecration to destruction. The momentary presence justifies the Lutherans in confining their worship of the eucharist to the moment of reception. The longer presence justifies the Catholics in worshipping it from the consecration to the digestion of the bread and wine. Leibniz assumes that Scripture and Church tradition will reveal Christ's choice in the matter, a naive assumption. Obviously he had much to learn in 1671 about mutual suspicion and hostility between the churches.

61. W. H. Barber, *Leibniz in France from Arnauld to Voltaire* (Oxford 1955), p.11.
62. 'Von dem Abendmahl des Herrn wird also gelehrt, daß wahrer Leib und Blut Christi wahrhaftiglich unter der Gestalt des Brots und Weins im Abendmahl gegenwärtig sei und da ausgeteilt und genommen wird.' *The Augsburg Confession: a collection of sources*, ed., Johann Reu (Chicago 1930), p.177. 'Principio docet sancta synodus et aperte ac simpliciter profitetur, in almo sanctae eucharistiae sacramento post panis et vini consecrationem Dominum nostrum Iesum Christum verum Deum atque hominem vere, realiter ac substantialiter sub specie illarum rerum sensibilium contineri.' Heinrich Denziger, *Enchiridion symbolorum, definitionum et declarationum* (Freiburg im Breisgau 1937), no.874.

The attempt to appease the more powerful church in the *System*, which he wrote fifteen years later, suggests a greater understanding of the difficulty involved in reunification of the churches. Here he confirms that his faith in transubstantiation had driven him to abandon extension as the substance of matter. He approaches the Catholic dogma too closely however for the comfort of the other churches, whose doctrines he systematically rejects. He denies that 'le corps du Christ est dans, avec et sous le pain' (*Système*, p.197), as Luther teaches,[63] or in the bread like coins in a purse. Likewise the Zwinglian objection that no body can be in heaven and on earth in several places at the same time. Likewise the Calvinist expedient of comparing the perception of the heavenly body by the elevated mind of the faithful with imaginary travel to distant lands, as when 'nous nous transportons par la pensée à Constantinople et à Rome' (*Système*, p.193). Likewise the Cartesianism of Calvinist theologians who, out of hostility to Catholicism, reduce accidents to inseparable modes of substance. None of these doctrines satisfies Leibniz's standard of belonging to the tradition of Christian antiquity, which interprets 'This is my body' as proof that a conversion really takes place. As usual he founds this conviction on the contemporary ignorance of eucharistic theology before Ambrose. He even implies that the Roman Church needed only to translate the Greek words for conversion in order to establish transubstantiation. This error alone would have sufficed to ruin the neutrality of the *System* if he had published it.

The nature of bodies, he concedes, necessitates extension unless God makes an exception. They consist of derivative active and passive energy produced by the primary active and passive energy of their substances. Derivative active energy manifests itself as the power of a body to act, and derivative passive energy, as its resistance to penetration. These secondary powers are not ordinary accidents or modes of substance, but real accidents that add something absolute to substance. Changing them changes the body, although the substance remains the same. Secondary powers result in dimensions (extension) and other secondary qualities. These may change naturally when some secondary powers replace others, but God can alter this replacement or prevent it, so that a substance will have no extension: 'D'après les règles de la raison, tout ce qui est distingué réellement peut être séparé par la puissance absolue de Dieu' (*Système*, p.209). God can assign various combinations of secondary qualities to a body and he can also assign one body to several substances. He can even sustain the secondary qualities of a body he has destroyed. But he cannot manipulate ordinary accidents, which are merely modes of substance or relations depending on real accidents by metaphysical necessity. Then how exactly does God transubstanti-

63. See my *Voltaire and the eucharist*, Studies on Voltaire 198 (Oxford 1981), p.65-66.

ate consecrated bread and wine into Christ's body and blood? Leibniz neither indicates nor suggests that he has adopted any particular solution to this problem. Perhaps he could not decide between the various solutions he proposes.

He did make the decision he had avoided in his letter to Arnauld. Should we worship Christ in the eucharist from the consecration to the digestion of the species or only at the moment of reception? The author of the *System* adopts the Catholic opinion and discards the Lutheran one. Either the words of the consecration are false, he argues, 'ce qu'à Dieu ne plaise' (*Système*, p.201), or the species become the body of Christ before manducation. Proponents of transubstantiation at the moment of manducation face 'difficultés repoussantes' (*Système*, p.201), so disgusting that he does not explain them, but he was probably thinking of Capernaitic consequences, however devious they may seem in this case. He advances another argument in favour of a lasting presence. The ancient Christians brought the eucharist to sick people who could not come to church and they took it with them when they travelled in regions where they could not obtain it. Obviously they thought Christ remained present from consecration until digestion. The example of the ancient Christians usually has decisive influence on Leibniz. A Protestant reflex, no doubt.

In the *System*, therefore, he advocates a doctrine of transubstantiation that conforms almost entirely to Catholic dogma. But several years before he composed the work, he wrote to bishop Spinola (1683) that the Protestants would demand the right to disagree with the dogma as a condition of reunification, if negotiations for this purpose should take place. Since the pope had mandated Spinola to investigate the possibility of such negotiations, the future author of the *System* would seem to be giving him a realistic warning of what to expect. Several years after the composition of this work, he wrote to the Catholic convert Pellisson (1691) that transubstantiation 'semble choquer les principes de la raison' (Foucher, i.228). He adheres to the Confession of Augsburg, he continues, and believes in the real presence. His correspondence with Pellisson, Bossuet and others explored the possibilities of reunifying the Lutheran and Catholic churches. Evidently, however, he no longer accepted transubstantiation and no longer thought that this doctrine and the real presence imply each other. Perhaps his warning to Spinola in 1683 conveyed personal doubt as well as the opposition of his fellow Protestants. After 1691, in any case, he discussed transubstantiation only in the interest of seeking church reunification or illustrating his monadic philosophy. Did he abandon his unqualified endorsement of the doctrine in the *System* because he realised that his fellow Protestants would never follow his example? Reunification certainly appears to have exceeded all of his other priorities, including his personal faith. He nonetheless emitted two further theories of transubstantiation, even though he had lost enthusiasm for the dogma.

The first theory remains within the bounds of phenomenalism. According to Broad's interpretation (p.125), we consciously misperceive the colour, texture and taste of bread (and wine), unconsciously the minute structure that stimulates these sensations. We misperceive them nonetheless, because both are merely the appearances of monads. When the celebrant says the words of consecration, Christ miraculously converts the minute structure to that of his body (and blood) without disturbing the colour, texture and taste of bread. While continuing to misperceive these qualities consciously, the communicants now misperceive the body of Christ unconsciously. So superficial an account could hardly have satisfied Leibniz if transubstantiation had still interested him. Nor did it satisfy Catholics like Des Bosses who, in his correspondence with the philosopher, urged him to formulate a profounder theory. Leibniz had excited the Jesuit's curiosity by boasting that he could found such a theory on monads. Yet he hesitated to do it for several years in the name of a Lutheranism admitting neither transubstantiation nor consubstantiation. As late as 1709 he wrote to Des Bosses that we perceive the body of Christ upon reception of the consecrated bread, a doctrine he calls transperception.

In 1712 be began to show him he could account for transubstantiation by means of substantial bonds. He regards bread and wine as organisms because, though unalive in the natural sense, they come from plants.[64] When a celebrant recites the words of the consecration, Christ destroys the substantial bond uniting the monads of bread and wine. He transfers these monads to the substantial bonds uniting the monads of his body and blood. The transferred monads continue to sustain the appearances of bread and wine, so communicants perceive no sensual change in the species. Yet they receive Christ's body and blood, the only remaining real composite substances. When Christ said, 'This is my body', he did not mean the monads of his body, 'sed substantiam per vincula substantialia ortum seu compositum' (Gerhardt, ii.459). For how could he have been thinking of monads? But how, we might retort, could he have been thinking of substantial bonds either? One seems as remote from Jesus's mind as the other. Des Bosses in fact raises the question of an alternative solution involving monads alone. Thus Leibniz satisfies his curiosity by supposing, in

64. 'Omnia corpora sunt ex viventibus aggregata, et vincula substantialia singulorum viventium componentium, substantiam eorum componunt' (Gerhardt, ii.482). 'It is only where you have a dominant monad and an organism of subordinate monads that it is plausible to suppose that there is a *vinculum substantiale*, which combines these subordinate monads into a genuine corporeal substance independent of the observer and his perceptions. How he reconciles this with his application to the theory to the bread and wine in the eucharist I do not understand' (Broad, p.127).

this case, that 'the monads of bread and wine are destroyed and the monads of [Christ's] body put in their place' (Loemker, p.607). Despite his detachment, however, he states his preference for a theory of transubstantiation based on substantial bonds. A few years later he informed Des Bosses that the substantial bonds of Christ's body exert the same influence on those of our body as those of bread and wine would have if Christ had not destroyed them,[65] so that 'we perceive the substance of the body and blood of Christ' (Loemker, p.614). Once the appearances of bread and wine undergo destruction, they cannot reappear as they were, but only as they would have become without destruction. Hence the natural results of digestion, even after communion on transubstantiated bread and wine!

This speculation on a supernatural process in which Leibniz no longer believed amounts to an exercise useful only in demonstrating the flexibility of his metaphysics. But why had he renounced transubstantiation after defending it so vigorously in earlier years? Pichler has found a few answers in Leibniz's unfinished *Annales Imperii Occidentis Brunsvicienses*.[66] an enormous project imposed on him by Duke Georg-Ludwig.[67] The author deplores bleeding communion wafers and the other superstitions inspired by transubstantiation. He emphasises that the early medieval disputes over the real presence, from which transubstantiation emerged, spawned this superstition. Furthermore, Paschase and Ratramn not only disagreed with each other, but Thomas and the Scholastics taught a doctrine different from theirs and even from that of the Roman Church in Leibniz's day. Although several centuries of controversy between learned Christians did not settle the issue, the Church imposed a partisan doctrine by decree. At Trent it even cursed the many Christians who could not accept this arbitrary decision.

Unlike the youthful Leibniz, the old man realised the impossibility of resolving the antagonism over transubstantiation by reinvestigation of its Biblical sources and the early Christian tradition. The Protestants, he now understood, would never concede the validity of a doctrine they had always scorned and resented. Since it nonetheless remained a major obstacle to reunification of Protestants and Catholics, he urged Bossuet to consider a suspension of the canons enacted

65. There is an error in Loemker's translation here: 'But the substantial chains of the monads of the body of Christ will have an influence upon the substantial chains of the monads of our body, which they would otherwise have had on the substantial chains of bread and wine' (Loemker, p.614). 'Sed vincula substantialia monadum corporis Christi eum in vincula substantialia monadum corporis nostri influxum habebunt, quem alias in ea habuissent vincula substantialia monadum panis et vini' (Gerhardt, ii.505). The final clause of the translation should read: 'which the substantial chains of bread and wine would otherwise have had on those of our bodies.'

66. Partial publications in 1843, 1846. See Pichler, ii.355-56.

67. Who became George I of England in 1714.

at Trent that condemned Protestant dissent from transubstantiation and other dogmas. He envisaged a preliminary stage of reunification in which both parties would tolerate each other's opinions until a council had settled their differences. Bossuet refused. Yet Leibniz suspected the Catholics of disagreeing with one another on other dogmas as radically as they disagreed with the Protestants on transubstantiation.

He saw a further stumbling block for reunification in the Catholic worship of the eucharist. In a letter to Bossuet's friend Mme de Brinon, he complained, 'quand on parle chez vous du bon Dieu [...] le vulgaire entend et adore un petit morceau blanc et rond qu'un prêtre porte' (Foucher, ii.83). From the negotiations for reunification, however, he knew that English and Polish Protestants as well as the Helvetian Confession kneeled before the sacrament. Protestants should therefore tolerate the Catholic worship of the sacrament, provided the pope declare Christ the unique object of worship. This declaration would alleviate their suspicions of idolatry.

But Leibniz wanted to reconcile the Protestants with each other as well as with the Catholics. Accepted by Lutherans and rejected by the Reformers, the real presence, among other things, threatened his intentions. During his early endorsement of transubstantiation, he settled for disapproval of the Reformers, whose eucharistic theology he knew poorly. Towards the turn of the century, however, he examined it for points in common with Lutheranism. He discussed the reunification of the two churches with the Calvinist Jablonski and the Lutheran Molanus, also a participant in the discussion with Bossuet. The presence of Christ's body in the eucharist divided the Reformers themselves between Calvinists and Zwinglians. Though conciliatory in the final period, Leibniz opposed Zwingli's purely symbolic presence throughout his career. It was rather his attitude towards Calvin's spiritual presence that changed. In 1669 he welcomed *La Perpétuité de la foi* by Arnauld and Nicole,[68] a reply to the Huguenot Claude, in which he saw definitive external proof of the real presence. He only needed, he thought, to complement their erudition by the definitive internal proof he attempted in his early writings on transubstantiation. Calvin's spiritual presence could muster no greater support than the absurdity of an extended real presence in the Cartesian perspective, which he meant to abolish.

In seeking an accomodation with the Calvinists, he turned to the example of the Anglican Church before 1714 when his patron became king of England. The latitude this church allowed its members, and laymen even more than clergymen, impressed him. In his correspondence with Jablonski he insists on the retention of the real presence, but denies that Lutherans believe in impanation or

68. Nicole is the true author.

consubstantiation, a common assumption among Calvinists. We can locate Christ's presence in the communion wafer no more precisely, he explains, than the soul in the body. It consists in the immediate application of substance or, in other words, active and passive force. Leibniz purports to reconcile Calvin with himself by interpreting the perception of Christ's body in his doctrine as the effect of this force. This interpretation should allay Calvinist fears of Capernaism, as Leibniz insinuates in a letter to Jablonski. Here he exposes a similar kind of presence in the twenty-eighth article of the Anglican Confession: 'Der Leib Christi [wird] wahrhaftig [...] gegessen [...] obschon auf eine himmlische [...] Weise; das ist nicht fleischlich.'[69] The Calvinists likewise fear reception by unworthy communicants, hence the requirement of faith. Rather than run the risk of symbolism, on the other hand, the Lutherans admit reception by the unworthy. Thus Leibniz proposes mutual concessions tending to a common position. The Calvinists should explicitly rule out the symbolic interpretation and the Lutherans, the possibility of any injury to Christ by unworthy communion. As if one could soil the sun by throwing mud at it (a traditional argument)! Both should agree that, while the unworthy can commune on the bread and wine, they do not receive the body and blood. Christ keeps them from receiving his body and blood, which he can present wherever he pleases. Leibniz's interpretation of the Calvinist presence should persuade the Reformers' followers that Christ's real body can be in heaven and on earth in many places at the same time. They should therefore accept the real presence, but the Lutherans must exclude Capernaism too.

Leibniz raises the question of Protestant differences again in the *Nouveaux essais* and the *Théodicée*. In the former work, Philalèthe assumes that the professors at Luther's university in Wittenberg teach consubstantiation. How can anyone with good sense believe flesh and bread to be the same thing? Lutheran theologians, Théophile replies, have denied many times that they believe in consubstantiation. 'En recevant les symboles visibles, on reçoit d'une manière invisible et surnaturelle le corps du Sauveur, sans qu'il soit enfermé dans le pain' (*N.E.*, p.456). Neither local, nor spatial, nor dimensional, this presence escapes detection by the senses. Yet it differs from the presence of Christ's body in heaven which has a locality suitable to the circumstances. The sacramental presence by which Christ governs the Church is not everywhere like God, but everywhere he wants it to be. Essentially Calvin agrees with Luther since he says that the symbols provide what they represent without 'la

---

69. *D. E. Jablonsky's Briefwechsel mit Leibniz, Acta et commentationes imp. universitatis Jurievensis*, ed. J. Kvacsala (Dorpat 1897), p.97. 'The body of Christ is given, taken and eaten in the [Lord's] Supper only after an heavenly and spiritual manner.' Quoted from E. S. Bicknell, *A theological introduction to the thirty-nine articles of the Church of England* (London 1955), p.382.

circonscription des lieux ou la diffusion des dimensions' (*N.E.*, p.457). They only disagree over the conditions of communion, perception of the symbols according to Luther and faith according to Calvin, who thus excludes the unworthy. And Calvin opposes the metaphorical presence of Zwingli.

The *Théodicée* repeats some of these opinions and adds others. The Lutherans distinguish themselves from the Reformers by their fidelity to the literal meaning of the institution words. The necessity for honouring Jesus's last wishes stiffens their resistance to absurd interpretations. 'Ils n'ont point recours à je ne sais quelle diffusion d'ubiquité qui [...] dissiperait [le corps du Christ] et ne le laisserait trouver nulle part' (*Th.*, p.62). Nor do they accept the multiplication of this body by replication as proposed by certain Scholastics. They profess a mysterious concomitance by which communicants receive the body at the same time as the bread but separately. After a restatement of the similarity between Calvin's theory of the presence and the Lutheran doctrine, Leibniz illustrates the latter by an analogy with immediate presence. This idea consists in the operation of one body on another at a distance from it. Immediate operation may in fact depend on a presence of one body to others achieved by divine power. Although many philosophers including Leibniz no longer accept immediate presence, Newton's theory of gravitation implies a renewal of the principle. Lutheran theologians submit, in any case, that God not only causes one body to operate immediately on others, but also to exist in their presence without intervals or dimensions.

Thus Leibniz adhered to the Lutheran doctrine of Christ's presence in the eucharist during his entire career, even though his interpretation of the doctrine evolved from consistency with transubstantiation to conflict with this dogma. In discussing reunification, he proposed compromises between the Catholic, the Lutheran and the Reform positions on worship of Christ in the eucharist, as I have mentioned. But did he have an opinion of his own on this issue? Perhaps. While early Christians did not worship the sacrament, he observes in the *System*, later Christians did and he approves their motives. Once the zeal of primitive Christianity had subsided, communicants needed a cult to ensure proper devotion. Furthermore, 'Dieu apparaissant dans la forme visible du Christ, la raison [...] nous ordonnerait de l'adorer' (*Système*, p.227). Leibniz is thinking of Irenaeus who describes Christ's humanity as 'the visible' of his divinity,[70] yet eucharistic theology limits this visibility to metaphor. Leibniz himself emphasises that communicants do not worship roundness, whiteness and the other accidents of the species, but rather the divine presence of Christ.

No more than Luther, on the other hand, does he admit the sacrificial aspect of

70. *Irenaeus against heresies* in *The Ante-Nicene Fathers* (Buffalo 1887), i.469.

the Catholic mass. His project for the foundation of a scientific academy, Pichler reports, would require the Lutheran members to accompany their Roman colleagues to mass. He would alter the Catholic cult only by substituting German for Latin as the language spoken by the priest. Yet he clearly regards mass as nothing more than a celebration of the eucharist: 'missa illa consistat celebratione sacramenti eucharistiae' (*S.S.*, iv.1.529).[71] He imagined this step towards reunification in 1670. In a later commentary on the Twenty-Second Session,[72] he suspects the fathers at the Council of Trent of standing on the shaky ground of Scholastic novelty rather than the firm foundation of ancient Christianity. They contradicted themselves by interpreting the sacrifice of mass as both a representation and a reproduction. In Leibniz's opinion, Jesus's words, 'Do this in remembrance of me',[73] refer to the celebration of the eucharist and not the offering of a sacrifice. He admits the idea of sacrifice only in the sense of symbolic edification. The papers that foreshadow the *System*, Pichler warns, show that Leibniz did not intend to endorse Trent in this work. The Catholic Broglie effectively mistranslates words in two key sentences quoted by Pichler in this context: *reproduit* for *repraesentat* and *reproduction* for *repraesentatione*:[74] 'Le Christ [...] reproduit et [...] confirme l'efficacité perpétuelle de son premier sacrifice [...] Mais il n'y a pas [...] de propitiation sans cesse répétée [...] Toute sa force consiste dans l'application, dans la reproduction du premier sacrifice sanglant.' How could this sacrifice reproduce the original one without repeating the original propitiation? Broglie follows in Bossuet's steps by trying to convert Leibniz to Catholicism.[75] Pichler nonetheless remarks that, in the *System*, he otherwise professes the Catholic dogma by his words if not by his thoughts. One could hardly dispute this opinion. Although Christ, according to the *System*, sacrificed himself once and for all on the cross, he offers himself perpetually by the ministry of priests. The self-sacrificing high priest belongs to the order of Melchizedek who 'évidemment' (*Système*, p.233) prefigures Christ![76] Concealed by the accidents of the species, the body and blood serve as a holocaust. Only the sacrifice of a perfect being can appease God, whose nostrils delight in the odour of a humble heart. Need we continue? Leibniz seasons this servile stew of traditional jargon by allusions to various authorities: Justin, Irenaeus, Augustine ... Here his yearning for reunification drives him to an extreme. In later writings he likewise considers the mass a representation and not a reproduction of Christ's original self-sacrifice, despite

71. See Pichler, ii.380.
72. See my *Voltaire*, p.70-71.
73. Luke xxii.19; 1 Corinthians xi.24.
74. Foucher, i.624; *Système*, p.235; Pichler, ii.381-82.
75. 'Comment se fait-il ensuite que Leibniz, arrivé jusqu'à ce point, s'y soit arrêté' (*Système*, p.xxvii)?
76. See Genesis xiv.17-20; Hebrews v.6-10, vii.1-17; my *Voltaire*, p.71-72.

his pleas for mutual tolerance between Protestants and Catholics.

The *System* treats private mass more indulgently than eucharistic sacrifice, while Luther, on the contrary, attacked the former more ruthlessly than the latter. Worse, the *System* reformulates the traditional apology of private mass: a sacrifice of Christ to God alone, such a mass merely honours the saint whose feast occasions it. The custom fosters worship of God that might not otherwise take place. To abolish it would deprive God of this honour and offend good Christians who believe in it. How many of them have the solid faith of ancient communicants? Only these could accept the restoration of the original simplicity, 'et plût à Dieu que le nombre en fût grand' (*Système*, p.243)! Although the Church did without private mass for a long time, the custom became a necessity when worship began to occur more frequently than the need for communion. Elsewhere Leibniz nonetheless disapproves of celebrating mass more than once a day in a given church, a Greek Orthodox rule.[77] The author of the System must have realised that the defence of a custom which had caused much corruption and superstition would scarcely have appealed to his fellow Protestants. Pichler has no doubt that, if Leibniz had published it, 'das *System* [...] schon wegen der glimpflichen Darstellung der [Privat]messe von der ganzen protestantischen Theologie mit Erbitterung zurückgewiesen worden wäre' (ii.383). After the *System* he continued to advocate tolerance of private mass, but he no longer sought to justify it. Although he refrained from condemning it in a letter to the Landgrave (1691), he declared it unprimitive and unnecessary. Aware that both private mass and eucharistic sacrifice threatened reunification, however, he subsequently tried to deflate these issues by relegating them to the status of semantic controversy. He insisted that Catholics and Protestants agreed on them essentially, yet he continued to adhere to the Lutheran position which no Catholic could accept. A convenient but unproductive hypocrisy.

Perhaps this tactic would better have suited the unending dispute over the lay cup, but he seems to have thought otherwise. He wrote to the Landgrave in 1683 that the Church had used its authority to impose a deviation from Jesus's recommendations at the Last Supper. Finding no good reason for this change, he suspects that the hierarchy acted in its own interest rather than the Holy Spirit's. This act did not justify a schism, in his opinion, but the Church should respect the legitimate desire of many good Christians who will return to it only on this condition. The fear of delighting its enemies seems to have kept it from making this wise concession. Generosity would save more souls than admission of an error would lose.

---

77. 'Only one divine liturgy can be performed on the same altar during a day.' Stan Carlson, *Faith of our fathers: the Eastern Orthodox religion* (Minneapolis 1968), p.55.

A more comprehensive and somewhat different treatment appears in the *System*. There is no doubt, he says, that Jesus shares both species of the eucharist with his disciples. Paul and the primitive Church followed his example, just as the Eastern Church does today. Yet the danger of spilling the wine or leaving a few drops in the cup eventually moved the Western Church to withdraw it from lay communion. A number of arguments support this decision. The risen Christ gave bread alone to his followers at Emmaus, an episode still interpreted as eucharistic in Leibniz's day.[78] Ancient bishops exchanged consecrated bread to attest their fraternal charity. Ancient communicants took the bread with them on travel to desolate regions. In neither case did wine accompany the bread. Leibniz cites several writers who attest the regression of the lay cup in the fourteenth century. Finally, the Council of Constance restricted lay communion to bread alone on the grounds that concomitance assures the presence of Christ's blood as well as his body under the single species of bread. The following point contradicts the letter to the Landgrave: if individuals had altered the sacrament instituted by Christ, they would have committed a grievous sin. In the present case, however, 'nous voyons, par l'usage que l'Eglise suit depuis tant de siècles, qu'on peut omettre le calice pour des raisons légitimes' (*Système*, p.219). The Church may do what individuals may not. Otherwise, the *System* elaborates on the letter to the Landgrave. Withdrawal of the cup, for instance, does not justify a schism, but the Church should bring schismatics back into the fold by making an appropriate concession. The precedents include those made to the Bohemians at the Council of Basel[79] and the Greeks under Venetian rule. Catholic princes such as the emperor of Germany, the king of France and the duke of Bavaria sought this favour from the pope and the Council of Trent.

Leibniz is firmer in 'Pour faciliter la réunion' (1698), which declares the perpetual right of laymen to both species a condition for the return of the Protestants to the Catholic Church. As an equivalent concession, he urges the Protestants to tolerate the continuation of lay communion under one species in Catholic churches. The permanence of this right to both species suggests that he withdrew his concessions on this point in the *System* as soon as he withdrew the others we have seen.

His discussion of the sacrament stems more from the desire to reunite the major Christian churches than the urge to illustrate his metaphysics by using it to solve theological problems, an important motive nevertheless. This urge predominates in his writings on the Trinity and the two natures, where the traditional Christ and the historical Jesus receive little attention. Did the threat

---

78. See my *Voltaire*, p.124.
79. Leibniz tried repeatedly but in vain to obtain an admission of this precedent from Bossuet.

he saw in Bayle's attitude towards the innocence of God alarm his faith? His defence of God's integrity implies a greater concern for trust in the metaphysical order and respect for the moral consequences. His zeal for Christian reunification resembles pan-German patriotism more than Christian piety. Papers beyond the purview of this study[80] reveal a hidden suspicion of French politics that contrasts with his open admiration for French thought. He was not one of those Germans who, fascinated by France, forgot cardinal Richelieu's intervention in the Thirty Years War on the pretext of defending Catholic unity. The advocate of metaphysical force conceived of religion as a powerful social and political force capable of destruction or construction depending on how it was used. However typical of his times and others, this conception scarcely harmonises with true Christianity. His abstinence from practice of the Lutheranism he professed confirms the convenience of his religion. How ironical that Bossuet should want to convert such a Lutheran!

80. 'Er sucht Ludwig XIV. zu einem Zug Ägypten zu veranlassen wodurch die Expansionsdrang Frankreichs in eine andere Richtung gelenkt werden soll.' Kurt Müller und Gisela Krönert, *Leben und Werk von Gottfried Wilhelm Leibniz* (Frankfurt am Main 1969), p.25.

# Locke

JOHN Locke found the Continentals presumptuous to assume that we participate in God's thought and share his knowledge. Although he likewise referred to the natural light, he could imagine nothing in common between human and divine intelligence. The discovery by scientists like his friend Newton of infinite and eternal relations between the parts of the universe implied no need for intervention by the Creator. God gives us an intelligence of our own. These objections appear in Locke's posthumous 'Examination of P. Malebranche's opinion' along with an attack on the Frenchman's use of the sun to illustrate his occasionalism. When the sun shines on us, Malebranche argues, we do not see it directly but rather in God. How, Locke objects, can he be sure the sun really exists? Why did God bother to create it? In a posthumous reply to the criticism of Malebranche's disciple John Norris, Locke cites the intricate structure of eyes and ears. Did God take such care in vain? Why do the blind not see in him too? The difference between God containing the essences of all things and being identical with all things seems tenuous to Locke. Thus resemblance to Spinoza continued to bedevil poor Malebranche. But Locke had an even more serious quarrel with him and with Descartes as well. He rejected their opinion that the senses are illusory.[1]

He nonetheless owed much to Descartes, whose philosophy he had ample opportunity to assess while living in France (1677-1679) and Holland (1683-1689). He may have come to France for secret negotiations on behalf of his Whig patron the first Earl of Shaftesbury,[2] but he also engaged in much scholarly activity, including study of the Bible. After his return to England, Charles II began to punish the Whigs for plotting against his Catholic brother and Locke fled to Holland. He devoted this exile to intellectual fellowship and the completion of several works, among them the first *Letter concerning toleration* and the *Essay concerning human understanding*. Both appeared in 1689, the year after the Glorious Revolution which had replaced James II by William and Mary.

---

1. 'While Locke's teaching is identical with Descartes' as to the subjective side of the experience, it is not so with regard to the objective. Here he is, I believe, in conscious opposition to Descartes.' Richard Aaron, *John Locke* (Oxford 1955), p.224.
2. 'Secret relations between the French court and the English opposition began in 1676 and lasted until the spring of 1679, when their object was accomplished and Danby removed from power [...] The curious thing is that Locke went to France just before the deal was made and he returned to England immediately its end was achieved.' Maurice Cranston, *John Locke* (London 1959), p.159.

Having participated in the negotiations that brought this couple to the English throne, he returned to London in Mary's ship. Henceforth he divided his time between working for the government in the city and writing in the country. The London air aggravated his asthma, thus forcing him to seek relief at Oates where Lady Masham welcomed him,[3] but recovery proved increasingly difficult. During this period he defended his philosophy from several adversaries, the most dangerous of whom was Bishop Stillingfleet. He also published *The Reasonableness of Christianity* (1695) and befriended the younger Anthony Collins, who would make a name for himself as a deist. Locke died in 1704.

Philosophy was only one of his interests. To those already mentioned we must add medicine, which he practised, and education, on which he wrote.[4] His ideal of toleration accounts for part of his diversity. His four letters on toleration proclaim the right of all men, with two exceptions, to practise the religion of their choice. He tolerates neither atheists, whom he considers legally irresponsible, nor members of a church controlled by a foreign power, in other words Roman Catholics. Aggravated by the rivalry between Protestant factions, the national hostility to Catholicism had erupted in much turmoil during his lifetime.[5] His political activity and many of his writings served a political party, the Whigs, and eventually a Whig government, both of which supported his conception of tolerance. One reason why he promoted tolerance was his conviction that men could never reconcile their religious differences no matter how hard they tried. The *Essay* evolved from a disagreement between friends in 1671 over 'the principles of morality and religion'.[6] To settle the issue apparently, Locke proposed to examine the human mind and determine the limits of what it can know.[7] He made an assumption that practically no one would make today. 'I thought all I would have to say on this matter would be contained in one sheet of paper' (*Essay* i.10). The remark seems naive precisely because his analysis revealed something of the enormous complexity we now take for granted. The more he worked on this project, the more he realised how much he had to do. 'Written by incoherent parcels and after long periods of neglect' (*Essay* i.10),[8] the first edition, which

3. The daughter of Ralph Cudworth (1617-1688), the Cambridge Platonist.

4. In particular, *Some thoughts concerning education (1693)* and *Of the conduct of the understanding* (1706).

5. The Stuarts' absolutist and Catholic ambitions resulted in persistent conflict and especially the Great Rebellion (1642-1646, 1648-1652).

6. 'According to his friend James Tyrrell, who was at the "meeting", the "difficulties" arose in discussing the "principles of morality and revealed religion".' Alexander Fraser (ed.), *An essay concerning human understanding* (New York 1959), i.9n. I will refer to this edition.

7. He says he intended 'to take a survey of our own understandings, examine our own powers and see to what things they were adapted' (*Essay*, i.31).

8. Written in 1671, two drafts are extant. Draft A is a short version of the entire work, and Draft B, a more fully developed version of the first three books. See R. I. Aaron and Jocelyn Gibb, *An*

appeared nineteen years later, consisted of four volumes. Locke published three further editions and his friend Pierre Coste published a French translation in 1700.

Whether we read the *Essay* in Locke's ponderous English or Coste's graceful French, the reasons for the impact of this work on the eighteenth century do not immediately occur to us. Why Voltaire's enthusiasm, for instance?[9] Although Locke took his cue from Descartes, making a systematic inventory and evaluation of one's own mind seemed original and appropriate to his contemporaries. 'My book [...] is a copy of my own mind in its several ways of operation,' he tells Stillingfleet.[10] He published it, he says, because he thinks 'the intellectual faculties are made and operate alike in most men' (*Works* iv.139). Even before publication, he adds, men who had read the manuscript confirmed this opinion. Not only does introspection reveal the structure and function of the mind, in his opinion, but it is also infallible, as he wrote Collins the year he died.[11] He claimed to have discovered the limits of human knowledge at a time of reaction to religious dogmatism and rational speculation, a time of enthusiasm over the promise of empirical science. Newton was eclipsing Descartes. Thus Locke provided Voltaire and the *philosophes* with weapons to destroy the old order and tools to build the new. A pioneer in a virgin field, he made mistakes increasingly evident to those who followed in his footsteps. The distinction, for instance, between speculative epistemology and empirical psychology, which he conflated, emerged only later. Yet the structure he perceived in the human mind played an essential part in the development of eighteenth-century thought.

The elusive intentions behind his procedure, which analysis of the *Essay* will reveal, justify use of the same order here. In the Introduction he proposes to identify the powers of the understanding and ascertain 'how far they reach, to what things they are in any degree proportionate [and] to stop when it is at the uttermost extent of its tether' (*Essay*, i.28). His purpose remains therefore much the same as in 1671, even though the project had grown to unforeseen proportions by 1689. Like Descartes he attributes man's superiority over the other 'sensible beings' (*Essay*, i.24) to the understanding, but he denies that beasts are machines without

*early draft of Locke's 'Essay'* (Oxford 1936). 'In 1671 [...] he brought out his *De Intellectu Humano*, where the reduction of all our ideas to simple ideas is presented, and in 1688 he published in Leclerc's *Bibliothèque universelle* a preliminary French sketch of his *Essay*.' Ira Wade, *The Intellectual origins of the French Enlightenment* (Princeton 1971), p.485.

9. 'Jamais il ne fut peut-être un esprit plus sage, plus méthodique, un logicien plus exact que M. Locke [...] Locke a développé à l'homme la raison humaine, comme un excellent anatomiste explique les ressorts du corps humain.' Voltaire, *Lettres philosophiques* (Paris 1964), p.82,84.

10. *The Works of John Locke* (London 1801), iv.139.

11. 'However I may be mistaken in what passes without me, I am infallible in what passes in my own mind' (*Works*, x.283).

feelings. He also follows Descartes in defining idea as 'the object of the understanding when a man thinks' (*Essay*, i.32). The concept is broad, however, for it embraces sentiments, desires, illusions and other mental phenomena not usually subsumed under ideas. Indeed O'Connor identifies five different connotations of *idea* in the *Essay*.[12] Locke's semantics are no more rigorous than Leibniz's. He has a definite concept in mind, however, for he believes he can separate ideas from each other and isolate them. Though fleeting, they may qualify as real beings.[13] The refutation of innate ideas in book I of the *Essay* prepares the analysis of ideas as such in book II. Ideas form propositions which constitute knowledge, but Locke treats the disparity between words and ideas in book III before he surveys the extent of knowledge in book IV.

Experience, according to book I, furnishes the 'empty cabinet' (*Essay*, i.48) of the mind with ideas, which it uses to form propositions or principles. Locke describes innate principles as 'characters [...] stamped upon the mind of man, which the soul receives in its very first being and brings into the world with it' (*Essay*, i.37). Note the Cartesian identity of mind and soul. There are no innate principles, Locke insists, but he does admit innate faculties that enable the mind to form speculative and practical principles. He cites universal consent as the usual argument in support of innate principles. Even if all men agreed on a principle, however, this agreement would not prove that it is innate. No principle has universal consent anyway. Children and idiots, for instance, do not know the speculative principles of identity and contradiction. Thus Locke rejects the naive version of innate ideas. Nor do children have such principles inscribed on their souls, so that they become aware of them at the age of reason. This is the dispositional version of innate ideas, which Locke also discounts. The mind, he objects, cannot be unaware of its own contents. In contrast with Leibniz he does not even consider the possibility of unconscious awareness. Although the mind knows truth, 'the capacity [...] is innate, the knowledge acquired' (*Essay*, i.41). If the mind contained innate truths eventually discovered by reason, it would have to know them and be ignorant of them at the same time, a commonsense impossibility. Since reason discovers truths that are not innate,

12. '"Idea" is used to mean [...] (i) the contents of our sense experience [...] (ii) [...] I have also a sense presentation of a physical object [...] And this too would be an idea, in another sense [...] (iii) Images whether they occur in memory or in imagination are a third kind of "idea" [...] (iv) He also uses the word to refer to characteristics or properties in a general sense which is not restricted to sense-qualities [...] (v) Locke has been accused [...] of using the word [...] to mean [...] the act of knowing itself. I have been unable to find any unequivocal examples of this use.' D. J. O'Connor, *John Locke* (London 1952), p.35.

13. 'Ideas may be real beings, though not substances; as motion is a real being, though not a substance, and it seems probable that in us ideas depend on and are some way or other the effect of motion, since they are so fleeting, it being [...] so hard and almost impossible to keep in our minds the same unvaried idea' (*Works*, x.256).

moreover, how could we distinguish between the two anyway? We could not, in Locke's view.

Speculative principles differ from practical principles by their self-evidence. 'Common sense' establishes, for instance, that 'it is impossible for the same thing to be and not to be' (*Essay*, i.68), the speculative principle of contradiction. It does not necessarily establish, on the other hand, that 'one should do as he would be done unto' (*Essay*, i.68), the Golden Rule. We must deduce this practical principle from an antecedent proposition, so it cannot be innate. Even thieves treat each other fairly, but convenience motivates them rather than any innate principle of justice, for they do not treat honest men fairly at all. Hobbes's followers keep their word for fear of punishment by Leviathan, Christians in the hope of an eternal reward, and the ancient philosophers because dignity requires it. There can be no innate principle here. Obedience to God, it is true, conforms with 'the light of reason' (*Essay*, i.70). The great majority of mankind acknowledge the law of nature, a rough equivalent of reason which O'Connor hesitates to define as 'a moral law self-evident to all rational creatures' (p.205). Few practise what they profess, however, and those who do are usually motivated by convenience or self-interest. No one enters this life with the law of nature engraved on his mind. Nor does conscience, which imposes different or even opposite rules of behavioir from nation to nation,[14] furnish any evidence of an innate moral law. To affirm such a law is as flagrant an error as to deny 'a law knowable by the light of nature [...] without [...] positive revelation' (*Essay*, i.78). To his refutation of innate practical principles, Locke nonetheless makes an exception of the desire for happiness and the aversion to misery. Since these tendencies are truly ageless and universal, he accepts them as innate practical principles. But he undermines this concession by declaring them '*inclinations of the appetite* [and] not impressions of truth on the understanding' (*Essay*, i.67). They neither *regulate* behaviour nor contribute to *knowledge*, as he interprets these terms. Though innate, therefore, they do not qualify as true practical principles according to his standards.

After eliminating innate principles, he turns to their components, innate ideas. We could hardly have innate principles, he remarks, if we are conceived with no ideas. Perhaps unborn infants have the ideas of hunger and warmth, but how can we tell?[15] They certainly do not have those of identity and impossibility, which they must make an effort to learn after birth. No one is born with ideas such as these. If any idea were innate, surely that of God would be, for we could never conceive of innate moral principles without it. Here

14. Locke relies on the very unscientific travel literature of his time for evidence of such variety.

15. 'Locke's opposition to the doctrine of innate ideas is not motivated by his conviction that they are necessarily non-existent, but that they are beyond the scope of his inquiry' (*Wade*, p.506).

Locke relies on the travel literature of the period for reports of atheistic nations in exotic lands.[16] This shaky evidence convinces him that the idea of God is not innate. He attributes its prevalence to the fact that we find it 'agreeable to the common light of reason and naturally deducible from every part of our knowledge' (*Essay*, i.99). Reason makes no more natural discovery than this one, in his opinion, so he cannot imagine a better candidate for innateness. Since it is not innate, he concludes, no ideas are.

We do not need to pursue his further arguments and examples in order to raise an essential question. Why does he attack innate ideas? His massive efforts suggest that his motivation surpasses the mere desire to correct a philosophical error. Towards the end of book I he censures self-appointed 'masters and teachers' who declare principles innate to protect them from investigation. They persuade their followers to accept their doctrines without questioning them: '*Principles must not be questioned.*' Deserting reason and judgement for 'blind credulity', these followers submit to 'the dictator of principles and teacher of unquestionable truths'. The indoctrination of innate principles may give one man no 'small power' (*Essay*, i.116) over another, an abuse deplored by Locke. The context implies a pedagogical or philosophical concern, but the overtones indicate hostility to religious hegemony.

Why? Who was advocating innate ideas? Whom was he attacking? Explicitly he mentions only the deist Herbert of Cherbury and only as an afterthought.[17] Leibniz and Voltaire assumed he was combatting Descartes and his followers, an opinion confirmed by critics like Aaron.[18] In Descartes's writings, however, one finds a clear equivalent of innate tendencies and only an obscure equivalent of innate dispositions, the milder form of innate ideas condemned by Locke. Since Locke knew Descartes's philosophy well, he probably did not regard him as his primary target. Some of the Cambridge Platonists, More and Cudworth for instance, tended to innate ideas, but surely not enough to provoke the massive reaction in the *Essay*. Locke's friendship with Lady Masham, Cudworth's daughter, was serene and durable. According to Yolton and others, a number of English academics and clergymen were promoting innate ideas in

16. 'Hath not navigation discovered, in these later ages, whole nations, at the bay of Soldania, in Brazil, in Boranday, and in the Caribee islands, etc. amongst whom there was to be found no notion of a God, no religion' (*Essay*, i.96-97)?

17. 'When I had written this, being informed that my Lord Herbert had, in his book *De Veritate* [1624], assigned these innate principles, I presently consulted him, hoping to find in a man of so great parts something that might satisfy me in this point and put an end to my inquiry' (*Essay*, i.80). Herbert did not change Locke's mind.

18. 'There is very substantial evidence that Locke was attacking Descartes and the Cartesians. But they were not the only people he had in mind' (Aaron, p.93).

128

either the naive or the dispositional sense.[19] Many were Schoolmen who had deviated from the traditional School and Locke had encountered some of these at Oxford, hence in part, perhaps, the ironical titles of *master* and *teacher*. Here there was a general tendency to declare the natural light innate, found first principles on it and deduce all other knowledge by syllogism.[20] Locke seems to have had this tendency in mind. Against innate ideas, in James Collins' opinion, he struck a blow from which they never recovered.[21]

Since we are apparently born without any ideas in our mind, we must acquire them after birth. 'EXPERIENCE' (i.122), according to book II, writes them on the 'white paper' (i.121) of the mind. There are only two sources of experience: sensation and reflection. Sensation consists in perception of external objects by the senses, and reflection, in the observation of mental activity. But reflection depends on sensation because the reflective mind observes its own treatment of ideas and these must derive, at least initially, from the senses. Reflection does not imply, as Tedeschi presumes, the pre-existence of reflective ideas in the mind, a clandestine innateness.[22] On the contrary, ideas of reflection originate in the mind just as ideas of sensation do, but without their external stimulation. Although the mind begins to have ideas as soon as it perceives, it does not necessarily continue to have them. Locke disputes the Cartesian theory that it begins to exist when it starts to think and never stops thinking after that. Nor can it have ideas without knowing about them. Awareness of one's own ideas or consciousness assures personal identity.

Ideas are either simple or complex to Locke. Complex ideas result, he believed, from the combination by the mind of simple ideas received from experience. He treated thought as his friend Robert Boyle was treating matter, by trying to break it down into its components. One cannot break it down any further than simple ideas, which are to thought as atoms are to matter. The mind can neither make nor destroy them, but merely derive them from sensation and reflection, from the five senses, in other words, and the inner sense. Clear, distinct and stable, each contains no more than '*one uniform appearance or*

19. 'It is very difficult to doubt that it was against this firm tradition in English moral and religious thought that Locke was writing.' John Yolton, *John Locke and the way of ideas* (Oxford 1956), p.30.

20. 'It was not [...] against any leading exponents of Scholastic thought that Locke wrote, but against the actual tendencies which he found around him.' James Gibson, *Locke's theory of knowledge and its historical relations* (Cambridge 1917), p.40.

21. 'The theory of innate knowledge never recovered its full strength, after his vigorous blows were delivered.' James Collins, *A history of modern European philosophy* (Milwaukee 1954), p.318.

22. 'Nous savons ce qu'il faut penser des expressions de Locke: idées innées, principes innés, propositions innées, facultés innées, nous avons vu qu'elles ne s'attachent qu'à ce qui n'est pas inné dans sa doctrine, tandis que, ce qui est inné dans cette même doctrine, a un autre nom (réflexion, raisonnement).' Paul Tedeschi, *Paradoxe de la pensée anglaise au XVIIIe siècle ou l'ambiguïté du sens commun* (Paris 1961), p.87.

*conception*' (i.145), a vague description supported by arbitrary examples. There are four kinds of simple ideas: (1) those that come from one sense (solidity); (2) those that come from more than one sense (space or extension, figure, rest and motion); (3) those that come from reflection alone (perception or thinking and volition or willing) and (4) those that come from both sensation and reflection (pleasure or delight, pain or uneasiness, power, existence and unity). In practice Locke forgets the distinction between simple and complex ideas when it tends to inconvenience or absurdity.

He warns us not to confuse simple ideas of sensation with the things we perceive. Some of the ideas do not resemble the things and others even refer to a lack of something, such as the idea of darkness. Locke attributes sensations to the impact of moving particles on the sense organs. According to Boyle's corpuscular theory, matter consists of particles in various modes of motion or rest. The idea of a colour, Locke infers, could not possibly resemble the particles that cause it when they strike the eyes. But how can the impact of particles on sense organs produce an idea in the mind? Locke borrows his solution from Descartes: 'Some motion must be [...] continued by our nerves or animal spirits [...] to the brain or seat of sensation, there to produce in our minds the particular ideas we have of them' (i.171-72). The things perceived agitate the animal spirits in different ways, thus producing various degrees and modes of movement in them. Like Descartes, however, Locke does not try to explain the transition between animal spirits and ideas, between matter and thought. He does examine the relationship between the ideas in the mind and the powers in the things we perceive to cause these ideas. He divides the qualities manifested by these powers into three types: *Primary qualities* are really in the things perceived and in every part of every one, whether we perceive them or not. Our ideas of these qualities resemble them so closely that we perceive the thing nearly 'as it is in itself' (*Essay*, i.178). Locke gives the examples of solidity, extension, figure, number, bulk, situation and motion or rest. *Secondary qualities* are not really in the things perceived, but they result from the powers of the things to produce sensations in us that do not resemble these powers. Examples: colours, sounds, tastes, smells and the pain of 'steel dividing our flesh' (*Essay* i.173). A *third sort*, which critics call *tertiary qualities*, are not really in things either. We perceive them when the powers in one thing cause changes in the primary qualities of another, so that the powers in this one produce sensations dissimilar to the primary qualities of both things. 'The sun has a power to make wax white and fire to make lead fluid' (*Essay*, i.179). While Locke tends to conflate tertiary with secondary qualities, he regards the latter as modes of primary qualities, the only ones that exist independently.

In an apparent transition from simple ideas of sensation to simple ideas of reflection, he designates the faculty of perception as 'the first and simplest idea we have from reflection' (*Essay* i.183). Yet his interest immediately shifts from perception as a simple idea to perception as a faculty of the understanding. In this faculty he sees an involuntary initial step towards the acquisition of knowledge and the exercise of judgement, which are voluntary. The passive mind becomes active when it confirms or interprets one perception by comparing it with another. It takes a second step towards knowledge and judgement by retaining an idea derived from sensation or reflection. Retention may assume the forms of contemplation or memory. Contemplation focuses on an idea for a period of time, while memory stores it for future use, retrieves it as needed and notes that the mind has already perceived it.[23] Neither memory nor retention seem like simple ideas, which Locke no longer mentions. Instead of returning to them, he introduces other faculties and defines these as operations of the mind: distinguishing between ideas or discerning, comparing them with each other, combining them or composition and abstraction which converts a particular idea into a general one representing all the other particulars of the same kind. Finally Locke justifies this impromptu discussion of faculties on three grounds: (1) their operation begins with simple ideas; (2) we understand them more easily when they treat simple rather than complex ideas and (3) they are themselves ideas derived from reflection and appropriate for consideration 'after the simple ideas of sensation' (i.211). But Locke does not consider them simple themselves and simple ideas of reflection remain somewhat vague for lack of discussion.

While the passive mind receives simple ideas from sensation and reflection, the active mind produces complex ideas, which fall into three categories: modes, substances and relations. Modes cannot subsist by themselves, for they depend on substances. Simple modes are variations of a simple idea, while mixed modes combine simple ideas of different kinds. Substances unite simple ideas thought to represent a thing subsisting by itself. Single substances exist separately from each other (a man, a sheep) and collective substances unite several single substances (a flock, an army). Relations compare one idea with another.

Locke cites space, time, number and infinity as examples of simple modes, for each of them, he finds, results from the accumulative repetition of a simple idea. Expansion produces space, duration produces time, multiplication

---

23. Locke added the last two points about memory to the initial one in the second edition of the *Essay* (1694). He also inserted the insinuation that ideas stored in the memory 'cease to be anything' (i.194) because they are not being perceived. This is an awkward reaction to Stillingfleet's objection that, if memory stores ideas, the mind has ideas of which it is unconscious. This implication contradicts an important point in Locke's refutation of innate ideas: the mind cannot have ideas of which it is unconscious.

produces number and unending multiplication, infinity. This time he illustrates ideas of reflection as well as ideas of sensation. From the simple idea of thinking, which he interprets as broadly as Descartes, he derives the simple modes of sensation, remembrance, recollection, contemplation, reverie, attention, intention or study, dreaming and ecstasy. In dreaming one has ideas while asleep, yet without any perception of exterior things, the senses being 'stopped' (*Essay*, ii.299). Ecstasy means dreaming with open eyes, and reverie, borrowed from French for lack of an appropriate English word, the floating of ideas in the mind! The exact distinction between ecstasy and reverie may escape us, but we can certainly understand why Locke classes them together with dreaming as modifications of thinking in the Cartesian sense. No ideas occur at all, he observes, 'in the dark retirements of sound sleep'. Thus thought 'is the action and not the essence of the soul' (*Essay*, i.301) in spite of Descartes. Both sensation and reflection provide the mind with the simple ideas of pain and pleasure. A hedonist, Locke defines good and evil in terms of pain and pleasure: good increases pleasure or decreases pain, while evil increases pain or decreases pleasure. Good and evil cause pain and pleasure, in his opinion, but he does not say what kind of ideas they are. He nonetheless describes all four as 'the hinges on which our passions turn' (*Essay*, i.303) and casts them in the role of simple ideas forming the modes of passion. Pleasure becomes love, pain becomes hatred, good becomes joy and evil becomes sorrow. After thorough treatment of simple modes, Locke dispatches mixed modes in a single chapter, but in anticipation perhaps of book III where he develops them more extensively.

Substances differ from modes by their independent existence. How do we know they exist independently? The mind consistently derives the same simple ideas from sensation or reflection and combines them in the complex idea of a substance. But how do we know the substance really exists? We cannot imagine that the powers producing these ideas support each other or subsist alone without support. We therefore suppose that they belong to a substance. What is a substance? The world rests on an elephant's back, according to an Indian (Hindu) philosopher, and the elephant stands on a turtle. What does the turtle lie on? '*Something* [the philosopher] *knew not what*' (*Essay*, i.392), says Locke. We do not know what substance is. We only know that something must support the powers that cause our perceptions of its qualities. Substances are material or spiritual, we assume, depending on whether the simple ideas that form the complex idea of substance derive from sensation or reflection. We can only conceive of body as the support of qualities affecting our senses, and spirit as the support of operations in the mind. To body we attribute '*the cohesion of solid and* [...] *separable parts* and *a power of communicating motion by impulse*'; to spirit, '*thinking* and *will* or a *power of putting body into motion by thought*' (*Essay*, i.407–

408). Yet we cannot understand how a substance imparts motion by impulse or thought. Nor can we extend our knowledge of substance beyond the combinations of simple ideas we derive from sensation or reflexion.

Relations are not obscure like substances. They compare one simple idea with another or with a complex idea. Any simple or complex idea may figure in an infinite number of relations, which account for a large portion of thought and language. Neither of the ideas in a relation refers intrinsically to a comparison of them, but the relation itself may be clearer and more distinct than either. Some words, however, not only indicate an idea, but also a relation, words like *'father, brother, king, husband, blacker, merrier*, etc.' (*Essay*, i.432). *Father* is more intelligible than *man* because we understand the relation of *paternity* better than the substance *humanity*. The relation of cause and effect troubled Locke. He complicated the matter by his attempt to distinguish between causality and power, which are practically identical in his thought. A short chapter in the *Essay* treats causality as a relation and a long chapter treats power as a simple mode, which nonetheless 'includes in it some kind of relation' (*Essay*, i.310). Locke acknowledges a further complication: power is a simple idea and the principal element in the complex idea of substance. His uncertainty about how to fit the concept into the structure of the mind as he saw it betrays his perplexity over the nature of causality itself. Indeed the difficulty he encounters reveals the excessive rigidity of this structure.

An elaborate description rather than a precise definition introduces his chapter on power. The senses, he observes, inform the mind of habitual exterior incidents in which one idea (quality) disappears and another appears. He does not call the disappearing quality a cause and the appearing quality an effect because of his awkward decision to consider power a simple mode and causality a relation. Yet he is referring to a habitual incidence of cause and effect in the material world, which results in the disappearance of one idea and the appearance of another in the mind. From reflection, he continues, the mind learns of other habitual events in which one idea disappears and another appears. Some of these result from the stimulation of the senses by qualities in material substances, the cause being physical and the effect mental. Others result from 'the determination of [the mind's] choice' (*Essay*, i.308), the cause being mental and the immediate effect mental too. In this case, the mind can cause a body to act and even to act on other bodies. The three kinds of habitual events described here persuade the mind that similar causes will always produce similar effects in the same way. In the chapter on modes, Locke refers to cause as an active power and effect as a passive power: 'the sun has the power to blanch wax and wax, a power to be blanched by the sun' (*Essay*, i.309).

What power does, he discovers, is less difficult to explain than how it operates.

Struck by a rolling ball, a stationary ball begins to roll. A power that produces no motion, but merely transfers it from one object to another is passive and not active. Everywhere in nature we witness the exchange rather than the origination of energy. Yet 'everything must have a cause', as Stillingfleet wrote to Locke.[24] And 'everything that has a beginning must have a cause' (*Works*, iv.61), as Locke replied. Although both were proving the existence of a Creator, Stillingfleet might have asked Locke how he knew that beginning requires a cause. Could he infer this principle from experience alone? Is it not an innate principle? Aware of the danger, Locke sought to found it on experience alone. In the *Essay* he first regards the idea of cause as simple and then as complex, but he consistently attributes it to experience. According to his chapter in book II on the relation of cause and effect, we see one substance produce another without understanding how. A chapter in book IV on the extent of knowledge tells us that the universal persistence of this phenomenon reveals a natural law, 'yet a law that we know not' (*Essay*, ii.222). Although we can say *that* effects come from causes, we cannot say *why*. From the collision of billiard balls we learn that bodies have the power to transfer energy by impulse. We know minds have the power to move bodies or stop them from moving by thought. Despite daily experience with both kinds of power, however, Locke finds one as incomprehensible as the other. Still, the power is passive in bodies and active in minds. We experience the operation of active power only by reflection, even though we cannot understand it. Perhaps cause is an attribute of spirit, and effect, an attribute of matter. This hypothesis, as Gibson remarks, approaches Leibniz's position.[25]

Identity, another complex idea of relation, received Locke's particular attention in the second edition of the *Essay*. We establish it when the comparison of a thing with itself as it exists at two different times proves it to be the same. Locke concentrates on the identity of substances, which he divides into three different kinds, God, finite spirits and bodies. One and only one of each can occupy the same place at the same time. Identity varies according to the nature of the substance. A particle of inorganic matter owes its identity to its position in space and time, which no other particle can occupy. A mass of particles keeps its identity as long as it gains or loses none, no matter how much we rearrange them. We identify a machine such as a watch by its mechanism, and machines differ from beasts only in that the former have an external source of energy and the latter an internal source. Although the particles of a living organism change constantly, the biological organisation, which remains the same, assures its

24. Stillingfleet, *The Works of that eminent and most learned prelate, Dr. Edw. Stillingfleet, late lord bishop of Worcester* (London 1707-1710), iii.508.
25. See Gibson, p.109.

identity. As opposed to that of a person, the identity of a man also consists in his biological organisation. Locke founds personal identity on the unity of consciousness, much to the chagrin of opponents like Stillingfleet, who thought he should found it on the soul for the sake of Christianity. Consciousness depends on the recognition of the same thought as one's own at different times and in different places. Founding personal identity on it helped to emancipate psychology from the tutelage of Christian theology.

Having classified ideas, Locke turns to the relationship between ideas and what they represent. In this connection he distinguishes between real and fantastic ideas, between adequate and inadequate ideas, between true and false ideas. Real ideas evoke things that exist or their archetypes, and fantastic ideas things that do not exist. All simple ideas are real because the Creator wanted them to correspond to the powers that produce them in the mind. Since the mind is passive in receiving simple ideas and active in forming complex ideas, it can only invent fantastic ideas of the latter type. The reality behind mixed modes[26] and relations exists nowhere but in the mind, so they serve as their own archetypes. Ideas of substance qualify as real or fantastic depending on whether the combination of simple ideas in the mind accurately represents a combination of powers outside of the mind. One creates fantastic substances by assembling simple ideas that do not belong together. The complex idea of a centaur, for example, combines the simple ideas of man and horse which remain separate in nature. Adequate ideas represent their archetypes completely and inadequate ideas represent theirs only partially. God made the powers in things, so that they cause the simple ideas we have of them, thus all simple ideas are adequate. Locke considers all ideas of modes and relations adequate too, but only because the mind forms them according to its own archetype and without any external reference. In ideas of substance, however, he sees the inadequate representation of external realities whose essence we cannot know. Mere perceptions of the mind, ideas are intrinsically neither true nor false but, extrinsically, they may be either one or the other. An idea may be true or false when one assumes that it conforms to (1) an idea known by the same name in other minds, (2) real existence or (3) the essence of anything. Locke finds most, if not all, ideas of substance false. All three imply the exercise of judgement, which he separates from the understanding.

In the fourth edition of the *Essay*, he added to book II a final chapter on the association of ideas. According to this chapter, reason justifies natural associations and condemns chance or customary associations. Children fear goblins at night, for instance, because they associate them with darkness. False associations

---

26. Locke does not mention simple modes here.

sometimes transform slight and innocent disagreements into bitter quarrels. Locke ascribes the mutual hostility of religious and philosophical sects to such errors. Education, custom and partisan rhetoric join unrelated ideas so closely that people can no longer tell them apart. They treat two ideas as if they were one. This illusion 'captivates their reasons and leads men of sincerity blindfold from common sense' (i.534). Thus uninhibited common sense or reason does not tolerate the sectarian association of unrelated ideas. Unfortunately Locke did not seize the opportunity to study associations of related ideas, a study which might have proved as valuable to him as it does to us today.

He had intended to investigate knowledge immediately after ideas, but he saw the intermediate need for an analysis of words, to which he devoted book III. A nominalist in the tradition of Ockham,[27] he finds that most words have a general meaning, and all things, a particular existence. Universals exist only in the mind which, having invented them, names them. It forms a general idea of particulars that resemble each other and assigns a name to this bundle (*Essay*, ii.31) for convenience in building and communicating knowledge. Without such abstraction the quantity and diversity of particulars would obstruct knowledge. Yet abstraction produces a nominal essence in the mind which does not necessarily conform to the real essences of the particulars to which it corresponds. The nominal essences of things represented by simple ideas and simple modes are always the same as their real essences, but those of substances, which vary from mind to mind, never. The names of mixed modes and relations designate their real essences because these exist only in the mind. Thus problems concerning the difference between nominal and real essences involve substances alone. Locke concludes book III by recommending various precautions against the illusions and abuses of words, the cause of much obscurity, confusion and error.

Book IV on knowledge and probability might have constituted the entire *Essay* if he had not felt the need for the detailed and tedious analysis of the first three books. Thoroughness is his greatest merit and fault. Concerned like Descartes with certainty, he admits nothing but certain information as knowledge and consigns the rest to probability. We arrive at knowledge by perceiving the agreement or disagreement, not *between*, but *of* ideas. Woozley interprets the latter preposition as evidence that ideas may also agree or disagree with things.[28]

27. 'Locke [...] was a nominalist. By "nominalism" I mean the thesis that everything which exists is an individual; moreover that everything is in itself individual, and has not needed to be made individual in any way whatsoever.' J. R. Milton, 'John Locke and the nominalist tradition', *John Locke: Symposium Wolfenbüttel 1979* (Berlin, New York 1981), p.129.
28. 'There is no doubt (1) that Locke believed that the second term of an agreement relation was sometimes something other than an idea [...] But it does not follow (2) that he believed that the agreement could be perceived in the case where the second term was not an idea [...] I am

Indeed Locke divides all agreement and disagreement of ideas into four kinds of which the fourth involves the relationship between ideas and their objects: (1) identity and diversity, (2) relation, (3) coexistence or necessary connection and (4) real existence. This classification satisfies no one, not even Locke himself, who concedes that (1) and (3) belong to the same general category as (2), since all three are relations, strictly speaking.[29] Aaron in fact discerns two theories of knowledge 'standing side by side' in book IV, 'the perception of relations between ideas' (p.241) and the perception of particular existences.

Locke nonetheless maintains his fourfold classification throughout his discussion of knowledge. He describes (1) as 'the first act of the mind', by which it identifies an idea and distinguishes it from all other ideas. 'Men of art' (*Essay*, ii.169) have codified this act as the laws of identity and contradiction, but he believes the mind performs this act long before it learns these laws, if ever it does. Perceiving the relation between any two ideas, his definition of (2), does not obviously imply mathematics, but later comment shows that he has mathematics especially in mind. (2) applies to all kinds of ideas, and (3), to substances in particular. The coexistence of ideas in a subject, the lack of it or their necessary connection (as in causality) figure in natural science and theology. Do the combinations in the mind, however, actually reflect exterior reality? This problem subsists. Thus (4), the real existence of things represented by the mind, appropriately follows (3), in Locke's opinion. In ordering the four kinds of knowledge, he proceeds from the mind in isolation to the mind in its relation to what exists outside of it. Temporal analysis adduces a further distinction between actual and habitual knowledge. In actual knowledge, the mind perceives the agreement or disagreement of ideas in the present; in habitual knowledge, it agrees to such a relation preserved by the memory of a former perception. It acquires habitual knowledge either by perceiving a relation again or recalling that it has already perceived this relation without remembering the intermediate ideas. Locke warns against error in the latter case.

He not only distinguishes between kinds, but also between degrees of knowledge. From Descartes again he borrows the distinction between intuition and demonstration. Unlike his predecessor, he admits the intuition of ideas from sensation as well as reflection. Intuition occurs, in his view, when the mind perceives the agreement or disagreement of two ideas immediately and without recourse to the perception of any other idea. It is instantaneous, infallible and

convinced that Locke did not believe (2).' A. D. Woozley, 'Remarks on Locke's *Account of knowledge*', *Locke on human understanding* (Oxford 1977), p.142.

29. 'Though identity and co-existence are truly nothing but relations, yet they are such peculiar ways of agreement or disagreement of our ideas, that they deserve well to be considered as distinct heads, and not under relation in general' (*Essay*, ii.171).

even irresistible, 'like bright sunshine' (*Essay*, ii.177). The certainty of all knowledge depends on it, because demonstration, as in Descartes's philosophy, consists in a series of intuitions. In demonstration or reasoning, the mind relies on relations between intermediate ideas to establish the agreement or disagreement of the terminal ideas. Unlike intuition, it does not exclude initial doubt, which it overcomes with time and application, nor does it result in knowledge as clear as that of intuition. It can also result in error, for one may omit or forget an intuition in the series, and the longer the demonstration, the greater the danger of such an error. In a premature conclusion, Locke relegates all information that comes neither from intuition nor demonstration to the status of opinion or belief.

He declares an immediate exception to this rule. When the mind perceives '*the particular existence of finite beings* [outside] *us*' (*Essay*, ii.185), it surpasses probability without attaining the certainty of intuition and demonstration. Locke assigns such information to the third or sensitive degree of knowledge. Might one not object that memory and dreams produce ideas of particular substances too? Yes, but the mind discriminates between these ideas and those obtained directly from sensation, which it recognises as authentic. Even a sceptic 'will allow a very manifest difference between dreaming of being in the fire and being actually in it' (*Essay*, ii.188). Nor could he ignore, we might add, the difference between a remembrance of being burned and this unpleasant experience itself. Yet the example presents too extreme an experience to prove his point adequately.

In an attempt to determine how much the mind can know, Locke reviews the degrees and kinds of knowledge. Our knowledge, he states, can neither exceed our ideas nor our perceptions of agreement or disagreement between them, whether we use intuition, demonstration or sensation. We cannot have an intuitive knowledge of the relations between all our ideas, because we cannot compare them all immediately with each other. Intuition tells us the difference between an acute and an obtuse triangle, but it does not tell us whether they enclose the same area. Nor can demonstration, for lack of intermediate intuitions, explore all the relations between our ideas. Limited to actually existing particulars, sensitive knowledge has an even more narrow scope than the other two degrees of knowledge. Real existence exceeds our ability to know, and the portion of real existence accessible to our ideas exceeds our actual knowledge. We will continue to learn, but we will never reach these limits. Despite the ideas we have of thought and matter, for instance, we do not know 'wherein thinking consists' (*Essay*, ii.193) and we shall never know whether matter[30] can

30. Locke replaced 'matter' (first edition) by 'material being' (*Essay*, ii.192) to avoid the implication of a material God.

think. Certainly the Creator could have instilled in it the power to do so. Stillingfleet accused Locke of undermining belief in the immateriality of the soul by this remark, despite an explicit disclaimer by the author of the *Essay*. For lack of evidence, however, the latter assigns this Christian principle to probability rather than certainty. In his reply to the bishop, he explains that, according to his principles, '[an] eternal, immaterial, thinking substance has put into us a thinking substance which, whether it be a material or immaterial substance, cannot be infallibly demonstrated from our ideas' (*Works*, iv.37) This secret lies beyond the reach of human knowledge.

Having explored the potential of every degree, the *Essay* considers the possibilities of each kind. We know by intuition the identity and diversity of all the ideas we perceive, but not their coexistence. The simple ideas forming a complex idea of substance yield no evidence that they belong together. We associate them with each other merely because we perceive them in combination. Most of them derive from secondary qualities, which depend on primary qualities or, as Locke adds, 'something yet more remote from our comprehension' (*Essay*, ii.200).[31] We do not perceive any necessary connection between primary and secondary or tertiary qualities. We have no proof that primary qualities coexist in the same combinations as the simple ideas forming complex ideas of substance. In this case we must rely on experience, which establishes no more than probability. In relations, on the other hand, Locke sees 'the largest field of our knowledge' (*Essay*, ii.207). The mind can explore this field to the limit of its sagacity or ability to discover intermediate ideas for use in demonstration. The field includes mathematics, of which Locke expects as much as Descartes, and he even proposes to extend it to morals. He limits real existence to sensitive knowledge, but with two exceptions. We have intuitive knowledge of our own existence and demonstrative knowledge of God's. Here again he follows Descartes.

At this point he shifts from an affirmative to a negative consideration of the same problem. What are the causes of our ignorance? He divides his answer into three sections and the first section into two subsections. (1) A lack of ideas causes ignorance. (A) We do not have enough senses and mental faculties to acquire ideas of all things. (B) We could perceive certain things with the senses we have, if they were not too remote or small. Locke also imagines an infinite

---

31. 'By this important qualification [...] Locke guards himself against the dogmatic assumption – that the innumerable secondary qualities and powers with which material substances are endowed and which give them their chief human interest, *must* be the issue of their primary qualities, i.e. of the variously modified and moved atoms of which each substance consists and by which it is objectively distinguished from other substances.' Thus Fraser (*Essay*, ii.200, n.5) explains Locke's distinction between his own theistic atomism and atheistic atomism.

number of spirits 'too remote from knowledge' (*Essay*, ii.219) for perception by our faculties. To be sure, he has no excuse for leaping from the literal to the figurative meaning of *remote*. (2) The inability to find connections between some of our ideas causes ignorance too. As examples Locke cites several kinds of cause and effect, including resurrection which depends 'wholly on the determination of a free agent' (*Essay*, ii.222), God. (3) Finally, ignorance comes from the failure to perceive ideas and relations between them that are perceptible to us.

But ignorance of what? 'The mind perceives nothing but its own ideas' (*Essay*, ii.228). Do they therefore conform to the things they represent? In book IV Locke considers a kind of truth different from the kind treated in II. It is more a matter of propositions than ideas. He defines truth as joining or separating the signs of things according to agreement or disagreement between them. These signs are words in verbal propositions and ideas in mental propositions. Since words designate ideas, however, truth consists essentially of relations between ideas that correspond to relations between their archetypes inside or outside of the mind. There is no such correspondence in false propositions. When general propositions express a relation between terms that we perceive between the ideas designated by the terms, we know them to be true. We find general certainty only in relations between ideas. We find no more than particular certainty in relations between things outside of the mind.

When we immediately consent to the relation between the ideas in a proposition (a maxim, an axiom, etc.), it is self-evident, but not innate. All propositions of identity or diversity, many of abstract relations (mathematics, morals), a few of coexistence or necessary connection and none of real existence except our own and God's are self-evident. Locke questions the value of such propositions, however, and he even devotes a chapter to those he finds trifling. The law of identity, for instance, seems useful to him only as a means of rebuking absurdity. 'Nobody', he comments, 'will so openly bid defiance to common sense as to affirm visible and direct contradictions in plain words' (*Essay*, ii.292). All trifling propositions either identify one abstraction with another ('gratitude is justice', *Essay*, ii.301) or predicate a part of a whole ('gold is a metal', *Essay*, ii.302). They contribute nothing to knowledge, Locke concludes.

He takes real existence more seriously. We know our own, he observes, by intuition, that of God by demonstration and that of other things by sensation. He merely condenses Descartes's proof of the first point and simplifies his proof of the second. The mind can do nothing without being conscious of itself. Since it exists, it must have begun to exist and only an eternal, infinite mind could have caused it to do so. In proving the existence of other things, however, Locke naturally parts company with Descartes. We know they exist, he asserts, because they stimulate ideas in our mind which we recognise as distinct from those we remember or dream of. He advances four arguments in support of this position: (1) People who do not have or cannot use the organs of a sense lack all of the ideas associated with it. (2) Those who have the organs cannot avoid perception of these ideas. (3) If pleasure or pain accompanies the perception of an idea derived from sensation, it does not recur when we remember the idea. (4) The senses confirm each other in reporting the existence of things outside the mind. Whenever our senses therefore stimulate an idea in the mind, we must accept that something outside it really exists at the time. Remembrance of such ideas perceived in the past assures us that things affecting our senses really existed then. In neither case, however, does knowledge register more than the momentary existence of these things. When we have ideas of spirits other than God, moreover, our senses cannot determine whether they really exist, so we must rely on faith and revelation.

The study of knowledge in book IV induces Locke to distinguish between two kinds of propositions. One raises the question we have just discussed: does the idea in my mind represent something that really exists? Except for myself and God, I know only of material particulars. The other kind of proposition, which may be certain and universal, expresses the relation between abstract ideas. Each kind suits a different type of investigation, so 'we must [...] adapt our methods of inquiry to *the nature of the ideas we examine*' (*Essay*, ii.346). Propositions about relations between abstract ideas teach us much about mathematics and morals, but little about substances. The study of natural science, on the other hand, requires propositions about the existence of material particulars. All knowledge nonetheless begins with particulars, from which the mind induces general ideas.

Locke does not believe, however, that we could live by knowledge alone. We must supplement it, he says, by probability. Judgement consents to probability or dissents from improbability. Thus the mind has two faculties: in knowing it perceives and in judging it presumes the agreement or disagreement of ideas. Demonstration proves the relation between two ideas by intuitions of the intermediate ideas. Probability is the appearance of a relation between two ideas sustained by the evidence of intermediate relations. When we assume something to be true on the strength of arguments rather than intuitions, we engage in opinion or belief. Since arguments are extrinsic, they do not prove the relation between ideas, but merely establish its probability. We cannot always remember the arguments that persuaded us to make a judgement we face again. There are often too many of them. If we have forgotten them, must we reproduce them before we make it again? No, we need only recall the judgement itself. Yet Locke does not condone reliance on a bad judgement or the delusion of a judgement never made. He blames these errors for many stubborn prejudices. Diversity of opinion is inevitable, however, so he recommends tolerance.

He founds probability on two criteria: (1) conformity with our knowledge, observation and experience; (2) testimony by others based on their observation and experience. The validity of testimony depends on 'the number, the integrity [and] the skill of the witnesses, the design of the author [in recorded testimony], the consistency of the parts and circumstances of the relation, and [confrontation with?] contrary testimonies' (*Essay*, ii.366). Probability comprises empirical propositions or matters of fact, to which one can testify, and unempirical propositions, to which one cannot. Empirical propositions attain the highest degree of probability when reliable witnesses testify to a matter of fact confirmed by the constant experience of men with such facts in all ages. Fire warms the body, melts lead and reduces wood to charcoal. We see so little difference between assurance, the first degree of probability, and certainty itself that we submit to the former almost as if it were the latter. The second degree or confidence differs from the first in that the fact attested by reliable witnesses conforms to what usually happens in this case according to universal and historical experience. 'Most men prefer their private advantage to the public', for instance, and, since all historians who write about Tiberius say he did so too, this 'is extremely probable' (*Essay*, ii.376). In third-degree probability witnesses report that something happened which might have happened otherwise. A bird, we know from experience, might fly this way or that and thunder might sound on the left or the right. We cannot avoid consent to any degree of probability but, when historians contradict each other or common experience, their testimony does not necessarily qualify as probable. We must resolve such conflicts by evaluating their arguments and weighing them against each other.

The more transmission from person to person removes the testimony from the event, the less convincing it becomes. English law admits the attested copy of a document as legitimate evidence, but not the copy of a copy, no matter how many witnesses attest it. In the minds of some men, he complains, transmission of opinions over a long period of time reinforces their authenticity: 'Propositions evidently false or doubtful in their first beginning come, by an inverted rule of probability, to pass for authentic truths' (*Essay*, ii.378). A patriotic but unorthodox Anglican, Locke is obviously thinking of Catholic dogma and unobviously of doctrines held by both the Catholic and the Anglican churches. We would expect him, as O'Connor remarks, to assign 'propositions known by religious faith' to unempirical probability, 'but this is not what he does' (p.191). In his view, such probability includes finite spirits outside of the mind (angels, devils, etc.), natural objects too small or remote for perception and the hidden causes of natural phenomena. One can determine unempirical probability only by analogy with knowledge. Since fire comes from rubbing sticks together, it must be the agitation of the particles that constitutes burning matter. He treats revelation as a class apart on the grounds that God can neither deceive nor be deceived. Truths revealed by him belong to the highest degree of probability whether 'they agree or disagree with common experience'. For fear of exposing 'ourselves to all the extravagancy of enthusiasm' (*Essay*, ii.383), however, we must make sure that they are authentic and that we understand them correctly. Faith in revelation cannot reasonably exceed the evidence of its authenticity. We must found faith on reason.

Why does Locke devote a chapter to reason late in book IV? He has already explained that by reason he means reasoning and by reasoning, demonstration. But even before the *Essay concerning human understanding*, the *Essays on the law of nature*, which he had written by 1664, showed that his conception of reason involves more than mere demonstration. Here reason, as he acknowledges himself, has two connotations. The word designates both the inborn faculty[32] used in demonstration and an acquired code of moral principles which he calls right reason or the law of nature. The faculty enables us to discover the law, so that we can regulate our own conduct. As in the *Essay* reason depends on sense experience, 'for the senses primarily supply the entire as well as the chief subject matter of discourse [demonstration]'.[33] Building on the foundations of sense perception, reason raises its edifice to the heavens. Sense perception and reason combined form the light of nature, which 'like sunlight [...] reveals to us by its rays the rest of reality' (*Essays*, p.137). It does not continually remind man of his duty and infallibly guide him through life. Nor is it an inward light illuminating the law of nature written, as it were, on our hearts, 'like a torch approaching a notice board hung up in darkness' (*Essays*, p.123). It does nothing more than enable every man to learn by himself the truth accessible to the human mind, provided he uses the light properly. The *Essay* refers to the same ability by a term borrowed from Proverbs xx.27.[34] 'The candle [...] set up in us shines bright enough for all our purposes' (i.30). The concept implies that all men have the light of nature, an implication acknowledged by the author of the *Essays*. But he denies that all men use it or use it as they should: 'Not even the sun shows a man the way to go, unless he opens his eyes' (*Essays*, p.115). In the later *Conduct of the understanding* (1706), which Locke had intended as an

32. 'The word "faculty" [...] means in Locke nothing more than a dispositional property of the mind' (O'Connor, p.195).
33. Locke, *Essays of the law of nature* (Oxford 1954), p.149. 'Reason is here taken to mean the discursive faculty of the mind, which advances from things known to things unknown and argues from one thing to another in a definite and fixed order of propositions' (*Essays*, p.149).
34. 'Man's spirit is the lamp of Yahweh, / searching his deepest self.'

addition to the *Essay*, he finds that the great diversity of men's understandings comes less from their natural faculties than their acquired habits.[35] In a letter to Collins he regrets that they agree no more with each other than with common sense.[36] Clearly a synonym of reason here, common sense characterises the spirit of Locke's writings if not his usual semantics.[37]

The chapter on reason in the *Essay* defines it as both demonstration and judgement, the source of probability. Unlike Descartes, Spinoza, Malebranche and Leibniz, Locke does not confine reason to certain truth. He does join them in identifying it as the faculty that distinguishes men from beasts. It consists of sagacity, the ability to discover intermediate ideas, and illation, the ability to discover connections between them. Together they form a logical series establishing the certainty or probability of a relation between the terminal ideas. Thus reason arrives at knowledge or opinion beyond the reach of simple intuition. Any one of five causes may nonetheless frustrate its efforts to achieve this purpose: a lack of ideas; obscure or confused ideas; the failure of sagacity to find intermediate ideas; the inability of the mind to extricate itself from difficulties, contradictions and absurdities; verbal confusion. We cannot blame the last two faults on reason, but only on ourselves. Locke accepts the Scholastic distinction between propositions according to (in agreement with) reason, above reason and contrary to reason. They agree with reason when they certainly or probably conform to experience; they are above reason when, experience being impossible, we know them to be certain or probable anyway and contrary to reason when they conflict with it. Locke gives the following examples: 'The existence of one God is according to reason; the existence of more than one god, contrary to reason; the resurrection of the dead above reason' (*Essay*, ii.413). He regrets the custom of opposing reason to faith, but he doubts that it can be eradicated. Belief without the support of reason is neglect of 'the light' (*Essay*, ii.413) which the Creator has given us to avoid error. Reliance on this light will satisfy him that we are seeking truth as he intended, even though it does not reveal all of this truth.

35. He associates common sense with knowing and thinking of 'things as they are in themselves.' *John Locke's Of the conduct of the understanding* (New York 1966), p.66.

36. They rebel aginst 'their half-employed and undervalued reason.' (*Works*, x.79). 'Le sens commun qu'on invoque se différencie de l'opinion vulgaire [...] Ce sens commun s'oriente vers une situation assez exceptionnelle, la situation du sage ou du petit nombre, sans cesser d'exprimer le sentiment de l'humanité [...] Ce paradoxe pourrait s'expliquer ainsi: les hommes diffèrent d'opinion sur ce qu'ils ont en commun, sur ce qu'ils ont de naturel et ils ne ressentent ce commun, ce naturel, que dans l'originalité et l'autonomie de leur pensée, de leur sensibilité' (Tedeschi, p.70,72).

37. 'Obwohl das Wort *common sense* noch keine zentrale Stelle in seiner Philosophie innehatte, finden sich bei ihm doch schon viele Momente, die sich später mit dem *common sense* verbanden' (Körver, p.91).

While Locke admits no conflict between 'Faith and Reason', the title of the next chapter, he does assign each to a separate jurisdiction. Hopeful of settling disputes over religion, he proposes to determine the 'boundaries' between the two 'provinces'[38] (*Essay*, ii.415). Sectarians welcome reason, he notes, insofar as it supports them, but reject it whenever it jeopardises their opinions, which they set above it. He defines faith as consent to any proposition 'on the credit of the proposer as coming from God in some extraordinary way of communication' (*Essay*, ii.416). However unnatural an original revelation may be, divine inspiration cannot enable a witness to communicate simple ideas to others who have not already acquired them from experience. He must use words that they understand, that convey ideas they all have in common. Although revelation may teach us the same truths as reason, we do not need it to learn them. How can we in fact be sure that it comes from God? We have surer knowledge of the relations between our ideas, for God gave us reason so that we may arrive at such knowledge by natural means. Intuition and demonstration yield the most certain knowledge we have except for direct revelation by God. Even in this case, however, our certainty depends on our knowledge that God is revealing it.

No proposition contrary to knowledge qualifies as authentic revelation. 'Faith can never convince us of anything that contradicts our knowledge' (*Essay*, ii.421). Unless God tells us we must believe a proposition in a book or the entire contents of the book, reason, not faith, must determine belief. Faith, on the other hand, concerns things above reason which God reveals, such as resurrection. 'God, in giving us the light of reason', has not abandoned the right to overrule by revelation 'the probable conjectures of reason' (*Essay*, ii.423). Since the mind is uncertain of whatever it cannot know, it must admit the probability of things above reason when God reveals them. It nonetheless retains the right to verify the claim of divine inspiration and reject anything contrary to reason. Failure to respect the boundaries between faith and reason[39] gives licence to

38. 'It seems to me that God has plainly set out the boundaries of our several faculties and showed us by which we are to conduct our lives, viz. by our senses in the cognizance of sensible objects, by reason in the deductions of discourses from perfect and clear ideas and by faith in matters that the senses nor reason will not reach to, and though reason often helps our senses, and faith our reason, yet neither the one nor the other invalidates the authority or destroys the evidence of the inferior and subordinate faculty.' Locke, *Journal* (28 Aug. 1676) in *Essays*, p.280-81.

39. 'Locke definiva la ragione e i suoi rapporti con la fede in modo da far valere i limiti alle possibilità della prima e alle pretese della seconda. La ragione, anziche una facoltà dogmatica, diventava una facoltà critica, le cui risposte univoche si ottengono, via via, attraverso una libera discussione della fede, che deve potersi manifestare liberamente per rendere possibili le scelte non prevedibili della ragione. Ma allora, proprio sulla base dell'impostazione razionalistica, nasceva la giustificazione della tolleranza religiosa, come l'unica sistemazione che potesse garantire il libero svolgimento della ricerca razionale sulla fede.' Carlo Viano, *John Locke: dal razionalismo all'illuminismo* (Torino 1960), p.368-69.

enthusiasm, whose extravagance the level-headed Locke deplores and fears. In an echo of his polemic against innate principles, he protests against the plea that faith can censure reason or that reason has nothing to do with religion. 'Men,' he complains, 'having been principled with an opinion, that they must not consult reason in the things of religion, however apparently contradictory to common sense and the very principles of their knowledge' (*Essay*, ii.426), succumb to whimsy and superstition, adopt opinions and practices unacceptable to God. Despite the rhetoric, which I have abridged, we can scarcely doubt Locke's confidence in reason or common sense (synonyms here) as a bulwark against charismatic exaltation. He concludes 'Faith and Reason' by rejecting the Augustinian apothegm, 'I believe because it is impossible' (*Essay*, ii.427).

Ever wary of enthusiasm, he inserted a chapter on this subject in the fourth edition of the *Essay*. Some people, he remarks, 'persuade themselves' (*Essay*, ii.431) that God causes them to think and act in certain ways, especially those they cannot explain by reason. The symptoms of their enthusiasm are melancholy, devotion and conceit. They flatter themselves that God's intimacy and favour raises them above other people. They even claim frequent communication with the Holy Spirit. Locke willingly concedes that God can dart a ray from his fountain of light directly into the mind, but he objects to enthusiasts attributing any impulse they may have to this source. He suspects them of yielding to their own inclinations on the pretext of divine inspiration: 'Strong conceit [...] carries all easily with it when got above common sense and freed from all restraint of reason [...] it is heightened into a divine authority' (*Essay*, ii.433). Once lazy, vain and ignorant men indulge in the illusion of privileged access to superior knowledge without effort, they make a habit of it. Already convinced, they see no need for inquiry and evidence to arrive at certainty. Reason has no influence on them, for they believe themselves above it. Why hold a candle to the sun? Locke does not question the effect of the heavenly light, but rather the privilege of enthusiasm. He prefers to accept persuasion as proof of divine inspiration. Revelations do not qualify as authentic because enthusiasts believe in them. They qualify as authentic because they are either self-evident to reason or founded on demonstration or judgement. '*Reason* is *natural revelation*': God conveys a portion of the truth to us by our natural faculties. '*Revelation* is *natural reason enlarged*': reason certifies that it comes from God. Even when he illuminates us with supernatural light, he does not extinguish reason. '*Reason must be our last judge and guide in everything*' (*Essay*, ii.438).

While the *Essay* admits doctrines above reason in theory, his *Reasonableness of Christianity* (1695) does not admit any in practice. This work, Westfall finds, eliminates 'everything above common sense'.[40] Under the cover of anonymity, Locke argues that, since God gave us reason, it dictates his law. Thus reason, in his opinion, not only condemns transubstantiation, but also original sin and even, despite his discretion, the deity of Jesus and the Trinity.

The Catholic Descartes adapted transubstantiation to his philosophy; the Anglican Locke used his philosophy to refute it, although both expressed themselves privately in this matter. Locke entered his refutation in his journal in 1676: only 'where the light of reason fails' (*Essays*, p.277) does faith intervene. Transubstantiation concerns philosophy and not faith, because the eucharist is accessible to our senses and knowledge. We know the real essence of bread by one collection of ideas and that of flesh by another. We confuse the complex idea of bread with that of flesh as easily as a man believes himself to be a loaf. Only custom and fear can persuade us that the substance of flesh underlies the accidents of bread. God reveals his doctrines by means of the senses he created in us; he does not confound them by miracles. The *Essay* comments on the role of custom in convincing Catholics of transubstantiation. After forty or fifty years of constant indoctrination, even an 'intelligent Romanist' (*Essay*, ii.405) will ignore the evidence of his senses when confronted with a more reasonable opinion. Another passage declares transubstantiation contrary to intuitive knowledge. The mind perceives the agreement between the ideas of one body and one place so clearly that it rejects the presence of one body in more than one place at the same time. The evidence should therefore dissuade us from assigning the dogma to God. 'Faith can never convince us of anything that contradicts our knowledge' (*Essay*, ii.42).

*A second vindication of the reasonableness* (1697) reminds us that transubstantiation is only one of several ways in which Christians interpret the eucharist. The Catholics believe that they commune on nothing but Christ's real body and blood; the Lutherans, on bread and wine as well;[41] the Calvinists, on the spiritual body and blood of Christ and the Zwinglians, on symbols of his body and blood. Voltaire would give a satirical twist to such enumerations.[42] Each of these sects demands consent to its own interpretation, and even by Christians belonging to the other sects who think Jesus intended a different one. By them, however, consent would imply that Jesus lied. Locke is answering John Edwards, a critic of the *Reasonableness* who objects to his unique article of faith, that Christ is the messiah. Edwards would require many others, including the Calvinist interpretation of the eucharist. Must one nonetheless agree with 'the creed-

---

40. Richard Westfall, *Science and religion in seventeenth-century England* (New Haven 1958), p.135.
41. Thus Leibniz correctly assigns this opinion of Lutheranism, which he denies, to Philalèthe, the disciple of Locke in his *Essais*. See p.138-39.
42. See my *Voltaire and the eucharist*, p.186, 196.

maker' (Edwards) in order to be a Christian? 'May not the old gentleman in Rome (who has somewhat the ancienter title to infallibility) make transubstantiation a fundamental article?' (*Works*, vii.393). Edwards deserved no gentler treatment. The idea of a simplified creed follows from the religious toleration advocated by Locke in the *Letters* he published on this subject. The *Third letter* (1692) rebukes Jonas Proast for advocating the cancellation of innkeepers' licences to sell ale when they fail to commune. Although Proast agrees with Locke that reason brings men to true religion, he thinks one must force most of them to use it.[43] Locke warns him against the consequences of forcing men without faith in the eucharist to commune. If this does not profane the sacrament, what will?

He thus joins most Protestants in condemning transubstantiation, stresses the futility of requiring belief in one of several different eucharists and opposes the coercion of negligent communicants. But which of the opinions enumerated in the *Second vindication* does he hold himself? Before his death, he received the sacrament from the Anglican priest of the parish at High Laver. On this occasion, however, he professed his 'sincere communion with the Church of Christ, by whatever name Christ's followers call themselves'.[44] From this and other evidence McLachland concludes that he was a unitarian. Yet one could be, as the critic remarks, both a unitarian and an Anglican in those days, despite the disapproval of more orthodox Anglicans. Locke's posthumous *Paraphrase and notes on the Epistles of St Paul* (1706) reveals his eucharistic faith. In his commentary on Paul's account of the Last Supper (1 Corinthians xi), he rephrases the traditional distinction between eating and drinking to satisfy hunger and thirst, and eating and drinking to achieve a more solemn purpose. Although he states this purpose as if it were also traditional, it is nothing of the kind for an Anglican: 'This eating and drinking [...] was instituted for another end, viz. to represent Christ's body and blood.'[45] Nor does he add anything,

43. 'If force be used not instead of reason and arguments, i.e. not to convince by its own proper efficacy (which it cannot do), but only to bring men to consider those reasons and arguments which are proper and sufficient to convince them, but which without being forced, they would not consider: who can deny, but that indirectly and at a distance it does some service toward the bringing men to embrace that truth.' Proast, *The Argument of the Letter concerning toleration briefly considered and answered* (Oxford 1690), p.4.
44. Reported by H. McLachland, *The Religious opinions of Milton, Locke and Newton* (New York 1972), p.107.
45. Article xxviii of the Church of England contains the following: 'The bread which we break is a partaking of the body of Christ; and likewise the cup of blessing is a partaking of the blood of Christ [...] The body of Christ is given, taken and eaten in the supper only after an heavenly and spiritual manner.' E. J. Bicknell, *A Theological introduction to the thirty-nine articles of the Church of England*, rev. by H. J. Carpenter (London 1955), p.382. Article xxviii also condemns transubstantiation.

except that Jesus intended the eucharist to 'show forth' (*Works*, viii.145) and commemorate his death, that we should eat and drink his sacramental body and blood in remembrance of him. Of the four alternatives with which he confronted Edwards, therefore, he secretly believed in symbolism, the least mysterious and most appropriate to his philosophy.

He spares some of the mystery in the fall by his respectful exegesis of the story in Genesis. In *The Reasonableness* he proposes a compromise between 'two extremes'. Some Christians consider 'Adam's posterity doomed to eternal, infinite punishment for the transgression of Adam, whom millions had never heard of and no one had authorised to transact for him or be his representative' (*Works*, vii.4) Others find this injustice so unworthy of God that they reduce the salvific mission of Christ to the mere restoration of natural religion. Here we recognise, on one hand, the orthodox theory of original sin held by Catholics and Protestants, and, on the other, the Socinian interpretation of the fall. In avoiding both positions, Locke submits that Adam merely fell from a state of perfect obedience. According to Genesis, God warns Adam that, if he eats the fruit, he will die that very day. Yet he eats the fruit and does not die. Instead of killing him, God expells him from paradise where the tree of life grows, so that Adam loses his immortality rather than his life. Thus Adam resembles 'a prisoner between the sentence and the execution' (*Works*, v.5-6). Locke acknowledges that this interpretation of death in Romans v.12 and 1 Corinthians xv.22 will not satisfy Christians who construe it as endless torture in hell. But they impugn God's justice and contradict themselves. By what law could a criminal who has received the death sentence 'be kept alive in perpetual and exquisite torments' (*Works*, vii.6)?

These Christians believe God has condemned us to sin perpetually. How could our righteous Creator force us to offend him forever?[46] Nowhere does the New Testament describe death as a form of corruption propagated by Adam's sin. By death Locke can only understand the loss of life, an end to action and thought. This is the kind of death that eventually came to Adam and comes to all of his posterity. Never would they have escaped from it if Christ had not redeemed them. Exile from the bliss of paradise and relegation to a life of misery are the legacy of his descendants. 'As Adam was turned out of paradise, so all of his posterity were born out of it, out of reach of the tree of life' (*Works*, vii.7). God does not treat them unfairly because he never granted them the privilege of immortality he had withdrawn from their original ancestor. He deprives them of no right and they obviously appreciate the temporary life

46. 'Much less can the righteous God be supposed, as a punishment of one sin, wherewith he is displeased, to put man under the necessity of sinning continually, and so multiplying the provocation' (*Works*, vii.6).

he gives them. 'Though all die in Adam, yet none are punished, but for their own deed' (*Works*, vii.8).

The commentary on Romans v.12 in the *Paraphrase* confirms that, when Adam broke God's law against eating the fruit, he 'forfeited immortality' (*Works*, viii.292) both for himself and his entire posterity, even though none of the latter had broken the law. His paraphrase of this verse describes death as punishment for the offence, thus implying that his innocent offspring suffer the consequences of the punishment. Yet in the language of the verse, he detects a metonymy substituting the effect for the cause: 'As by one man sin entered the world, and death by sin; and so death passed upon all men, for that all have sinned' ('Text', *Works*, viii.293). In other words, according to Locke, all men inherited the effect of sin and are therefore mortal. Paul does not mean to attribute actual or impugned sin to them, but rather death. Romans v.13 refers to the period between Adam's sin and the promulgation of the law by Moses.[47] Locke interprets it as follows: 'Mankind, without the positive law of God, knew, by the light of nature, that they transgressed the rule of their nature, reason, which dictated to them what they ought to do' (*Works*, viii.294). Yet Paul does not seem to have had anything like the natural light in mind when he wrote these verses. Unwittingly, no doubt, Locke is reading into the text a rationalist mentality entirely remote from Christianity in the time of Paul.

Obviously he did not believe in original sin. But he did not consider withdrawing from the Church of England either. As he admits in the *Third letter on tolerance*, the thirty-nine articles of the Anglican faith include this doctrine.[48] He insinuates, however, that a member of the church 'sincerely seeking the truth' (*Works*, vi.411) will encounter staggering difficulties if he carries investigation of original sin very far. A latitudinarian, to say the least, he did not find an exact profession of the official faith necessary for membership in what amounted to a national institution.

He deviated even more significantly from Anglican orthodoxy by his secret unitarianism. He had many unitarian friends. In Holland he met Remonstrants like Limborch and Leclerc with whom he corresponded after his return. In England he frequented unitarians like Firmin and Nye, and left a favourable account of the latter's *Discourse concerning natural and revealed religion* (1696) in his papers. Likewise a secret unitarian, Newton sent him his negative appraisal

---

47. 'Until the law sin was in the world; but sin is not imputed when there is no law' (*Works*, viii.293).

48. Article IX: 'Original sin [...] is the fault and corruption of the nature of every man that naturally is engendered of the offspring of Adam; whereby man is very far gone from original righteousness and of his own nature inclined to evil [...] and therefore in every person born into this world, it deserveth God's wrath and damnation' (Bicknell, p.171).

of 1 John v.7 and 1 Timothy iii.16 as evidence of the Trinity.

In the *Reasonableness of Christianity* Locke advocates a unique article of faith, that Christ is the messiah, and leaves the rest to individual conscience. He loads the work with quotations from Scripture which, he endlessly insists, prove this point. He divides the proof into three kinds: 'miracles', 'phrases and circumlocutions', 'plain and direct words' (*Works*, vii.32-34). After a mere page on each of the first two, he devotes the rest of his work to an explanation of why Jesus never called himself the messiah in plain and direct words. With tiresome docility he echoes the early Christian propaganda in the gospels intended to obfuscate Jesus's failure by the distinction between the temporal messiah whom the Jews expected and the spiritual messiah who had appeared. No authentic pre-Christian tradition justifies spiritual messiahship, invented no doubt to explain the crucifixion away. A Scripturalist,[49] Locke endorses all of Mark's excuses for the messianic secret without suspecting that the evangelist was trying to divorce Jesus from the Jews and Judaism. How often does he remind us that Jesus said nothing about his messiahship to avoid sedition and politics? Few serious scholars still accept this excuse. The naive determination to prove that Jesus is the messiah[50] seems to have distracted Locke from the necessity of defining this title. His interpretation of Matthew xi.27[51] reveals no more than his belief that the messiah is 'by birth' the Son of God who inherits immortality by 'natural right'. We are sons of God and his brethren 'by adoption' (*Works*, vii.107), so we share in his inheritance.

'A discourse of miracles', which Locke wrote in 1701, furnishes more

49. Words embroil us in difficulties, obscurities and disputes, according to part III of the *Essay*. No wonder 'the will of God, when clothed in words, should be liable to that doubt and uncertainty which unavoidably attends that sort of conveyance, when even his Son, whilst clothed in flesh, was subject to all the frailties and inconveniences of human nature, sin excepted' (*Essay*, ii.120)! The passage implies that the flaws of language detract from Scripture as much as from any text. Does Locke also believe that Jesus's human frailties included the deficiency of language? The more optimistic *Reasonableness* affirms that a commonsense exegesis will restore his message in all or nearly all of its original simplicity. Furthermore, the sentence following the one quoted from the *Essay* here exhorts us to amplify the universal message which Jesus expressed in 'such legible characters' and with 'so sufficient a light of reason' (*Works*, vii.120) that no one could really doubt it. Consequently Locke does not seem to suspect Jesus's language of human deficiency, but rather the sophisticated interpretations of theologians. The clarity of the message stems from the natural light with which the incarnate Son of God appropriately enlightens his fellow men.

50. 'Although the statement "Jesus is the messiah" is neither a self-evident truth nor deduced from self-evident truths, it is a proposition obtained through a comparison of well-attested sources. The probability of its truth is sufficiently high for any rational being to be able to stake his eternal salvation on it.' Peter Schouls, *The Imposition of method: a study of Descartes and Locke* (Oxford 1980), p.229.

51. 'Everything has been entrusted to me by my Father; and no one knows the Son except the Father, just as no one knows the Father except the Son and those to whom the Son chooses to reveal him.'

information about the first kind of proof that Christ is the messiah. A miracle occurs, in the author's opinion, when witnesses judge an event to surpass 'the force of nature in the established, steady laws of causes and effects' (*Works*, ix.256). A miracle certifies the divine mission of the man who performs it, unless another man does a greater miracle. Christ's miracles prove that God sent him. If his mission had dishonored 'the one, only, true [...] God' (*Works*, ix.261) in any way, it would not have been divine. After revealing 'the unity and majesty of his eternal Godhead, and the truths of natural religion and morality by the light of reason, [God] cannot be supposed to back the contrary by revelation' (*Works*, ix.261-62). That would frustrate his gift of reason by which we must distinguish between 'divine revelation and diabolical imposture' (*Works*, ix.262). Christ's teaching harmonises with the light of reason,[52] so we recognise him as God's missionary, but not necessarily as God himself.

Yet his resurrection, which Locke considers a historical fact, demonstrates his immortality. According to the *Second vindication*, this miracle especially proves that Christ is the messiah. In the controversy with Stillingfleet, Locke and the bishop agree on the resurrection of Christ's crucified body. Locke nonetheless disputes Stillingfleet's assumption that the bodies other men actually had at death will also rise. The bishop objects to the definition of personal identity in the *Essay* on the grounds that it conflicts with bodily resurrection. Personal identity, we read in the *Essay*, consists in the recognition of oneself as the same thinking thing in different places and at different times. In the passage that offends the bishop, Locke suggests that a person's resurrection does not involve the same body, but rather the same consciousness. In his reply to Stillingfleet, he makes two distinctions between the resurrection of Christ's body and that of other men's bodies: (1) Christ rose from the dead before his body had decomposed, while those of other men will be little more than dust by judgement day. Thus Locke sees no harm in putting them back together again. (2) The identity of Christ's risen body and his crucified cadaver convinced his disciples that his resurrection was no illusion. He proved that he had risen from the dead by eating in front of them and letting Thomas stick his fingers in the wounds (John xx.27-29). Locke foresees no such necessity on judgement day, but he refrains from further speculation because Scripture does not say what bodies will appear then.

Christ's sensationist demonstration for the benefit of Thomas and the other disciples illustrates the reasonableness Locke finds in Christianity. Sticking one's fingers into the wounds of a crucified man and watching him eat are

52. 'Le Christ de Locke est un maître de l'âge des lumières, dont l'enseignement ne peut être disjoint du bon usage de la raison critique.' Georges Gusdorf, *Les Sciences humaines et la pensèe occidentale* (Paris 1966-1982), iii.116.

simple modes derived from the simple ideas of feeling and seeing: 'The *resurrection* was a species of mixed modes in the mind before it really [took place]' (*Essay*, ii.45). The disciples represent the vast majority of mankind who cannot follow the subtle logic of rational argumentation. They need empirical evidence.

They are among the many witnesses to the resurrection appearances by Christ noted in 1 Corinthians xv.5-8. This passage convinces the author of the *Paraphrase* that the resurrection actually happened. He described it in fact as 'one of the most fundamental articles of the Christian religion' (*Works*, viii.348). It not only proves that Christ is the Son of God, but also that God will raise us from the dead too, provided we believe in it. Thus we will become members of Christ's heavenly body or subjects in his heavenly kingdom. Locke warns against confusion of the heavenly and the earthly kingdoms of God, for he identifies the latter with the Church. He has not the faintest insight into the Jewish kingdom Jesus actually envisaged. Indeed he swallows the traditional Christian propaganda interpreting Old Testament prophecy as a miraculous anticipation of the spiritual messiah. He typically faults the Jews on their ignorance of their own revelation and the illusion of a messiah who would drive the Romans out of Israel. Instead of a king reigning over a liberated homeland, they saw the crucifixion of a humble provincial: 'a dead man could not be the messiah or deliverer even of those who believed in him' (*Works*, viii.347). Unwittingly Locke falls victim to his own irony.

In Christ he sees the messiah, the Son of God, but does he also see God himself, a person in the Trinity? Does he believe in the Trinity? Under the titles of 'Unitaria' and 'Trinity', which he dates 1661, he compiles elements of a negative answer. According to 'Unitaria', the pre-Nicaean fathers resemble the Arians more than they resemble the Athanasians, for they do not treat Christ and the Holy Spirit as God. 'Trinity' names several papists (Hosius, Bellarmino, etc.) who admit that Scripture does not justify the Trinity. The Trinitarian contemporaries of Nicaea believed in a union rather than the unity of the three persons in God. Locke follows the Arminian Courcelles (1586-1659) in his erroneous attribution of Trinitarian unity to the Scholastics instead of Augustine. For an account of the original Trinitarian doctrine, he recommends Cudworth, the Cambridge Platonist. Tending to modalism himself, Cudworth compares the Christian and Platonic trinities in *The True intellectual system of the universe* (1678). Lactantius, Pétau and Huet, Locke continues, suggest that no one believed in the deity of the Holy Spirit before the fourth century.

From the 1691 edition of Bidle's unitarian *Confession of faith touching the Holy Trinity according to Scripture*, Locke took copious notes under the following titles, each on a separate sheet of paper: 'Christus merus homo, Christus non merus homo, Christus Deus Supremus, Christus non Deus supremus, Trinitas, Non Trinitas, Spiritus Sanctus Deus, Spiritus Sanctus Non Deus.'[53] Bidle exploits the Biblical evidence against the two natures and the Trinity, so that the papers with the diminutive titles are nearly empty and those with the augmentative titles, substantially fuller. 1 Peter i.11 furnishes the only argument he finds to support 'Christus non merus homo': 'his spirit was in the ancient prophets'.[54] He would continue to accept the claim now discredited that Old Testament prophecy announces Christ, but Christ the messiah, in his opinion, and not a Trinitarian person. Among the many arguments in favour of 'Christus merus homo' are references to New Testament passages calling him a man, such as Matthew ix.6-8, 1 Corinthians xv.21-22,[55] etc. When the Jews accuse him of pretending to be God in John x.33-35, his answer implies that he has no divine nature, but merely a human nature sanctified by God.[56] The three reasons for 'Christus Deus Supremus' include a quotation from Romans ix.5 in Greek implying that *theos* refers to Christ. Yet 'Christus non Deus supremus' notes that *theos* has no article here, 'so [it] signifies not the supreme deity' (King, p.546). Locke's *Paraphrase* of the passage tends to separate Christ from God: 'Christ is come, he who is over all, God be blessed for ever, amen' (*Works*, viii.338). The passage, in other words, thanks God for the advent of Christ who is 'over all'. Locke borrows another antinomy on this subject from Bidle. 'Christus Deus Supremus' argues that Christ must be God to satisfy for our sins. 'How can God satisfy God?' (King, p.345) retorts 'Christus non Deus supremus'. Furthermore, one Trinitarian person who satisfies for another remains unsatisfied himself, unless he forgives the offender. In the preponderant 'Christus non Deus supremus' we also discover a fourfold refutation of the two natures: (1) God does not make this distinction (in Scripture); (2) it supposes what is in question; (3) it implies two persons in Christ; (4) the Son himself, and not merely his human nature, submits to God in Philippians ii.7.[57]

In one of three points 'Trinitas' cites the plural subject of Genesis i.26, 'Let us make man.' In Locke's day, apologists interpreted this plural as evidence of

53. Lord King (ed.), *The Life and letters of John Locke* (London 1858), p.342, 344.

54. Bodleian Library, ms. Locke C.43, p.29.

55. 'He said to the paralytic – "get up and pick up your bed and go off home." And the man got up and went home. A feeling of awe came over the crowd when they saw this and they praised God for giving such power to men' (Matthew ix.6-8). 'Death came through one man and in the same way the resurrection of the dead has come through one man. Just as all men die in Adam, so all men will be brought to life in Christ' (1 Corinthians xv.21-22).

56. 'The Jews answered him: [...] "You are only a man and you claim to be God." Jesus answered: "Is it not written in your law: *I said you are god?*" So the law uses the word gods of those to whom the word of God was addressed and Scripture cannot be rejected' (John x.33-35).

57. '[Christ] emptied himself to assume the condition of a slave, and became as men are, and being as all men are, he was humbler yet' (Philippians ii.7-8).

the three persons in God. 'Non-Trinitas' denies that the plural proves the speaker himself to be more than one person. God's employment of another person to help with the creation does not establish the Trinity. 'Non Trinitas' likewise enumerates passages that conflict with the dogma, which it condemns as tritheism. 'Spiritus Sanctus non Deus' rejects the distinction between person and essence on the grounds that Scripture does not authorise it, that it evokes 'no distinct conception but of ye sounds' (C.43, p.31), that it implies two infinities and hence two Gods, that it partially depersonalises the deity. Scripture distinguishes the Spirit from God, subordinates him to God and Christ, and even mentions several spirits including evil ones. The allusion to the Father, the Son and the Holy Spirit in Matthew xxviii.19[58] does not found the Trinity, an objection to one of the two statements in 'Spiritus Sanctus Deus'. The other infers the deity of the Spirit from his omnipresence, but 'Spiritus Sanctus non Deus' protests that Satan is omnipresent too. 'The spirit dwelleth in the gh [Godhead] by his gifts and effects, but not by his substance' (C.43, p.31), for otherwise his substance would fill the Word and all men. Since Locke borrowed all of this material from Bidle, we have no reason to examine it more thoroughly. King, who edited some of it, introduces it as the preliminary stage in a project entitled 'Adversaria theologica' which Locke carried no further. He made no attempt, therefore, to rectify the imbalance between pro and con by compiling further arguments from Trinitarian apology.

One can easily imagine why he abandoned the 'Adversaria'. Under latitudinarian influence, the Church of England had begun to tolerate private, but not public heterodoxy by its aristocratic laymen. It would ignore the anonymous deism of Locke's friend Collins, a landed magistrate, and discipline the avowed Arianism of Samuel Clarke, an Anglican clergyman. Thus Locke felt free to oppose the compulsory profession of orthodoxy by laymen. In the *Third letter on toleration*, he asks Proast whether he expects ploughmen and dairymaids to understand the Athanasian Creed. Athanasian in name only, this creed, which dates from the fifth or sixth century, proclaims the Augustinian Trinity and Christology. Salvation in Proast's view requires an explicit faith in these difficult doctrines, which he thinks everyone can learn if he tries. Learned men interpret the creed in many different ways, Locke replies, and some confess that they cannot understand it: 'Is it necessary to your or my salvation that you or I should believe and pronounce all those damned who do not believe [...] every proposition in [that creed], which I fear would extend to not a few of the Church of England?' (*Works*, vi.410). Proast could hardly have doubted who Locke had

---

58. 'Go, therefore, make disciples of all the nations; baptize them in the name of the Father and of the Son and of the Holy Spirit.'

in mind. The author of the *Third letter* does not believe he has the right to endorse the anathemas against such people in the creed. He would never have gone this far if he thought it exposed him to rebuke by the Church of England, for he valued his political career and social prestige, both of which depended on membership in the national church.

When he proposed in *The Reasonableness* a unique article of faith, that Jesus is the messiah, the Calvinist John Edwards protested against the omission of another article, that Jesus is God. In the *Vindication of the reasonableness* Locke ridicules Edwards's objections without admitting that he does not believe Jesus to be God. Edwards accuses him of naming both Christ and Adam sons of God in the same sense as the Racovians or Polish Socinians do. He has never read the Racovians, Locke replies, and he has drawn his conclusions from his own study of the Bible. If he retracted, it would not be because they say what he says, but rather because someone had convinced him he was wrong. As if to taunt Edwards, however, he confesses to Socinianism ironically. The Socinians, he adds, happen to be right about the Jews calling the messiah the Son of God (an error). Since the late archbishop of Canterbury had the same opinion, he must have been a Socinian too. Edwards also complains that the Apostles' Creed contains more than Locke and his 'brethren'[59] will agree to. 'The unmasker', as Locke names him, therefore implicates the compilers of the creed in the charge of Socinianism against Locke for, no more than the philosopher do they declare: 'Christ is the Word of God [...] Christ was God incarnate; the eternal and ineffable generation of the Son of God [...] The Son is in the Father and the Father in the Son.' (*Works*, vii.281). Locke delivers this cunning blow in the *Second vindication*. Usually, however, he prefers to bury a major point by quibbling over minor ones which he distorts and derides. We do not forget, as he apparently assumes we will, that Edwards has accused him of saying, 'Christ is not above the nature of a man' (Edwards, p.54). Instead of answering the charge, he ridicules others concerning his 'Mohammedanism', which he associates with it.

The debate over the equivalence of messiah and Son of God continues in the *Second vindication*. The Sanhedrin, according to Luke xxii.67, asks Jesus whether he is the messiah in hopes of obtaining an admission that would set Pilate against him. Aware of the trap, however, Jesus describes himself as the son of man. After many others, Locke interprets this statement as an acknowledgment of messiahship that the Jews could understand, but not the Romans. Unsatisfied, the Sanhedrin substitutes a synonym (actually a false

59. John Edwards, *Socinianism unmasked: a discourse shewing the unreasonableness of a late writer's opinion; concerning the necessity of only one article of religion* (London 1696), p.48.

synonym) by asking him whether he is the Son of God. How could anyone infer, Locke demands, that they wanted to present Pilate with a confession of claiming to be God? 'Common sense, as well as the current of the whole story, shows the contrary' (*Works*, vii.370). They wanted rather to persuade Pilate that Jesus was claiming to be the messiah, a more plausible threat to Roman power. Son of God meant the messiah to them (an error). In the gospel, 'Jews, heathens, friends, enemies, men, women, believers and unbelievers' (*Works*, vii.370-71), in short many different people call Jesus the Son of God. Did they all understand this title to mean that he is God by dint of eternal generation from the Father? No, in Locke's opinion. Yet the unmasker translates the (apocryphal) profession of faith by the Ethiopian eunuch[60] as 'I believe the Son of God to be Jesus Christ.' This profession would amount to an 'absurd tautology' (Edwards, p.87) unless it identified Christ with the messiah and the messiah with the Son of God. And Edwards interprets the second point as recognition of Christ's deity. Locke denies the tautology on the grounds that the titles *Jesus* and *Christ* had become a name. He chides the unmasker for reducing the articles of faith to only two and omitting such essential doctrines as the Trinity. As this irony suggests, he responds to Edwards by polemical evasion rather than refutation of his charges.

He had more of a debate than a dispute with Edward Stillingfleet, bishop of Worcester. Stillingfleet's *Discourse in vindication of the Trinity* (1696) implied that Locke's *Essay* weakened the credibility of this doctrine. After all the precautions Locke had taken to hide his antitrinitarianism, this allegation came as a shock. He tried to persuade Stillingfleet to withdraw the charge, but the bishop wanted him to recant. Locke's first letter (1697) was obsequious and patient. In his reply, however, Stillingfleet made his suspicions more explicit. Locke's second letter (1697) was polite, but firm. This time Stillingfleet broadened his accusations. Thus Locke's third letter (1699) was stubborn and resentful. Then the bishop died and the controversy came to an end.

The *Essay* contains nothing against the Trinity, Locke complains, yet the *Discourse* will persuade people to the contrary. Far from jeopardising this or any other Christian mystery, his philosophy concerns an entirely different subject. Stillingfleet implicitly concedes that the *Essay* does not discuss the Trinity; but the philosophy in it, he insists, undermines this doctrine. He finds that, in *Christianity not mysterious* (1696), John Toland converts the philosophy into a critical tool useful to the Socinians who, according to the bishop, have no philosophy of their own. He holds Locke responsible for Toland's book, even

60. Acts viii.37 'is a very ancient gloss: [...] [the eunuch:] "I believe that Jesus Christ is the Son of God."' Matthew viii.36, note 'n'.

though Locke disapproves of it, and hence for the author's alleged support of the Socinians, from whom Locke nonetheless dissociates himself. In vain the philosopher protests against the injustice of guilt by association, for it seems entirely legitimate to Stillingfleet. Anxious to impose his authority, the bishop urges him to profess the doctrine of the Trinity taught by the church. Locke realised that Christian polemicists had always treated such professions as a surrender. 'A worthy proof!' he scoffs in a letter to Peter King (*Correspondence*, vi.522). In his third letter to Stillingfleet, he objects to the *sanbenito* that the inquisitorial bishop wants him to wear.

He declines to profess the Trinity on the pretext that he does not know 'how the doctrine [...] has been always received in the Christian Church'. Perhaps, in other words, it has not always been received. 'A poor ordinary layman' (*Works*, iv.197) feels that he has gone far enough by professing the Trinity in Scripture. Just five years earlier, however, as we have seen, he had found few passages in the Bible supporting the doctrine and many conflicting with it. His reading notes reveal that he knew the historical development of the Trinity better than ordinary laymen and even many clergymen. The conflict between public necessity and private conviction imposed this hypocrisy. In his third letter Locke disapproves of forcing people to profess what they cannot understand. He confesses that he cannot understand his lordship's explanation of the Trinity in the *Discourse*, 'the most unintelligible thing [...] I ever read' (*Works*, iv.198).[61] Intelligent men and even divines of high rank and reputation do not understand it either. Locke reminds Stillingfleet that in the bishop's reply and in his book, he did not doubt the philosopher's faith in the Trinity.[62] Both writings state, on the contrary, that others borrowed from the *Essay* for purposes unintended by the author, for polemic, that is, against the Trinity.[63] Locke compares the bishop's relentless suspicion to that of the Inquisition.[64] Did Locke nonetheless

61. This particular charge seems unfair, since Stillingfleet defines the Trinity as three persons in one nature several times. His discussion nonetheless involves endless quibbling and appeals to Fathers.

62. Since Stillingfleet seems constantly to do just that, it is not clear exactly what Locke had in mind. He may have been thinking of the following passage in which Stillingfleet quotes from his first letter: 'But you say you own *the infallible truth of the Scriptures, and that where you want the evidence of things there is ground enough for you to believe, because God hath said it.* I do verily believe you, because I have a far greater opinion of your sincerity and integrity than I see reason for as to [Toland]' (Stillingfleet, iii.531). In his *Answer* to Locke's second letter, he declares, 'I do not go about to accuse you of denying [the Trinity and incarnation]' (Stillingfleet, iii.577). Yet the context continues to belie this intention.

63. Stillingfleet cites 'the ingenious author of *the Essay of Human Understanding* (from whence these notions are borrowed to serve other purposes than he intended them)' (Stillingfleet, iii.505, 530).

64. 'Not that you need be afraid of the Inquisition, or that I intend to charge you with heresy in denying the Trinity; but my present design is to show that your mind is so entangled and set fast

realise that he was frustrating the bishop's ambition to 'convert' a famous philosopher? The remark about the *sanbenito* suggests that he did, but he does not seem to have enjoyed the victory that contemporaries awarded him, for he had no great sense of humour. Gentle irony would have taught Stillingfleet a better lesson than the honour of arguing with him.

He succeeded in forcing Locke to defend two aspects of his philosophy from the charge of antitrinitarianism, the inevitable human ignorance of substance and the relationship between substance and person. He thought Locke's scorn for speculation on substance struck at divine consubstantiality. In the *Discourse* he accuses him of eliminating the concept of substance from philosophy on the pretext that neither sensation nor reflection reveals it. Locke denies this accusation, refutes it by passages quoted from the *Essay* and reaffirms that no simple idea or sensible quality could exist without a substratum in which to inhere. It is not true that he has 'almost discarded substance out of the reasonable part of the world' (Stillingfleet, iii.503) as Stillingfleet insists. He quotes passages from both the *Discourse* and the *Essay* that agree on the necessity of a substratum for support of what Stillingfleet calls modes or accidents and Locke, simple ideas or sensible qualities. Since his lordship confirms the proposition in his defence of the Trinity, it could hardly undermine this doctrine. Stillingfleet wrongly interprets the remark about an elephant on a turtle on I know not what as a denial of substance. Locke quotes from the *Essay* to show what he did mean: we know what substance does, but we do not know what it is.

While refuting most of the bishop's objections to his treatment of substance, he has no effective answer for one of them. Since neither sensation nor reflection yields any information about substance, we have no simple idea of it. We form a complex idea of it, Locke affirms, by putting simple ideas together. A complex idea, Stillingfleet objects, cannot contain any more information than the simple ideas that form it. How can we discover unknown information by the assembly of known information unrelated to it? We cannot, in effect. The bishop wins this argument because he leaves Christianity out of it. He can scarcely forget his theology, however, when Locke refuses to deny the possibility of thinking matter. Stillingfleet's faith not only commits him to the immateriality of a thinking substance, but also to that of the Trinitarian substance. Locke assures him that his philosophy establishes the certainty of an immaterial divine substance and the highest probability of an immaterial thinking substance in man. The *Essay* confirms both points and we have already discussed the second (p.138-39). The first appears in book IV: an incogitative being, which the author

by your notion of ideas that you know not what to make of the doctrines of the Trinity and incarnation' (Stillingfleet, iii.563). It is clear that Locke is no heretic, but unclear that he believes in no heresy!

defines as necessarily material, cannot produce a cogitative being. Thus God could not have created man unless he were an immaterial substance. Despite Stillingfleet's Scholastic prejudice, Locke's philosophy does not impugn the divine substance. But it does allow him secretly to disbelieve the Trinity.

The bishop's only effective argument against Locke's conception of substance proves less effective when he uses it against his alleged failure to respect the distinction between nature (substance) and person. He fears that Locke's philosophy will detract from the doctrine of the three persons in one nature. Without 'clear and distinct apprehensions concerning nature and person' (Stillingfleet, iii.509), the identity and diversity of the Trinity will blur. Sensation and reflection yield no simple ideas of nature and person, so clear and distinct complex ideas of them are impossible.[65] In his first letter the philosopher agrees that whoever writes about the Trinity should have clear and distinct ideas of nature and person. Whether he himself has such ideas or not, however, the *Essay* does not discuss this doctrine. A unitarian might as well accuse him of expressing his principles imprecisely. In writing the *Essay*, he did not consider the dispute over the Trinity. If there are no clear and distinct ideas of nature and person in it, he is 'a mistaken philosopher' (*Works*, iv.68) and not a heretic. One might drag the author of any secular work into a theological quarrel on the pretext that he could be interpreted in a way detrimental to some Christian doctrine. To make matters worse, Stillingfleet himself advances contradictory ideas of nature, for he identifies it both with essence and substance. Although, in practice, he limits himself to the latter, Locke exploits his apparent ambiguity.

Stillingfleet's dissatisfaction with the Trinitarian consequences of the *Essay* stems in part from the conflict between his realism and Locke's nominalism.[66] The bishop regards nature and person as real essences created by God, while the philosopher considers them nominal essences or complex ideas assembled in the mind. Such assembly seems unreliable to Stillingfleet, who assumes that it would produce arbitrary combinations of simple ideas. Could clear and distinct apprehensions of nature and person come from such a source? Of course not. Locke agrees that a nominal essence varies with the selection of qualities from the real essence on which it depends. Real essence does not vary, but we have no idea of its inner constitution. How could nature and person be two beings

65. 'Stillingfleet wendet sich [...] nicht nur gegen Lockes Anschauung über die Entstehung der Ideen des Wesens und der Person, sondern Lockes Begriffe des Wesens und der Person selbst lassen es ihm unmöglich erscheinen die Trinität zu verteidigen; denn Locke betrachtet abstrakte Ideen als bloße Erfindungen des menschlichen Geistes, für die es keine Vorbilder in der realen Welt gibt.' Walter Dahrendorf, *Lockes Kontroverse mit Stillingfleet und ihre Bedeutung für seine Stellung zur anglikanischen Kirche* (Hamburg 1932), p.51.
66. 'Dies ist der wahre Kern in Stillingfleets philosophischer Polemik gegen Lockes Empirismus' (Dahrendorf, p.32).

that exist independently of the names we assign to them? The philosopher cannot imagine what Stillingfleet has in mind. Nor can he understand his efforts to distinguish between nature and person in the *Discourse*.[67]

In his second letter he expresses his dismay over the bishop's reply to his first one. On his many pages demonstrating that the *Essay* does not concern the Trinity, Stillingfleet comments, 'let it be so. But it concerns the matter I was upon' (Stillingfleet, iii.548). It threatens the Trinity even it if does not refer to it! Apparently the bishop had not read these pages very carefully. If nature and person are merely terms meaning nothing in themselves, he argues, the Trinity is impossible to defend.[68] Impossible? Should he persist in this opinion, Locke warns, people will take him literally and assume that he himself has abandoned the doctrine. The bishop's extreme realism flies in the face of common sense: 'This notion of nature and person, that they are two words that signify by imposition, is what will hold in the common sense of all mankind' (*Works*, iv.153). Ever a nominalist, Locke distinguishes between terms and ideas. But does the defence of the Trinity necessarily depend on the intrinsic meaning of nature and person required by Stillingfleet? Perhaps he endangers the doctrine by setting unreasonable standards for its defence. In the *Discourse* he calls Locke a sceptic for failing to understand the distinction between nature and person. The philosopher answers with many pages of testimony by unnamed others who support and even surpass his criticism. The anonymity of this testimony naturally results in blunter language. Towards the end of the letter, however, Locke strikes the most damaging blow himself. His lordship persistently denies that the ideas of nature and person derive from simple ideas of sensation and reflection, but he never explains where he thinks they do come from. Does he think they are innate? Perhaps the assault on innate ideas in the *Essay* deters him from advocating the origin he had in mind.

In his reply to the philosopher's second letter, he extends his defence of the Trinity to cover the incarnation, by which he means the two natures in one person. Locke's rebuttals do not shake his conviction that the new philosophy precludes a sure distinction between nature and person, because sensation and reflection furnish no simple ideas of them. If his lordship had said that this philosophy precluded simple ideas of nature and person, the philosopher would have agreed. A rainbow consists of several colours, Locke remarks, and a

---

67. Yet Stillingfleet's distinction is entirely traditional. He defines nature as follows: 'There must be a real essence in every individual of the same kind, for that is what makes it to be what it is' (Stillingfleet, iii.510). For his conception of person, see p.135.

68. 'If [your notions of nature and person] hold, I do not see how it is possible to defend the doctrine of the Trinity. For if these terms really signify nothing in themselves [...] one nature and three persons can be no more' (Stillingfleet, iii.549).

complex idea of several simple ideas. There are no simple ideas of nature and person. Nor does he agree with Stillingfleet's contention that sensation and reflection do not provide us with the simple ideas we need to compose the complex ideas of nature and person. He challenges him to produce an 'intelligible' (*Works*, iv.335) definition of nature or person that does not break down into simple ideas. He even juxtaposes existing definitions of person by himself and the bishop:

[Locke:] a thinking intelligent being that has reason and reflection, and can consider itself as itself, the same thinking thing in different times and places. [*Works*, iv.335]

[Stillingfleet:] a complete intelligent substance with a peculiar manner of subsistence. [Stillingfleet, iii.511]

Locke submits that all of Stillingfleet's objections to Locke's definition apply to Stillingfleet's definition too. Locke also invites his opponent to demonstrate, if he can, that Locke's definition conflicts with the incarnation in a way that Stillingfleet's does not. The bishop, according to Locke, now admits that the word *person* has no natural (intrinsic) meaning and his definition implies that it designates 'a general abstract idea' (*Works*, iv.336).[69] Thus *person* is no less a notion in his mind than in Locke's, and *nature* as well. Yet the bishop suspects him of thinking that *person* means whatever one may wish, a horse, a tree or a stone. This was true only before usage had associated the word with the idea. We must use words so that they recall the usual ideas to the minds of those with whom we communicate.

Impatient with Locke's resistance, the bishop finally resorts to the accusation that he doubts propositions appearing in Scripture. The philosopher, who has read his Bible thoroughly, replies that it does not contain the doctrines of the 'three persons in one nature' and the 'two natures in one person'. 'My Bible is faulty', he says, 'for I do not remember that I ever read in it either of these propositions in these precise words' (*Works*, iv.343). Until his lordship shows him one that does, he will have to assume that whoever assigns them falsely to Scripture fabricates a new scripture not dictated by the Holy Spirit. Thus Locke sprang a trap from which the bishop could scarcely have escaped with his dignity intact if the controversy had continued. Yet he couched his firmest rebuke of Stillingfleet in language that exposed him to no legitimate complaint. It would have been difficult to convict him of the unitarianism we know he privately embraced on the evidence of this statement, which nonetheless ruins his lordship's case against him. Although each had aggravated the other by his

69. Stillingfleet may not have intended this interpretation: 'Nature and person can [only] be [...] abstract ideas, *according to your own plain expressions*; and if they are so, they are no more than notions of the mind' (Stillingfleet, iii.576). The italics are mine.

persistence, the continuation of the controversy had worked to Locke's advantage. Death afforded the bishop a graceful exit.

However one may judge the discrepancy between Locke's public and private opinions, his controversies with Proast, Edwards and Stillingfleet reveal an unusual polemical skill and determination. He proves most resourceful in defending his public statements without compromising his private faith. This performance harmonises with his theory of tolerance, for he was exercising his right to the liberty of conscience by keeping his unitarianism secret and his civic responsibility by defending his publications from insinuations of heresy. In this way he demonstrated that his philosophy of reason had a practical as well as a theoretical value. Westfall finds (p.135) that he admitted the Christian mysteries above reason in theory, but accepted none in practice. Yet Locke certainly accepted an implicit one. Although he refused to say that Christ is God, he implied that he is more than a man. Since he nonetheless refrained from stating his position, we cannot tell whether he considered him an angel or a subordinate god. The latter alternative would confirm McLachland's opinion that he was an Arian,[70] but nothing indicates that he ever made this distinction. He did believe in the resurrection,[71] on the other hand, and even found a place for it in his philosophy. In his interpretation of the fall, reason imposed a compromise, for he agreed that Adam's sin had caused human mortality and denied that it had contaminated the entire race with the urge to sin. In reason Locke saw a more versatile tool than his predecessors. Judgement reinforces intuition and demonstration, so that reason embraces probability as well as certain knowledge. This versatility could not accommodate transubstantiation, however, not in a Protestant mind conditioned by a traditional hostility to the Roman manipulation of sacred mystery.

70. 'Locke did not allow that he was a Socinian, not because he was orthodox like Stillingfleet, nor a Sabellian, like Stephen Nye, but because he was an Arian, like Samuel Clarke' (McLachland, p. 91).

71. 'Until almost the middle of the last century unitarians generally believed in the virgin birth, the resurrection from the dead and the "divinity" (not the deity) of Christ' (McLachland, p.90).

# Buffier

'[LA] philosophie [de Locke] semble être [...] par rapport à celle de Descartes et de Malebranche, ce qu'est l'histoire par rapport à un roman.'[1] Voltaire borrowed this parallel[2] from Claude Buffier, one of his Jesuit teachers.[3] Although Buffier learned much from Descartes and especially Locke, his philosophical common sense does not lack originality.[4] His Jesuit flexibility enables him to steer a somewhat independent course without alarming his Order,[5] which had resisted Descartes and now resisted Locke. He founded his philosophy on common sense or the natural light, which are synonyms in his vocabulary. They designate what he considers a precise concept and a stable phenomenon. Nor does he doubt that common sense tends unequivocally to Christianity. In the *Exposition des preuves les plus sensibles de la véritable religion* (1732), he asserts that no other ideology[6] has ever brought so many great minds together from so many different countries for so many centuries. 'Une telle autorité n'est-elle pas ce qu'on appelle le sens commun' (*Cours* col. 1319)? The natural light inspires the choice of Christianity over all other religions. Buffier thanks God: 'c'est donc vous qui m'y avez porté selon les règles de la prudence et de la lumière naturelle du bon sens' (*Cours*, col. 1320). In the natural light he sees a Christian privilege unavailable to ancient poets like Homer, who could not extricate themselves from the monstrous obscurity of paganism. He even exhorts us to an incidental

1. Claude Buffier, *Cours de sciences sur des principes nouveaux et simples* (Paris 1732), col. 731. This edition contains most of Buffier's works.
2. 'Tant de raisonneurs ayant fait le roman de l'âme, un sage est venu, qui en a fait modestement l'histoire' (*Lettres*, p.83).
3. Buffier held the position of scriptor at the Collège Louis-le-Grand in Paris from 1701 until his death in 1737. Voltaire attended the Collège from 1704 until 1711. Later both frequented the house of président de Maisons. Buffier collaborated with other masters of Louis-le-Grand in editing the Jesuit *Mémoires* and *Dictionnaire de Trévoux*.
4. 'Buffier can be seen as the inheritor of both Descartes and Locke, but principally of Locke. The principle by which he arrives at true judgments, the *sens commun*, is however, neither Cartesian reason nor Lockian empiricism. It is a concept which, during the period of his writing, was held by him alone. In this sense one must acknowledge his originality.' Kathleen Wilkins, *A study of the works of Claude Buffier*, Studies on Voltaire 66 (Genève 1969), p.68.
5. 'Un malin pourra dire que Buffier fut assez ingénieux pour avoir cherché un fondement épistémologique à l'art jésuite de l'équivoque [...] [il] reconnaît que le sens commun lui-même est engagé dans la relativité des opinions [...] à l'encontre de la plupart des tenants d'un appel au sens commun, en philosophie, [il] prend au sérieux l'ambiguïté même du sens commun et sa structure paradoxale.' Louise Marcil-Lacoste, 'La logique du paradoxe du père Claude Buffier', *Dix-huitième siècle* 8 (1976), p.121, 124. This opinion seems oversubtle to me.
6. 'Nulle suite ou même nul système d'opinions' (*Cours*, col. 1319).

appreciation of Christianity in *Homère en arbitrage* (1715), a naive attempt to arbitrate the quarrel between Mme Dacier and La Motte over the relative merits of ancient and contemporary culture.[7] His Christian faith consists at least in part of faith in common sense.

Just as the *Exposition* advocates his Christianity, his philosophical works justify faith in common sense as he understands it. They ignore the repertory of 'opinions and prejudices'[8] in the vulgar connotation of the term. They treat it rather as a valid synonym of reason in both the subjective and the objective sense, between which they do not explicitly discriminate. At times they attribute it to all men and at others, to the majority, according to potential or actual use. The *Traité des premières vérités* (1724) tells us, 'L'auteur de la nature avait imprimé dans tous les hommes ce qu'il fallait pour atteindre à la vérité, autant que leur condition les en rend susceptibles (*Cours*, col. 580). He gave them liberty too, however, and they made such poor use of it that their judgement deteriorated, hence their strange ideas, their vain prejudices, their misconceptions, their idiosyncracies and their other abuses of common sense. Buffier's disapproval of these deviations from his intellectual norm identifies him as a proponent of French classicism. He even professes to know the kind of deviation caused by each degree of deterioration. The complete deterioration of common sense results in extravagance; a slight deterioration, in perfectionism; partial deterioration, in eccentricity and the advanced deterioration of a few elements, in a madness confined to a particular thing (obsession). The only advantage over Buffier enjoyed by modern psychology is scientific evidence. He also enumerates the motives he sees behind deviations from common sense: exaggerated curiosity about things beyond the limits of knowledge;[9] the vanity of distinguishing oneself by the peculiarity of one's thought; sectarian or party bias; logical concatenation obscuring a bad point of departure or a secret interest in avoiding inconvenient truth. The preponderance of wilful motives implies that we can foresee and avoid deviation from his common sense, a typical Enlightenment attitude. In his *Eléments de métaphysique* (1725) Eugène asks Téandre how we can be sure that all men share an opinion when we know so

7. The second phase (1714) of the quarrel between the ancients and the moderns involved Anne Dacier, a translator of Homer, and the poet La Motte Houdard.

8. 'Buffier takes his notion to be above the capacity of the vulgar. In fact, the *Traité [des premières vérités]* persistently disconnects common sense from vulgar opinions and prejudices [...] Buffier fully legitimates philosophic objections against common sense taken as a vulgar notion. Public opinion, in his mind, has nothing to do with it.' Louise Marcil-Lacoste, 'The epistemological foundation of the appeal to common sense in Claude Buffier and Thomas Reid', Diss. McGill 1974, p.61.

9. '[La raison doit se contenter de] proposer ses propres lumières, répandues dans tous les hommes, pour rejeter ce qui ne s'y accorde pas, et qui ne s'est formé que dans les écarts de quelques cerveaux malades tel que celui d'un Spinoza' (*Cours*, col. 932).

few of them. Téandre replies by asking Eugène how we know all men need food to live, even though we have not seen them all. Thus common sense spontaneously extrapolates the greater unknown from the lesser known. Buffier effectively takes universal consent for granted in such cases.

According to his philosophy human nature[10] compels universal consent to basic notions like the necessity of food and the desirability of happiness. What he calls the sentiment of nature in the *Traité des premières vérités* would confound anyone, he affirms, who denies these notions. Wherever we find the sentiment of nature, we likewise discover true evidence and a necessary rule of truth. 'C'est donc la nature et le sentiment de la nature que nous devons reconnaître pour la source et l'origine de toutes les vérités de principe' (*Cours*, col.579). We intuit truths of principle and infer truths of consequence. Buffier cannot imagine our nature misguiding us when it induces us to make a judgement. If it did, he submits, we would not even know what we are and what we must think, desperate alternatives to his mind. 'Si le sentiment de la nature raisonnable n'est pas une règle de vérité, nous n'en avons donc aucune' (*Cours*, col.579). We would succumb to the worst kind of scepticism, to a fanatical inability to ascertain anything (Pyrrhonism). This would be the direst of fates, the ultimate evil for a man of faith like Buffier. He often shrinks from desperate alternatives, a reflex of his common sense.

Within the sentiment of nature, he distinguishes between two sources of truth: intimate sense and common sense. Intimate sense produces truths about one's own mind, and common sense truths about everything else accessible to it. Although each has its own kind of judgement, both constitute the sentiment of nature. Then why distinguish between them? Aguilar explains that no one cast doubt on internal truths in Buffier's times, while several philosophers such as Descartes, tentatively, and Berkeley, definitively, doubted external truths.[11] There was no need to prove the existence of internal truths, but there was a need, and especially an apologetic need, to prove the existence of external truths,

10. 'A cette disposition [Buffier] donne le nom de "sens commun". Par là est affirmée l'existence au moins virtuelle d'une nature humaine *identique* chez tous, alors que la philosophie de Locke avait semblé faire éclater la notion de cette nature en expliquant sa formation par la suite des expériences sensibles constituant l'histoire de chaque individu.' Roger Mercier, *Les Sciences de la vie dans la pensée française du XVIIIe siècle* (Paris 1963), p.242. I would replace *identique* (my italics) by *semblable*. See note 15.

11. 'Basta su simple lectura para darse cuenta de que en él se atacan constantemente dos posiciones filosóficas distintas: el racionalismo cartesiano, con su principio de la idea clara y distinta, y el idealismo empirico de consecuencias acosmistas, más o menos afín a Berkeley, que pone en duda o niega la existencia de la realidad corpórea exterior a nuestro yo. Ahora bien, los filósofos representantes de estas dos posiciones filosóficas no niegan el valor del testimonio del sentido íntimo. Por ello Buffier no siente la necessidad de justificarlo.' Juan Aguilar, *El Sentido común en las obras filosóficas del P. Claude Buffier S.I.* (Barcelona 1957), p.56.

hence the Jesuit's theory of common sense. He nonetheless acknowledges the priority of the intimate sense, which he describes as the primary source and first principle of all truth, and even the foundation of all external truth. The conviction that the object of our thought really exists depends on the prior conviction that our thought itself exists. 'Notre pensée et le sentiment intime que nous en avons ne sont réellement que nous-mêmes qui pensons' (*Cours*, col.557). The intimate sense yields truths guaranteed by the most conclusive evidence possible, since it is metaphysical or absolute in nature. Haunted like many of his contemporaries by the *cogito*, Buffier proposes his own version of it: '*je pense, je sens, j'existe*' (*passim*). Though true and legitimate, it amounts to no great discovery in his view. Yet it has never occurred to an infinite number of people, so he excludes it from the first truths of the intimate sense. Nor does he have much to say about first truths of this kind. Descartes also declared that the mind thinks constantly, but Buffier denies that we can tell. Apologetic necessity convinces him only of the 'fact' that it can think independently of all bodily relations. God subjects it to a partial dependence on the senses for the duration of its union with a human body. Our Jesuit may have intended this remark as a rectification of Locke. His discussion of the intimate sense does not include a more thorough attempt to justify the status he gives it as the primary source and foundation of all truth. The contrary opinion seems so absurd to him that he does not bother to refute it. On the priority of the intimate sense, he is in agreement with Descartes and Berkeley.[12]

It was in reaction to the privileged status they assigned to the intimate sense that he embarked on a philosophy of common sense. According to Berkeley, he complains, we have no certain evidence that bodies exist, even our own body. Obviously 'la nature fait porter aux hommes qui ont atteint l'usage de la raison des jugements sur des choses que nous ne connaissons point par la perception intime de notre propre expérience' (*Cours*, col.565). Buffier stresses the absurdity of denying the truths produced by these judgements, which he considers infallible. Not only do they preoccupy us far more than introspection, but they also govern our lives. He concentrates on them because others ignore or neglect them. As usual, however, he has another reason for defending them: divine revelation and human authority (particularly that of the Church) depend on the testimony of our senses.

He attributes the confidence we have in our judgements of external phen-

12. 'Buffier's own commitment to the internal sentiment can be missed in the language he uses against the dogmatism of internality and there is no clear assurance that ultimately his defence of common sense could not be said to be a new version of the ontological argument itself, where we would pass from the sentiment of our existence to the sentiment of the existence of others and, therefrom, to the existence of God.' Marcil-Lacoste, 'The epistemological foundation', p.133.

omena to a rule of truth distinct from the intimate sense. He calls it the common sentiment of nature or common sense. Although his conception of it varies,[13] a thorough and emphatic definition in the *Traité des premières vérités* eclipses all the others (*Cours*, col. 564):

J'entends donc ici par le SENS COMMUN la disposition que la nature a mise dans tous les hommes ou manifestement dans la plupart d'entre eux pour leur faire porter, quand ils ont atteint l'usage de la raison, un jugement commun et uniforme sur des objets différents du sentiment intime [...] jugement qui n'est point la conséquence d'aucun principe antérieur.

Thus common sense disposes us to make judgements that the intimate sense cannot make. Most of us make them when we reach the age of reason and the exceptions, whom Buffier calls monsters,[14] only prove the rule. Despite the final clause in the quotation, common sense depends, as we have seen, on the intimate sense, although both stem from the sense of nature. While the intimate sense yields certain truth, common sense produces truth only of the highest probability. By uniformity of judgement, Buffier means similar rather than identical powers. 'N'est-ce pas toujours', Eugène asks, 'la même faculté de raisonner qui est dans tous les hommes?' (*Cours*, col. 909). Yes, Téandre replies, if the same implies a resemblance. But no, if it implies identity, for that would tend to Spinozism, a great evil.[15] Earlier in the dialogue, Eugène himself observes, 'le sens commun n'est guère commun' (*Cours*, col. 927). Men's opinions are as diverse as the variety in their faces, yet all have eyes, ears, noses and mouths.

The diversity of common sense does not detract from its potential, which inspires Buffier's optimism: 'Il n'est point de connaissance si profonde et si élevée où l'on ne puisse conduire toutes sortes d'esprits, pourvu qu'ils aient l'usage de la raison avec la mémoire' (*Cours*, col. 850). This optimism reminds one of Descartes, whose good sense Wilkins compares with Buffier's common sense.[16] According to the *Eléments*, common sense inclines us to consider all the evidence available, whatever it may be. Philosophy does not authorise us to abandon it when we exercise that discipline. It seems vulgar and superficial to

13. 'Never is [common sense] explained in crystal-clear terms: it seems at one time a natural feeling [...] at another a spontaneous and uniform way of judging [...] Occasionally Buffier equates it with its popular meaning of good sense or reason' (Wilkins, p.70).
14. 'Un homme qui dans ses sentiments et ses pensées n'aurait rien de semblable aux autres hommes passerait pour un véritable monstre; et il le serait effectivement' (*Cours*, col. 928).
15. 'Cette équivoque du mot *même* est le fondement du misérable système de Spinoza qui suppose une *même* substance dans tous les êtres, parce qu'ils ont quelque chose de commun, savoir, d'exister. Mais en répondant à Spinoza que ce qu'il prend pour le *même* et le *commun* n'est que le *semblable* et qu'il prend l'identité de *ressemblance* pour l'identité de *substance*, le système en même temps se trouve réduit en fumée' (*Cours*, col. 911).
16. 'Cartesian reason, as *bon sens*, can, in a sense, be approximated to Buffier's *sens commun*; in both cases, it is the faculty by which all men may arrive at truth' (Wilkins, p.86).

philosophers fond of subtlety, who suspect clarity achieved at the expense of their cherished terms and rules.[17] Buffier disagrees with them, but he also acknowledges that one needs more than common sense to practise philosophy. As a philosopher he should have distinguished between the subjective and objective aspects of common sense.[18] He sometimes treats it as a faculty, as we have seen, and sometimes as the product of this faculty, an elementary wisdom shared by all men. Téandre describes this wisdom as '*le sentiment qui est manifestement le plus commun aux hommes de tous les temps et de tous les pays, quand ils ont atteint l'usage de la raison et des choses sur quoi ils portent leur jugement*' (*Cours*, col. 926). We recognise the consensus by its universality and permanence in the minds of our fellow men. Buffier probably did not realise the democratic implications of this thought. He makes a further comment on objective common sense by characterising it as 'ce que pensent le plus communément les hommes dans les choses où ils sont également à portée de juger avant tout raisonnement' (*Cours*, col. 587). While common experience conditions objective common sense, reasoning exceeds the capacity of subjective common sense. Buffier limits the faculty to a spontaneous apprehension of sense data similar to empirical intuition in Locke. He does not regard it as an equivalent of reason, but rather, with intimate sense, as one of its two faculties.

The judgements of common sense are the first truths to which he devotes the *Traité*. These self-evident propositions satisfy three conditions: (1) a first truth is so clear that we can neither prove nor disprove it by a clearer proposition; (2) at least ninety-nine of every one hundred people in all countries and ages accept it; (3) even when someone denies it, he behaves as if he believed it. Buffier considers the second condition fulfilled when many different kinds of people make the same judgement. He recommends that we respond to the eccentricity mentioned in the third by ridicule and indignation. A philosopher who doubts a first truth faces a hundred thousand other philosophers, because he is no more competent in this matter than they are. If the first truth of one philosopher conflicts with that of another, 'le sentiment le plus répandu dans tous les hommes et à quoi ils se rendent le plus naturellement' (*Cours*, col. 611)

17. 'Ceux qui par leur profession se donnent pour maîtres dans les matières abstraites méconnaissent parfois les vérités les plus importantes, quand elles ne sont pas revêtues de formalités et d'expressions autorisées parmi eux: et qu'espérer de gens qui trouvent un ouvrage superficiel parce qu'ils n'y trouvent rien que d'intelligible, qu'on écarte les fausses subtilités et qu'on en abrège la pratique et les règles' (*Cours*, col. 555)?

18. 'El uso prevalente del término *sentido común* en su acepción subjetiva o en la objetiva es una de las notas que pone de manifiesto el cuño proprio de cada una de las diversas versiones de la filosofia del sentido común. Buffier pasa constantemente de una a otra acepción. Sin embargo en su filosofia el sentido común es fundamentalmente el sentido común subjetivo, siendo el objetivo su consecuencia o efecto' (Aguilar, p.73).

prevails. Thus Buffier's opinion that the mind causes the movement in the body triumphs over Malebranche's opinion that a spirit cannot affect a body.

Further examples of first truths appear in the *Traité*: there are other things and other people in the world beside myself; there is truth, wisdom and prudence in other people; they are not all in a league to deceive me; I consist of a mind and a body which have no properties in common; what is not intelligence cannot produce the effects of intelligence; pieces of matter cannot assemble themselves in a device with a regular movement like a clock. Buffier adds another thought without actually declaring it a first truth: if a clock reveals the existence of a clockmaker, the creation proves the existence of God. Elsewhere he does call the existence of God 'une sorte de première vérité' (*Cours*, col. 1264) which, though revealed by the sentiment of nature (intimate or common sense?), can be demonstrated by reflexion (reasoning) too. Human freedom, on the other hand, meets his three requirements for status as a first truth. This example and the others above are general in nature, since they concern all reasonable men in all situations. Another kind of first truth involves particular tendencies or circumstances. When particular knowledge, experience or habit attain uniform acceptance, they become particular external first truths, but Buffier does not explore them. He also neglects internal first truths and apparently because of the thorough treatment they receive from Cartesians.

Does sense perception determine external first truths? A disciple of Locke would agree and a disciple of Descartes would disagree. Where does Buffier stand? The *Traité des premières vérités* states that the senses always report faithfully whatever appears to them. It is the mind that confuses appearances with reality. Yet the *Suite du Traité*, which Buffier also entitles *Traité des vérités de conséquence* (1731), cites 'le rapport de nos sens' (*Cours*, col. 751) as one of the most frequent sources of false ideas. He may have meant that false ideas result from misinterpretation of sense data, but nothing in the passage either supports this hypothesis or indicates that he has changed his mind. What appears to the senses, according to the *Traité des premières vérités*, nearly always conforms to the truth about the conduct and ordinary needs of life. If reason contradicts a sensory appearance on the strength of fact and reflexion, it is not necessarily right. A present appearance may conflict with a past one, for instance, when the object of sense perception changes or when it becomes more or less perceptible. If my perception disagrees with that of others as acute as I am or, above all, with that of all the others in contact with me, I should admit that they are right and I am wrong. A sense perception contradicted neither by reason, nor by a previous perception, nor by the perception of another sense, nor by the perception of other people qualifies as a kind of first truth. Sense perception does not inform the mind of such a truth, but rather activates a pre-existing tendency to make the judgement that reveals it. In the *Principes du raisonnement* (1714) Buffier implies that sensory stimulation precipitates the discovery of abstract first truths, another kind. For 'toutes les opérations de l'esprit [...] sont la suite et le résultat d'une impression causée plus ou moins immédiatement par les objets sensibles' (*Cours*, col. 853-54). The *Traité des premières vérités* confirms, in effect, that the primitive ideas of all that we know come to us through sensation and experience.

Yet Buffier likewise speculates on the possibility of ideas completely independent of sensation. He concludes that only the example of a man without any senses could settle the issue. His equivocation raises the question of the relationship between first truths and innate ideas. In this connection, the *Traité des premières vérités* distinguishes between idea, an actual thought, and commonsense judgement, the tendency to think a certain way in a certain situation. While an idea merely represents something, judgement discovers a first truth. If people insist on referring to first truths as innate ideas, however, Buffier will not quibble over terms. 'Ils ne pourront se dispenser d'admettre avec moi le *sens commun* pour première règle de vérité' (*Cours*, col. 567). Buffier comments on Locke's refutation of innate ideas in an appendix to the *Traité*. If Locke means ideas of which we are constantly aware, innate principles deserve his scorn because experience shows otherwise. But if he means first principles, it is insane to deny them 'et je l'ai montré' (*Cours*, col. 732). In the *Traité des premières vérités* no doubt. Innate ideas tempt Buffier again in the *Traité des vérités de conséquence*. If there ever were such a thing, he imagines, it would be the idea of God or the identity principle. These things do not occupy our mind continually, so they cannot be innate. Buffier therefore distinguishes himself from both Descartes and Locke on this point.

He nonetheless conceives of ideas in the Cartesian manner, defining them as modifications of a thinking soul or mind. An idea is to the mind as a movement to the body. Ideas represent mental or physical objects, but our Jesuit takes a greater interest in the latter. Against the Cartesian suspicion of sense data, he argues that ideas derived from vivid sensations evidently represent more than mental objects. Such ideas prove the existence of extramental things which we call bodies. If awake and lucid, one does not confuse them with the phantasies of dreams and madness as Descartes fears. Buffier follows both Descartes and Locke in limiting the senses to the perception of appearances that do not necessarily convey any information about the internal organisation of material objects. The arrangement and movement of the smallest parts escapes detection by the senses and even reason. Buffier adopts the distinction between real and nominal essences advanced by Locke, except that he names the latter *essences représentées*. Common sense only discerns the representative essence and not the real essence. The *Traité des premières vérités* describes the representative essence as 'le sentiment que la nature a mis dans les hommes pour porter tel jugement sur l'existence des objets qui sont également à la portée de tous' (*Cours*, col.585). But no more than that, since it does not enable them to ascertain the internal organisation of matter.

Nor indeed the intimate nature of God, which belongs to the jurisdiction of faith. Yet these limitations do not, in Buffier's opinion, frustrate the pursuit of natural and religious science. Like most Christians in his day, he founds theology on the testimony of ancient witnesses recorded especially in the New Testament. The importance of this testimony to him explains his choice of two first truths as examples in the *Traité des premières vérités*: the existence of other men besides myself and the impossibility of a conspiracy by all other men to deceive me. He has the traditional faith in the numbers of witnesses agreeing on the authenticity of an event: 'un fait attesté par un très grand nombre de gens sensés qui assurent en avoir été les témoins ne peut sensément être révoqué en doute' (*Cours*, col. 933). In practice, however, he typically takes the good sense of witnesses who support dogma for granted. His apologetic bias also conditions his advice not to disagree with a majority of one's intellectual peers. Common sense would not be common sense unless it dictated belief in any event, even a miracle, witnessed by many reasonable men. Distinction between the natural and the supernatural by an intelligent majority is an infallible rule of truth instilled in us by our Creator. Buffier identifies it in fact as a first truth guaranteed by common sense.

Human authority qualifies as a first truth when it meets four conditions: (1) the witnesses have access to knowledge of the truth; (2) There are so many of them that one could not reasonably expect more; (3) no grounds for suspicion of their integrity exist; (4) no one contradicts their testimony, not even people who have an interest in doing it. The first condition, which does not specify how we can determine such access, is conveniently loose. While the others seem strict enough, Buffier apparently fears that they would jeopardise dogma. Once he has stated his four conditions, he supposes that any one of them and particularly the last one might not be necessary. If a proposition satisfies all four, 'c'est une règle de vérité si certaine qu'aucun homme sensé n'en disconviendra jamais' (*Cours*, col. 603).

Buffier disputes Locke's contention that no one inspired by God can reveal any truth contrary to intuitive knowledge (see p.45). Why does this Englishman admit the testimony of his eyes and deny 'le témoignage unanime de tous les hommes' (*Cours*, col. 604)? Aside from this exaggeration, the apologist assumes what is in question. In a manuscript passage quoted by Wilkins (p.78), he de-emphasises Locke's statement on the pretext that it does not harmonise with the context in the *Essay*. More plausibly he complains that it undermines the Christian mysteries and reduces the faith to belief in the empirical facts. An orthodox Christian, to say nothing of a Jesuit, could obviously tolerate neither tendency. Yet Buffier admits that much of revelation is probable and not certain. His extensive and somewhat vulnerable analysis of the probability he finds in the testimony of Christian witnesses does not concern us here. His rebuttal of another statement by Locke does, however. Each successive transmission of testimony, the *Essay* affirms, diminishes its probability (see p.142). On the contrary, Buffier protests, the greater the number of enlightened, judicious and intelligent men who verify the original testimony, the greater the probability of the information transmitted. The argument may be clever, but the naivety of ascribing scientific virtues to all of these men contrasts with Locke's well founded realism. Probability decreases with each successive transmission because the possibility of negligence and the opportunity for fraudulent alteration recurs each time. And Locke has no reason to share Buffier's faith in the scruples of Christian scribes.

'Dieu ne peut parler contre la raison', proclaims the *Exposition*. How could the source of all reason, the divine essence, contradict itself? One cannot imagine such a thing 'sans détruire' (*Cours*, col. 1278) the very ideas we have of God and reason. People who try to set reason against revealed truth are wrong. To be sure, God says and does things above reason. Experience teaches us that we must believe what we cannot understand. Although we do not know the extent of natural forces, 'la lumière du sens commun' (*Cours*, col. 1351) persuades us that they lack the power to restore vision to the blind and life to the dead. We know by reason that, if God did not authorise such miracles, he would be using the light of common sense to deceive us. This hypothesis is unthinkable because it negates our natural idea of divine providence. Yet some of Buffier's contemporaries did not shrink from such a consequence and they joined others in using the same argument against the authenticity of miracles.

Begging the question of authenticity, he insists that dogma conforms to reason.[19] What could be more reasonable than to believe what God or Christ his minister has said? The author of the *Exposition* wields this argument as if it should silence all objections. He never considers the difficulty of proving that they said such things. In his *Sentiments chrétiens sur les principales vérités de la*

---

19. 'Buffier est profondément pieux. Pour lui, les vérités de la religion chrétienne et catholique ne font jamais aucun doute. Il interprète tout à leur lumière [...] même lorsqu'il s'écarte inconsciemment des croyances orthodoxes vers un vague déisme. Certaines idées en elles-mêmes sont loin d'être celles d'un prêtre attaché à ses devoirs. Poussées à des conclusions logiques, elles sont contraires à la religion que le P. Buffier tient surtout à répandre. Mais jamais, doit-on dire, il n'a conscience de cette erreur.' Frances Montgomery, *La Vie et l'œuvre du père Buffier* (Paris 1930), p.181.

*religion* (1718) he urges us to take the Church's word for it. No other system of thought has ever united so many great minds. Common sense compels submission to such an authority. Although the *Exposition* restates the authority of the Church, it contains a passage undermining this statement. We could have done without a supernatural revelation, Buffier concedes, but not 'la raison qui est elle-même la religion naturelle' (*Cours*, col. 1228). Then why do we need a church dedicated to revelation? The Jesuit does not explain. The divine gift of reason and the legitimacy of natural religion incline him to deism, despite his commitment to Catholicism. In reviews of his books by fellow Jesuits, Marcil-Lacoste finds euphemisms implying reservations about his orthodoxy. His ideas seemed 'original, singular and audacious' to them.[20]

The theological implications of his philosophy must have disturbed them and not his treatment of dogma, with which he takes no liberties. They could hardly censure his neglect of original sin, which the Jesuits largely ignored anyway.[21] Nor could they object to his comments on the Trinity, Christ and transubstantiation. He includes the Trinity among the things that God has told us. Since God would never deceive us, reason tells us to believe what it cannot understand. The Socinians violate the rules of the natural light when they regard the Trinity as a contradiction. The nature of God infinitely exceeds our comprehension, so 'la lumière naturelle nous apprend a ne point juger [ce mystère]' (*Cours*, col. 644). Reason can extract no distinct idea from the propositions that God is three persons and three persons are one God. Reflection nonethless convinces reason that they express truths and reality. Buffier offers the analogy of a blind man who can see colours only through the eyes of other men. Thus we depend on revelation for faith in the existence of the divine substance and its three persons. We cannot reasonably doubt that God consists of three persons in one substance, and Christ, of one person in two substances or natures, despite our inability to comprehend these dogmas. In the *Histoire du Nouveau Testament* Buffier declares Christ all-powerful by virtue of his eternal generation from and hypostatic union with God. His obedient death proved him worthy of this power, which enabled him to rise from the dead. Analysis of the proposition '*Dieu s'est fait homme*' in the *Traité des premières vérités* (*Cours*, col. 726) yields three component ideas: God, man and the union of the two natures. The first two

20. 'One can expect some ambivalence toward a Jesuit perceived as fond of Locke, not radically against the Cartesians, clearly deist and, on the whole, rather sceptical.' Marcil-Lacoste, 'The epistemological foundation', p.29.

21. 'The catechism used in Jesuit colleges was that of Canisius [...] Original sin has only a small place, the doctrine of the redemption is not vital and there are few references to Christ. The passion is not related and the eucharist is defined without any mention of what it commemorates. Its doctrines are lax in comparison with Bossuet's catechism (1687)' (Wilkins, p.80). Wilkins is referring to Pierre Canisius, *Le Catéchisme catholique* (Paris 1565). First edition (in Latin) in 1558.

are accessible to the human mind, which infers divine qualities like immortality from one, and human qualities like mortality from the other. But reason cannot penetrate the mystery of the two natures in one person and therefore should not try. The authority of God makes this naturally unbelievable idea entirely believable.

Buffier founds his Christology on Jesus's miracles and, in particular, the resurrection. In the *Exposition* he applies his theory of historical probability to testimony by witnesses of both the empty tomb and the resurrection appearances. He emphasises the posting of guards around the tomb to prevent any act that might accredit the accomplishment of Jesus's prophecy that he would rise from the dead. Despite this precaution, the tomb was empty three days later. The risen Christ appeared many times in many different places over a period of forty days. After talking and dining with him, his followers watched him ascend to heaven. Buffier echoes the traditional exaggeration of the risk the disciples ran by testifying to the resurrection and in vain if they were lying. He stresses the number and variety of the witnesses, including the five hundred mentioned by Paul (1 Corinthians xv.6). How could so many different men have been wrong? Recalling Descartes's definition of good sense, Buffier notes, 'la raison humaine consiste à discerner ce qu'on doit juger vrai d'avec ce qu'on doit juger faux' (*Cours*, col. 1329). Reason judges the resurrection to be true because: (1) seeing, hearing and touching an object; (2) many people seeing, hearing and touching an object and (3) doing it many times over a period are for Buffier irrefutable proof. Down through the centuries, he submits, Christian scholars have verified the authenticity of the testimony and the competence of the witnesses, thus reinforcing this proof. He does not doubt their scientific detachment.

He illustrates his position by supposing what would happen if a modern equivalent of the resurrection occurred in Paris. A man put to death on the wheel in front of many spectators disappears from a tomb guarded by many soldiers. His accomplices insist that he has risen from the dead, thus fulfilling a prophecy he had made. Since his resurrection, they have seen him and eaten with him several times. For two or three years before his death, he had performed various miracles, healed incurable diseases and once, even fed thousands of people with five loaves of bread. Many Parisians watched him resuscitate a few of their fellow citizens. If this miracle were a hoax, Buffier triumphs, 'pourrait-on venir à bout de le faire croire à des gens raisonnables' (*Cours*, col. 1334) living in Paris at the time of the event? But how do we know that this eighteenth-century conjecture corresponds to a first-century event that really took place? And even if it did, would any of the conditions imagined by Buffier resemble original circumstances? Did Jerusalemites in Jesus's day have a conception of reason and respect for it similar to those of Buffier's fellow Parisians? Almost certainly not. Yet our Jesuit was not alone in ignoring such problems.

If the miracles in the gospel are true, he affirms, God has authorised Christianity. They must be either true or false and, if they were false, they would constitute an obvious and crude imposture. There is nothing subtle, imperceptible or abstract about them. If Jesus deceived the gospel witnesses, they had no incentive to publicise his miracles and yet they convinced an extraordinary number of people. The propagation of belief in them amounts to another miracle. Would God have allowed Jesus to do these miracles and establish a new religion in his name without his permission? 'C'est là ce que notre raison dans toute l'étendue de ses lumières ne se persuadera jamais' (*Cours*, col. 1307). Buffier interprets the kingdom of God proclaimed by Jesus as the Church. According to modern exegetes, the term probably meant a messianic revolution involving the intervention of God. Buffier sees it differently. The foundation of an eternal world kingdom in just three years by a man who had never left his homeland raises his enthusiasm. The gospel miracles more than confirm his apologetic faith in Jesus's essential message: '[Il] donna ce qu'il enseignait comme émané de Dieu même et comme la parole de Dieu, au nom duquel il l'annonça et la répandit' (*Cours*, col. 1283) Few would question the fact, but many would doubt the consequences drawn by Buffier. Although he devotes the entire *Histoire du Nouveau Testament* to Christ, he gives him relatively little space in his voluminous works. The trivial orthodoxy of this work deserves Montgomery's contempt: 'Le livre est dénué d'intérêt' (p.33). The heresy that tempted Buffier and his fellow Jesuits was neglect of Jesus.

Did Jesus teach that his body is really present in the eucharist? Catholics say yes and Protestants, no. Speaking on God's behalf, Jesus could scarcely have declared the same thing to be true and untrue at the same time. God does not contradict himself. So many people and so many sects profess faith in Jesus's teaching without really believing in it. Only the Church defends his authentic doctrine. Thus Buffier reaffirms the real presence. He discusses transubstantiation in the *Traité des premières vérités* and, particularly, the accidents of bread and wine that subsist after the consecration. Since the Council of Trent did not decide whether they are absolute, he refrains from expressing an opinion. But these species, as the Council calls them, are in a supernatural state, and ordinary accidents, in a natural state.[22] He disagrees with Cartesians who deny absolute accidents on the grounds that they cannot understand them. Although he cannot understand them either, he finds the Cartesians in error because God does

22. 'Leclerc dans sa *Logique* a très mal choisi pour exemple de contradiction la multiplication d'un même corps telle que les Catholiques [...] croient au mystère de l'eucharistie. Parce que c'est là un objet surnaturel dont nous ne pouvons naturellement juger' (*Cours*, col. 644-45). Buffier is referring to Jean Leclerc's *Logica sive ars ratiocinandi* (London 1692).

things no one can understand. Absolute accidents do not imply a contradiction as they maintain. Heresy hardly tempts him here.

He evidently took less interest in theology than philosophy. Even in the *Exposition des preuves les plus sensibles de la véritable religion* he neglected the dogma. When he carried his treatment of Catholicism beyond matters closely related to his philosophy, he reverted to apologetic stereotype. His attempt to equate Christianity with common sense tended to replace revelation by natural religion. He also accelerated the shift from metaphysics to natural philosophy initiated by Locke. Voltaire and the *philosophes* would follow him in discarding speculative systems like those of Leibniz and Malebranche. The deists among them would identify the natural light with common sense as he did. All of them appealed to the universal and eternal reason with which he credited the vast majority of men.[23] Yet his contribution to the Enlightenment was more timely than substantial, for he merely anticipated a trend by saying the right things at the right time. He hardly ranks with the other philosophers in this study. His thought suffers from the simplistic and superficial assumptions to which he had recourse whenever faced with difficulties that would only have whetted Leibniz's appetite.

23. 'Proclamer en philosophie le sens commun comme autorité unique et suprême, n'est-ce pas proclamer la souveraineté de cette raison qui est commune à tous les hommes? n'est-ce pas rejeter toutes les vieilles autorités, toutes les subtilités de l'école pour en appeler de la vérité et de l'erreur à la conscience du genre humain?' Francisque Bouillier (ed.), *Œuvres philosophiques du père Buffier* (Paris 1843), p.xliv.

# Berkeley

DIFFICULT problems inspired George Berkeley with radical solutions. An Anglican clergyman, he thought Enlightenment science and philosophy threatened religion. Newton had naturalised the Creator, Locke had hidden the creation from us, Bayle had fomented scepticism about them both and Malebranche had encouraged men to intrude on the mind of God. Nor did Spinoza's 'atheism' escape the Irish Anglican's misgivings. Berkeley's reaction to these dangers resulted in the most radical philosophy of the Enlightenment. Christians like Augustine had always incriminated matter, but Berkeley was the first to abolish the source of evil. His common sense exposed the illusion.

An immaterialist philosophy evolved from the 'arguings'[1] that preoccupied him when he was a fellow of Trinity College, Dublin, in 1707-1708. He recorded them in two notebooks published long after his death under the title of *Philosophical commentaries*. He chose not to burden his first published work, the *Essay towards a new theory of vision* (1709), with the risk of revealing his immaterialism, but some aspects of this philosophy appear in the text. Part I of *A treatise concerning the principles of human knowledge* (1710), which propounds the immaterialism, encountered so much opposition that, in order to defend himself, he wrote *Three dialogues between Hylas and Philonous* (1713), the clearest exposition of his early philosophy. No further parts of the *Treatise* ever appeared and Berkeley says he lost the manuscript of part II, on psychology and ethics, during a tour of Italy in 1716. An unsuccessful attempt to found a college in Bermuda brought him to Rhode Island where he wrote *Alciphron or the minute philosopher* (1732), a dialogue defending Christianity from the freethinkers. Returning to Great Britain, he became bishop of Cloyne (southern Ireland). In 1744 he published *Siris*, which begins with a recommendation of tar water, a cure-all, and ends with a review of ancient emanationism that implies a change in his philosophy. How profound a change? The critics disagree.

While *Siris* lavishes praise on ancient philosophy, the *Philosophical commentaries* propose to banish contemporary 'metaphysics [...] and [recall] men to common sense' (*Works*, i.91). The *Treatise* describes this metaphysics as a series of mazes leading eventually back to the point of departure or trapping the speculator in 'a forlorn scepticism'. The speculator's attempts to correct 'prejudices and errors of sense' by reason lure him into 'uncouth paradoxes, difficulties

---

1. *The Works of George Berkeley, Bishop of Cloyne* (Edinburgh 1948-1957), i.265.

and inconsistencies'. Intense reflection and meditation on 'the nature of things [raise] a thousand scrupules' in his mind. Never should he have abandoned 'sense and instinct' to embark on such an adventure. Satisfied with the evidence of their senses, 'the illiterate bulk of mankind [walking] the high road of plain common sense'[2] have no trouble understanding their familiar world. Turning from metaphysics to common sense has 'strangely enlightened'[3] Philonous, who speaks for Berkeley in the *Dialogues*. Now he easily understands many things that were mysterious to him before. Yet he has lost none of the sagacity he had learned by metaphysical speculation. Such metaphysics, in Berkeley's view, tends to scepticism, a threat to Christianity. For this disease he prescribes the sure remedy of common sense. His brand of common sense nonetheless seems ambiguous and inadequate for the task he assigns to it.

The reputation enjoyed by Locke's empiricism at Trinity College invited scrutiny by iconoclastic students. If objects outside of the mind cause sensation in the mind directly and indirectly, as he had believed, we perceive these sensations alone and not the objects themselves, which remain unknown to us. In the separation of a sensation from its object Berkeley sees an abstraction unjustified by reality as we experience it. 'Making the objects of sense to be things utterly insensible or unperceivable seems to me contrary to common sense' (*Works*, i.258), he objects in the *Essay toward a new theory of vision*. This separation confronts us with a choice between scepticism and blind faith in the existence of the objects perceived, so that belief in the revelation suffers. The *New theory* appeals 'to the experience of the first man you meet' (*Works*, i.258), who will probably identify an object of sense with what sense actually perceives rather than anything imperceptible or unknown. Philonous cannot 'abstract [...] the existence of a sensible thing from its being perceived' (*Dialogues*, p.76). In any perception the sensation and the object perceived are one and the same thing, which Berkeley calls an idea of sense.[4] Philonous insists that he perceives 'real things' (*Dialogues*, p.76). Each of these things is an immediate perception or what he actually sees, hears, smells, feels or tastes at the moment and nothing else.

Immediate perception excludes all inferences. One does not really hear a coach passing in front of the house, but rather the noise of the wheels grinding across the cobblestones and the hooves of the horses striking them. From this noise and this noise alone one infers the wheels, the horses and hence the passing coach. Each perception is not only immediate, but also separate from

---

2. George Berkeley, *Treatise concerning the principles of human knowledge* (New York 1957), p.5.

3. George Berkeley, *Three dialogues between Hylas and Philonous* (New York 1954), p.10.

4. 'The identity of an idea with the perception of it welds ideas to individual perceivers.' S. A. Grave, 'The mind and its ideas: some problems in the interpretation of Berkeley', in *Locke and Berkeley: a collection of critical essays* (Notre Dame 1968), p.297.

all of the others, whether they stimulate the same or other senses. As one approaches a distant tower, the form and colour change according to each successive perception. One sees a bent oar under water and feels a straight one, although, as Acton objects, common sense does not support Berkeley's interpretation of this discrepancy.[5] If a man born blind can distinguish between a sphere and a cube by touch, an operation restoring his vision will not enable him to make the same distinction by sight until he has learned to do it. The *New theory* denies that any quality can be determined by any combination of senses: 'there are in reality no such common ideas' (*Works*, i.265). The mind itself assembles intrinsically unrelated ideas according to extrinsic spatial and temporal relations. Although these collections refer to no empirical unity, Berkeley opposes the separation, comparison and combination of the constituent ideas. Abstractions, he emphasises, do not have any reality in experience. Nor does Newton's prestige deter him from condemning absolute space, time and movement, which he regards as terms with no conceivable meaning. He leaves unresolved the conflict between separate perceptions and the inseparable qualities of the thing inferred from them.

Perception discovers the existence of the thing perceived, for we could not otherwise know that it exists. Yet Berkeley leaps to a further conclusion: 'wood, stones, fire, water, flesh, iron and the like' (*Dialogues*, p.76) exist because they are perceived. They cannot exist unless someone perceives them. How does Berkeley arrive at this conclusion? As his disciple Philonous argues: things perceived by the senses are immediately perceived; and things immediately perceived are ideas; and ideas cannot exist [outside] the mind; their existence therefore consists in being perceived (*Dialogues*, p.76). He simply ignores the alternative possibilities. His arguments do not convince Locke's disciple Hylas, who objects that all men distinguish between the perception and the existence of a thing. This is common sense in the manner of Locke. Philonous in turn appeals to 'the common sense of the world', the Berkeleyan counterpart: 'Ask the gardener why he thinks yonder cherry tree exists in the garden and he shall tell you, because he sees and feels it' (*Dialogues*, p.81). Hylas might have pointed out that Philonous is not explaining why the tree exists, but rather how the gardener knows it. Instead he makes an unnecessary partial concession that implies a full concession: 'the existence of a sensible thing consists in being perceivable, but not in being actually perceived' (*Dialogues*, p.81). Berkeley seems to have considered the first possibility himself before discarding it for

5. 'This implies that our perceptions of such things as oars, as distinct from our perceptions of colors and pressures, are not direct as common sense supposes.' H. B. Acton, 'Berkeley', *Encyclopedia of philosophy* (New York, London 1967).

the second.[6] Hylas's unlikely cooperation with his opponent reminds us that, in philosophical dialogues, the author's doctrine seldom meets stiff resistance. Despite his concession, Hylas finds the equivalence of existence and immediate perception contrary to common sense. Philonous should ask the gardener 'whether yonder tree has an existence out of his mind' (*Dialogues*, p.81). The gardener, Philonous replies, would say that it does.

Now Philonous shifts his standard of judgement from common sense to Christianity. The following proposition, he affirms, would not shock a Christian: 'the real tree existing [outside the gardener's] mind is truly known [...] (that is, exists) in the [...] mind of God' (*Dialogues*, p.81). He might not understand it at first but, once he did, he would not deny it. This retreat to Christianity seems unnecessary, for surely common sense would admit the same possibility. Critical reason, on the other hand, raises several difficulties. Do we perceive the same ideas as God? No, says Berkeley, our ideas come to us independently of our will, so they are passive while God is active. Do we perceive ectypes of the archetypes in his mind? So Philonous says, but these ectypes exist only when we perceive them, while the archetypes have an eternal existence. Yet what we perceive really exists and continues to exist when we are not perceiving it.[7] Thus the distinction between our ideas and God's conflicts with the identity of what we perceive intermittently and he, continually. Although he has no senses, he knows our ideas and 'exhibits' them or 'excites' (*Dialogues*, p.58) them in our minds.[8] But how can he know pain without feeling it and sensations without having them? Common sense disagrees with Berkeley here. If we perceive the real thing, why does my perception differ from yours? Each perception is distinct in Berkeley's opinion. He does not face this problem either.

Although we know real things by perceiving them, neither sense nor reason tells us that a material substance supports them. 'I have no reason', says Philonous, 'for believing the existence of matter' (*Dialogues*, p.79). Implicit from Descartes to Malebranche, scepticism about the existence of matter became explicit with Locke. But this trend hardly justifies Berkeley's conclusion that

6. 'I think that the interpretation of the existence of an unseen thing in terms of possibility of perception is a residue from Berkeley's earlier way of thinking.' Konrad Marc-Wogau, 'The argument from illusion and Berkeley's idealism', in *Locke and Berkeley*, p.325.

7. A different account appears in the *Treatise* (p.48): 'Wherever bodies are said to have no existence without the mind, I would not be understood to mean this or that particular mind but all minds whatsoever. It does not therefore follow from the foregoing principles that bodies are annihilated and created every moment, or exist not at all during the intervals between our perception of them.'

8. Berkeley keeps his distance from Malebranche, however: 'I do not say I see things by perceiving that which represents them in the intelligible substance of God. This I do not understand; but I say the things by me perceived are known by the understanding and produced by the will of an infinite spirit' (*Dialogues*, p.59).

matter does not exist. 'What we know', as Watson comments, 'is all that exists. Since we cannot know matter, it cannot exist.'[9] Philonous refuses to believe what he sees no reason to believe, an inference more appropriate to free thought. Would a philosopher, he asks Hylas, or even a man of common sense believe in something unknown and unknowable? Philonous does not think so, yet Hylas finds immaterialism 'repugnant to common sense' (*Dialogues*, p.10). The opposite opinion, Philonous warns, implies even greater 'repugnance to common sense'. They nonetheless agree to adopt the opinion that proves, 'upon examination [...] most agreeable to common sense' (*Dialogues*, p.11). Thus Philonous badgers Hylas into several admissions of the doctrine that had raised such a furore when the *Treatise* appeared: 'Some truths there are so near and obvious to the mind that a man need only open his eyes to see them. [In particular:] All the choir of heaven and furniture of the earth [...] have [no] substance [outside] a mind' (*Dialogues*, p.25-26). Readers were willing to believe that the choir of heaven is spiritual in nature, but not the furniture of the earth.[10]

While Berkeley thought their ignorance of the unknown should persuade them, he gave other reasons as well. Since we only perceive ideas, which would have nothing to do with matter if it existed, they cannot derive from a material substance. The arguments Locke uses to show that secondary qualities do not inhere in the objects to which they refer apply to primary qualities too. Philonous forces Hylas to admit that primary qualities vary according to the perceiver and the perception, just as secondary qualities do. A body may appear to move slowly or rapidly depending on the observer. Locke finds that the primary quality of movement, both slow and fast in this case, inheres in the moving body: 'How is this consistent [...] with common sense?' (*Dialogues*, p.31). Hylas cannot say, yet he might have objected that common sense also balks at Philonous's interpretation. Common sense could account for the difference in speed by the entirely conventional distinction between appearances and reality, which Berkeley rejects. Philonous convinces Hylas that, since primary qualities vary as much as secondary qualities, 'all sensible qualities are alike to be denied existence [outside] the mind' (*Dialogues*, p.35). They cannot inhere in matter, therefore, and a substance without accidents implies a contradiction.[11]

As already stated, however, Berkeley had apologetic reasons for denying the

9. Richard Watson, *The Downfall of Cartesianism 1673-1712* (The Hague 1966), p.13.
10. George Pitcher shows that Berkeley's system can be reconciled to some extent with common sense on the basis of theoretical phenomenalism: 'On this view, physical objects, like physical forces, would be theoretical entities, conceived not realistically, but instrumentally [...] I cannot here enter into the complex question of just how sound the doctrine of theoretical phenomenalism is; but it is a position that Berkeley really *must* take, and it is one, moreover, that he has the materials at hand to defend.' *Berkeley* (London, Boston 1977), p.162.
11. Like any Anglican, Berkeley rejects transubstantiation.

existence of matter too. The latent scepticism about matter which Bayle had detected in Malebranche and Descartes worried him. He was afraid this scepticism would threaten belief in the creation and hence Christianity itself. Immaterialism eliminates the danger, for scepticism about matter does not concern an immaterial creation. Spiritualising the world should frustrate infidels and atheists who undermine creation from nothingness by advocating the eternal existence of matter. The creation of matter from nothing is 'so contrary to reason', Philonous admits, that many ancient philosophers and even some who believed in God 'thought matter coeternal with the deity' (*Dialogues*, p.106). The immateriality of the creation should facilitate belief in it. Thus Berkeley opposes immaterialism to the deism unwittingly inspired by Newton and Locke, and to heresy, infidelity and atheism. He typically suspects all deviation from the Anglican orthodoxy of tending to atheism. 'How great a friend *material substance* has been to atheists in all ages,' he laments in the *Treatise* (p.68). The elimination of matter would solve all the problems besetting Christianity down through the ages: 'Matter being once expelled out of nature drags with it so many sceptical and impious notions, such an incredible number of disputes and puzzling questions, which have been thorns in the sides of divines as well as philosophers' (*Treatise*, p.69). The author's espousal of immaterialism had resulted from the desire for a philosophical panacea that would cure all the theological ills plaguing Christianity. He would succumb to this kind of temptation again. Evidently the theological advantages outweighed the philosophical disadvantages in motivating his commitment to this theory.

We have no control over ideas of sense, he affirms, because God prints them on our mind. We produce or forget ideas of imagination at will, but they represent ideas already perceived either in the same or a different combination. For instance: 'The idea of the man Jones, whom I saw yesterday', as Park illustrates, 'or of the centaur Jones, whom I have never seen'.[12] Still, I have seen both men and horses. How then do we distinguish between ideas of sense and ideas of imagination? Berkeley seems to have realised that we do not always notice whether our perception is passive or active. He considers ideas of sense more vivid and distinct than ideas of imagination, and they necessarily conform to the laws of nature established by God. Yet these criteria do not adequately explain our confidence in the distinction we constantly make between reality and imagination.

Ideas of sense occur to us in an order and in combinations that correspond to the laws of nature or God's rules. We associate separate and immediate

12. Desirée Park, *Complementary notions: a critical study of Berkeley's theory of concepts* (The Hague 1972), p.38.

perceptions with each other according to these rules, which we have learned by experience. We complete the ideas of sense we have perceived by ideas of imagination suggested by our memory of such combinations experienced in the past. 'A cherry', submits Philonous, 'is nothing but a congeries of sensible impressions or ideas perceived by various senses [and] united into one thing [...] by the mind, because they are observed to attend each other' (*Dialogues*, p.97). The redness, roundness, juicyness and sweetness of the cherry have no more in common than a habitual association determined by the divine rules. Philonous and Hylas do not perceive the same cherry, strictly speaking, because each forms his own mental image of it. Since the same rules govern the formation of these separate images, however, they understand each other when they refer to the 'same' cherry. Needless to say, this ingenious theory hardly obtains the approval of common sense which, on the contrary, can only condemn it. Nor does it comfort belief in the creation, as a doubtful inquiry by the wife of Berkeley's friend Percival demonstrates. In his reply (6 Sept. 1710), the philosopher interprets the creation as an act of God's will making things he already knew to be perceptible by other spirits. As Philonous explains, 'God decreed they should become perceptible to intelligent creatures in that order and manner which he then established and we now call the laws of nature' (*Dialogues*, p.102). The context implies that God also created spirits so that they might perceive nature in keeping with these laws. Berkeley replaces the traditional conception of nature as a system of causes and effects by a theory of signs and things signified. The natural relations between the signs and the things signified are the laws of nature decreed by God.

Ideas do not account for all that exists according to Berkeley, since perception requires a subject as well as an object. Ideas are the things perceived and spirits, the perceiving things. 'I [...] a spirit or thinking substance exist,' testifies Philonous, 'as certainly as I know my ideas exist. Further, I know what I mean by the term I and myself immediately and intuitively' (*Dialogues*, p.78). Knowledge of one's spiritual existence derives from one's awareness of perceiving ideas. One knows one's own spiritual essence intuitively. One infers the existence of other spirits including God from awareness of the ideas they excite in one's mind. The *Treatise* defines spirit as a 'simple, undivided, active being' (p.35), whose understanding perceives ideas of sense and whose will produces and uses ideas of imagination. Like Descartes Berkeley looks upon the human soul as a spirit or mind that never stops thinking, hence its immortality.[13] All

13. 'Nothing can be plainer than that the motions, changes, decays and dissolutions which we hourly see befall natural bodies [...] cannot possibly affect an active, simple, uncompounded substance; such a being therefore is indissoluble by the force of nature; that is to say, the soul of man is naturally immortal' (*Treatise*, p.95).

spirits form a unique substance and yet each consists in its own activity or perception. Berkeley would have had to resolve this conflict if he had pursued his project to develop a philosophy of mind in part II of the *Treatise*. He postponed the project and, after the loss of his manuscript, abandoned it on the pretext that it would be disagreable to treat the same subject twice. Warnock and Tipton suspect that he failed to complete it because the difficulties discouraged him.[14] In the second edition of part I (1734), on the other hand, he introduced 'notions,' which refer to spirits and relations.[15] We can have no ideas of the latter because they are active and ideas, passive.[16]

The *Treatise* and the *Dialogues* recommend a philosophical panacea for all the ills afflicting Berkeley's Christianity. He answers the 'materialist' threat to his faith by amputating matter[17] and spiritualising the creation. Nothing exists but passive ideas and the active spirits that perceive them. Real ideas depend on the mind of God, who exhibits them to other minds, and imaginary ideas, on the created minds that produce them. All activity reduces to thought. Although some aspects of this philosophy reappear in *Alciphron*, Berkeley devoted this dialogue to Christian apology and polemic against the deism of Mandeville and Shaftesbury. The debate confronts the Anglicans Crito and Euphranor with the freethinkers Alciphron and Lysicles, who are visiting Crito on his country estate. Each side undertakes to convert the other, but the manifest superiority of the Christians limits all suspense to the manner in which they will finally prevail.

Both sides found their arguments on reason and they agree on the nature of reason. In the first dialogue Alciphron acknowledges that reason is natural in man, but he describes nature as 'original, universal and invariable' (*Works*, iii.55). He excludes the influence of custom and education, which he considers

14. 'It is perhaps permissible to guess that the long delay in publication of his projected second volume, of which so many years later he lost the unfinished manuscript, was due in part to his inability to harmonize the outlook of his early work with his theological and metaphysical beliefs.' G. J. Warnock, *Berkeley* (Baltimore 1969), p.197. 'It is very difficult to escape the conclusion that Berkeley would have found it far from easy to produce this volume, and that he was genuinely worried about paradoxes and serious problems arising from what he wanted to say.' I. C. Tipton, *Berkeley: the philosophy of immaterialism* (London 1974), p.260.

15. 'In the first edition of the *Principles* he did not recognize [notional] knowledge at all; it made its embarrassed appearance only in the second edition. The appearance is embarrassed because in the meantime Berkeley had come to see that with his earlier simple empiricism he had no right even to speak of God, of whose existence the whole *Treatise* was supposed to be a proof.' Warren Steinkraus (ed.), foreword, *New studies in Berkeley's philosophy* (New York 1966), p.vii.

16. Hylas plausibly objects: 'You admit [...] that there is spiritual substance, although you have no idea of it; while you deny there can be such a thing as material substance, because you have no notion or idea of it. Is this fair dealing?' (*Dialogues*, p.79).

17. 'Berkeley is an amputated Descartes, matter having been lopped off [...] There is more than a little truth in the view of Berkeley as a truncated Descartes – as a castrated Cartesian without matter.' Willis Doney, 'Is Berkeley's a Cartesian mind?' in *Berkeley: critical and interpretive essays* (Minneapolis 1982), p.273, 274.

unnatural. Yet Euphranor dissuades him from confining nature to the immediate product of birth, on the grounds that natural traits often develop later. Leaves, blossoms and fruit appear on apple trees long after they have sprouted from seeds. Orange trees grown in the north or south of England or in Portugal or Naples produce different results. Euphranor infers 'that things may be natural to human kind and yet neither found in all men nor invariably the same where they are found' (*Works*, iii.56). He forces Alciphron to admit that natural traits are not necessarily original, universal and invariable. On the contrary, proper education and cultivation result in a mature thought that qualifies as the highest achievement of reason. Thus reason endorses Christianity.

In answering commonsense objections to Christianity by Alciphron, Crito assigns two meanings to common sense in the sixth dialogue. It means 'either the general sense of mankind or the improved reason of thinking men' (*Works*, iii.241). Evidently Alciphron's objections belong to the first category, and Crito's apology to the second. Alciphron disputes this conception of reason and complains that his opponents are trying to reason him out of reason. Since God has given him reason to make judgements, 'I will judge by that unerring light, lighted from the univesal lamp of nature' (*Works*, iii.251). While Crito does not dispute this assertion, he insists on the distinction between reason and superior reason. Here Berkeley considers in sum two kinds of common sense and two kinds of reason. The parallel suggests the identity of general common sense with ordinary reason and of improved common sense with superior reason, but he does not specify.

In the fifth dialogue Crito names God 'the common father of lights'. Whether natural or revealed, all knowledge flows from 'the same source of light and truth' (*Works*, iii.182). This point seems so obvious to him that he sees no need for evidence to support it. The light of reason, he continues, reveals and proves natural religion to those who can understand it, but others need a revelation. The preface to the *Dialogues* affirms that the 'parts of revelation [lying] within the reach of human inquiry are most agreeable to right reason'. They should incline 'prudent unprejudiced persons to a modest and wary treatment of [...] sacred mysteries [...] above the comprehension of our faculties' (p.7). In *Alciphron* Crito urges in fact that, when some tenets of revelation appear good and useful to reason, others recommended along with them deserve the same trust. If reason can neither explain nor account for something, according to Euphranor, it may not be divine, but then it may also be divine. Thus we should use caution. The idea of revelation by God implies information different from and superior to common experience. In view of such statements Hedenius concludes: 'the whole of Berkeley's thought is pervaded by the conviction that reason both can and ought to corroborate the truth of the Christian religion'.[18]

In *Siris* he no longer tries to build a philosophical vehicle for his Christianity, but rather to demonstrate that the ancient philosophers, whom he admires, foreshadow the Trinity. While this work does not contain a systematic account of his current philosophy, it does reveal important changes. Critics who ignore or minimise these changes seem overcommitted to the more original philosophy of his youth.[19] Mabbott, on the other hand strikes a convincing balance. He discovers 'a new world' in *Siris*, which he finds 'poles apart from the other works'.[20] But he does not go as far as Rossi who distinguishes between Berkeley's first and second philosophy.[21] Jessop, the editor of the *Siris* in *The Works of George Berkeley*, divides the changes into three groups: corporeal relations, the value of sensation, and the metaphysical order.[22] For the first time Berkeley admits causal relations between bodies, though only in the scientific part of the work. His philosophical immaterialism remains intact.

Although the senses continue to perceive things as they really are, reason alone has access to knowledge. The senses, which Berkeley slights in Platonic fashion, can only apprehend effects, while reason discovers causes. His metaphysics shifts from sensationism to emanationism but, as Jessop cautions, one cannot easily discriminate between his admiration for the ancient philosophers and his espousal of their philosophy.[23] Yet his review of ancient metaphysics yields more than praise. From the Egyptians, Pythagoreans, Platonists and Stoics he borrows the great chain of being. He applies this theory to the human mind as follows (*Works*, v.140):

Sense supplies images to memory. These become subjects for fancy to work upon. Reason considers and judges of the imaginations. And these acts of reason become new objects to the understanding. In this scale, each lower faculty is a step that leads to one above it. And the uppermost naturally leads to the deity.

If he had chosen to complete part II of the *Treatise*, he could have added this idea to the philosophy in part I without distorting it. At the time, however, he

18. Ingemar Hedenius, *Sensationalism and theology in Berkeley's philosophy* (Uppsala 1936), p.153.

19. The most persuasive of these may be I. C. Tipton, 'The "Philosopher by Fire" in Berkeley's *Alciphron*', in *Berkeley: critical and interpretive essays*, p.168-69: 'What I am suggesting [...] is that, for Berkeley in *Siris*, there is nothing corporeal that is "insensible", except in the sense that, because it is "inconceivably small" [...] it lies, and may always lie, beyond the range of our most powerful microscopes. (One would expect Berkeley to hold that if no human will ever perceive the ether, other spirits can or could.) And this means that his acceptance of very minute particles in *Siris* provides no support for the view that he could or would have accommodated atoms or corpuscles such as those postulated by Boyle and Locke.'

20. J. D. Mabbott, 'The place of God in Berkeley's philosophy', in *Locke and Berkeley*, p.377.

21. Mario Rossi, *Saggio su Berkeley* (Bari 1955). See p.255-58.

22. T. E. Jessop (ed.). See *Works*, v.13-16.

23. See *Works*, v.16.

apparently saw no need for it. In the early works he also ignored the ancient sources from which he derives it in *Siris*. Consequently, the ascending dynamic of the faculties probably represents a departure from the philosophy in the *Treatise* and the *Dialogues*. A persistent inquirer 'ascends from the sensible into the intellectual world.' Here he discovers that the substances and causes he had assigned to matter 'are but fleeting shadows; that the mind contains all and acts all, and is to all created beings the source of unity [...] order [and] existence'. The mind of God operates and controls the macrocosm by means of a subtle fire that pervades it. Berkeley accepts the 'promiscuous' (*Works*, v.137) equivalence of fire, light and ether assumed by the ancient philosophers. The human mind operates and controls the microcosm by means of ether or animal spirits.

The health of the human body depends on the evacuation of poison. All illness results from insufficient evacuation, for which Berkeley prescribes tar water. It not only acts as a laxative when drunk, but also unclogs the pores. How can it do that? Tar water is made by infusing water with pine or fir resin and siphoning the essence from the surface. This essence contains the solar energy absorbed by the trees from which the resin comes. Drinking tar water therefore increases the animal spirits in the body, so that they dissolve the impurities clogging the pores. Once the body has evacuated the poison, it returns to health. However ridiculous this theory may seem to us, Berkeley and many of his contemporaries took it seriously. The metaphysics involved raises as many questions as the alchemy and the physic. The bishop succumbs to the apologetic fallacy of accrediting a legend on the strength of the endorsements it has received down through the centuries. In his day already, such traditions of belief no longer silenced the sceptics. The transitional state of the ether in the macrocosm and the animal spirits in the microcosm provides spirit with a medium through which it influences matter. Since Berkeley denies the existence of matter in the same work, however, there is no need for such a medium. The justification of his panacea seems to have embroiled him in a gratuitous speculation sustained by his fascination with the ancient philosophers.

His commitment to the medical panacea of tar water parallels his commitment to the philosophical panacea of immaterialism. He liked sweeping solutions for the great problems that nagged him. The hell-fire that threatened the souls of the American Indians inspired his project to found a college in Bermuda, where they might receive a Christian education. He promoted this panacea as vigorously as the other two, but he may have regretted his choice of site. For the money voted by the English Parliament, he waited in Rhode Island instead of Bermuda. It never came because the prime minister Robert Walpole blocked the expenditure. All Berkeley achieved by this generous adventure was the composition of *Alciphron* which, like *Siris*, has its value. *Siris* sold well, better in fact than his other works and, although tar water could have effected no more than laxative or psychosomatic cures, it did little harm. His earliest works, on the other hand, are his greatest achievement. Despite the flaw in the immaterialism of the *Dialogues* and the *Treatise*, they have had a major impact on modern philosophy.

He would have preferred to exert a religious as well as a philosophical influence and reverse the tide of free thought. Yet theology did not interest him much, except in relation to philosophy and morals. Crito acknowledges that we cannot form an abstract idea of original sin or the manner of its transmission. He shares Berkeley's disapproval of abstraction anyway. Faith in original sin, he nonetheless believes, instils in us a healthy awareness that we are unworthy and the redeemer is kind. Thus faith supports morals. After a mature interpretation of Scripture, faith derived 'from common sense and common use' does not tend to controversy over 'the wording of [such] a mystery' (*Works*, iii.302). A docile acceptance of the orthodox tradition therefore suits the Berkleyan Christian.

Berkeley gives original sin more comprehensive treatment in a sermon from the same period which he preached in Boston.[24] Even among the pagans, he asserts, wise men perceived the depravity of human nature. 'The light of reason in all times and places finds [this] nature debased and corrupted [for] having lost that rectitude and perfection' (*Works*, vii.86) the Creator had just granted it. Though aware of their wretched state, all men do not realise that they have fallen from grace. Scripture accounts for their predicament clearly and positively, but not adequately and fully. God created our original ancestors innocent and happy. Tempted by Satan, they promptly fell from that state. Just as a father's treason forfeits his children's birthright, the guilt of the original ancestors affects all mankind, who therefore incur the same punishment. Our preacher interprets the death to which God condemns Adam and Eve as a continuous fear of death and as an early end to life. He considers the estrangement from God and his grace even worse than death itself. Nor does he forget the suffering that follows banishment from paradise. In his opinion the mutual reinforcement of guilt and sin resulted in a proliferation of idolatry, paganism and wickedness, which caused vice, injustice and violence. Again he extracts a moral lesson from his discussion of original sin. This text, however, is more valuable as documentation than as edification.

It also advances the conventional argument that the guilty mass needs a redeemer. But the bishop's attitude towards the alleged founder of his religion is not less ambivalent than that of other Christian intellectuals in his day. His reverence for Christ generates little curiosity or enthusiasm. In *Alciphron* he

24. In King's Chapel on 12 September 1731.

strives rather to confound free thought than to win allegiance to Christ. Crito makes the usual assumptions about the spread of Christianity in the early centuries, the authenticity of the apostles' message and the testimony of sincere witnesses to Jesus's miracles and resurrection. He reaffirms this threadbare propaganda as if he expected Alciphron to accept it at face value. Although he concedes that the passage in Josephus praising Jesus may be fraudulent, he maintains that able critics defend it. Josephus's allusion to Jesus as the one called Christ, he insists, proves that the historian at least knew of him and had a neutral attitude towards him.[25] It takes Berkeley a few pages, however, to explain Josephus's neglect of Jesus away. Alciphron believes we should judge revelation by the probability or possibility that God would have made it. He defies 'the wit of man to contrive anything more extravagant than [...] apparitions, devils, miracles, God manifest in the flesh [...] self-denial [and] resurrection' (*Works*, iii.239). Berkeley includes self-denial because Mandeville had jeered at the clergy's claim of practising this virtue in his *Fable of the bees* (1714).[26] Any freethinker independent of Berkeley's will could have refuted his charge easily by citing contrary examples. Instead Alciphron exposes himself to Euphranor's irony over his presumption to know what God would do.

Berkeley is more interesting, if not more convincing, when he uses his philosophy to support his apology. The equivalence of light and ether in *Siris* suggests an allusion to the transfiguration.[27] The philosopher may wish to imply that the light shining on Jesus transfers divine power directly from the Father to the Son.[28] The theory that material things depend on perception for existence enables him to explain the conversion of water into wine by Jesus at the marriage feast in Cana (John ii.1-10). According to the *Treatise*, Jesus needed only to create the appearance or idea of wine, so that the guests could see, smell and taste it. Since matter does not exist, he did not have to make a material conversion.

In *Alciphron* Lysicles refuses to believe that 'the Son of God was born upon earth in a poor family, was spit upon, buffeted and crucified, lived like a beggar and died like a thief' (*Works*, iii.247). Common sense tells us, he maintains, that

25. No serious historians now admit the authenticity of this passage in Flavius Josephus's *Antiquities of the Jews* (*c*.94 AD).

26. In an allusion to the archbishop of Canterbury, Mandeville notes, 'humility is so ponderous a virtue that it requires six horses to draw it'. *The Fable of the bees* (Oxford 1924), i.163. *Humility* is a synonym of *self-denial* in the context.

27. Mark ix.2-8; Luke ix.28-36; Matthew xvii.1-8.

28. 'At the transfiguration, the apostles saw our saviour's face shining as the sun and his raiment white as light; also a lucid cloud or body of light, out of which the voice came; which visible light and splendour was, not many centuries ago, maintained by the Greek church to have been divine and uncreated, and the very glory of God' (*Works*, v.94).

the Son of God on a mission from heaven would arrive with even greater fanfare than a prince or ambassador. In view of the gospel accounts, Jesus's triumphant arrival in Jerusalem[29] must have been a paltry affair. Euphranor reminds Lysicles, however, that we do not know how God would behave on this or any other occasion. (Thus Euphranor spontaneously identifies Jesus with God.) Crito illustrates his point as follows (*Works*, iii.248):

If a man should make his entrance into London in a rich suit of clothes, with a hundred gilt coaches and a thousand laced footmen, [would this] be a more divine appearance [...] than if he had power with a word to heal all manner of diseases, to raise the dead to life and still the raging of the winds and seas?

Simple superhuman acts are more convincing evidence of the divinity than elaborate natural acts. However impressive, the arrival in London of a man who has performed no miracles would hardly compare with that of Jesus in Jerusalem.

Unconvinced, Lysicles complains that the death of a man who could resurrect other men offends common sense. Jesus's resurrection does not dissipate the mystery of why he had to die in the first place, why a just man had to die for unjust men and the Son of God for the wicked. Why Jesus, moreover; why this individual in that place at that time? And why did he not preach his gospel to the whole world? Would that not have been fairer? Lysicles urges Crito to reconcile these formidable discrepancies with 'common sense and the plain sense of mankind'. Yet Crito merely cautions against denying the unknown. One should not dismiss everything foreign to 'the vulgar sense of man' (*Works*, iii.248). Thus Berkeley abandons common sense when one would expect a decisive reply. Elsewhere he argues that men do not die for lies. Confusing the Christian martyrs with the actual witnesses of Jesus's miracles and resurrection, Crito denies that they could have been imposters. 'The evident light of sense', he contends, will certify 'sensible effects and matters of fact such as the miracles and the resurrection' (*Works*, iii.279). He considers them as certain as any other historical facts transmitted from age to age. The account of the resurrection in the *Treatise* resembles that of the wine made by Jesus, but the presentation is different. An immaterial resurrection, the author remarks, answers Socinian objections to the existence of the same body in both a mortal and an immortal state. If body means 'what every plain, ordinary person means by that word, to wit, that which is immediately seen and felt, which is only a combination of sensible qualities or ideas' (*Treatise*, p.69), the distinction does not matter very much. An immaterial body will exist as long as God perceives it. The parallel syntax of the last two clauses in the quotation implies that common sense equates

29. Mark xi.1-11; Luke xix.28-38; Matthew xxi.1-11; John xii.12-16.

the perceptural appearance of the body with its immaterial existence.[30]

Pretending 'to demonstrate or reason anything about the Trinity is absurd', Berkeley warns in Notebook A. 'Here an implicit faith becomes us' (*Works*, i.73). One must believe it without trying to understand it. The Trinity nonetheless confronts the philosopher with a conflict between the requirements of his orthodox faith and his hostility to abstractions. Is the Trinity not an abstraction and hence an illusion according to his philosophy? No, he tells himself. Euphranor insists that 'the same rules of logic, reason and good sense [...] obtain [...] in faith and in science.' If one believes in triangles, one should also believe in the Trinity. Alciphron accepts 'the rules of right reason', but he denies that they impose faith in mysteries and 'least of all the Trinity' (*Works*, iii.296). Euphranor replies – for the Christians always have the last word – that terms may refer to truth without conveying any distinct ideas to the human mind. Does Scripture not reveal 'that the Father, the Son and the Holy Ghost are God and that there is but one God' (*Works*, iii.297)? Euphranor has no doubt. The authority of Scripture, in his opinion, and the moral impact of the Trinity on life and conduct likewise justify belief in the doctrine. Christ's divinity inclines the believer to do good deeds and think good thoughts. We do not have to understand the two natures in one person of Christ in order to believe in them and derive moral inspiration from them. How and why? Euphranor does not explain and, in fact, sees no need for explanation. Instead he exorts us to 'untie the knots' (*Works*, iii.298) of human individuation before trying to elucidate the persons in the Trinity.[31] For he disagrees with Locke's theory that personal identity consists in the continuity of self-consciousness.

Alciphron insinuates that abstractions caused the disputes culminating in the councils and, in particular, the first one at Nicaea. He cites the subtle distinction between *homoousios* and *homoiousios* as an example. Thinking wishfully, Crito answers him with an obviously erroneous conjecture: the councils could not have sought to dictate abstract ideas of the sacred mysteries to ordinary Christians, 'this being impossible' (*Works*, iii.300). Instead they merely excluded the unacceptable extremes of Sabellianism and paganism: this point is entirely correct. Berkeley rejoices in the Hellenistic experimentation with trinities that

---

30. 'One of my earliest inquiries was about time, which led me into several paradoxes that I did not think fit or necessary to publish, particularly the notion that the resurrection follows the next moment to death' (*Works*, ii.293). 'Berkeley is apparently prepared to allow that on his doctrine there can be no period between my death and resurrection because my conceiving such a period would involve my conceiving time passing with no succession of ideas in my mind.' Tipton, *Berkeley*, p.279.

31. 'I must own myself very much surprised to find [Whiston] espouse such an odd paradoxe as adoration and prayer are not due to the Son and Holy Ghost, though he acknowledges their divinity' (viii.29).

foreshadowed the Nicaean doctrine. Augustine, he notes, finds the creation of the world by the Son of God in Hellenistic philosophy as well as Christianity. The author of *Siris* would like to credit the Christian God with the inspiration behind the Hellenistic trinitarianism: 'Perhaps [...] those sublime hints, which dart forth like flashes of light in the midst of a profound darkness, were [not] struck from the hard rock of human reason, but rather derived at least in part [...] from the author of all things' (*Works*, v.162). In this case God would have inspired these trinities directly rather than indirectly through pagan borrowings.[32] In reviewing them, Berkeley stresses the details that recall his own theory of ether. He reproduces for instance, the analogy between the Father, the Son and the Holy Spirit, on one hand, and sun, light and heat, on the other. *Siris* concludes with this discussion and the final paragraph contains a revealing sentence: 'Truth is the cry of all, but the game of a few' (*Works*, v.164). Berkeley thinks the Hellenistic philosophers sought and the Christian Fathers found.

Although he disliked transubstantiation as much as any Protestant, he wrote little on the subject. Notebook B rejects 'the excuse' (*Works*, i.42) of embracing this dogma on the grounds that our mind is finite and cannot reconcile the contradiction it implies. In the same passage, however, he admits that the Trinity, which he accepts, implies a similar contradiction[33] and he makes no attempt to solve this dilemma. According to the *Treatise*, one begins to believe in transubstantiation and the infinite divisibility of matter only by 'gentle and slow degrees' (p.86), an allusion to Leibniz perhaps. Prejudices in any case usurp principles. Alciphron protests that Euphranor could justify anything and even transubstantiation, but Crito denies the charge. Euphranor, he observes, does not advocate articles of faith unsupported by Scripture, repugnant to reason, implying a contradiction or leading to idolatry. Thus Berkeley, who has forgotten the Trinity, insinuates his condemnation of transubstantiation on all of these counts. He apparently thinks none of them apply to the Anglican eucharist, of which he has little to say. In his Boston sermon he borrows two eucharistic ideas from Augustine, the outer sign of the inner charity uniting all Christians and the Church body consisting of communicant members and Christ, the head. Here the preacher is merely doing his duty to indoctrinate the public with routine theology.

A dedicated clergyman, he sought to justify faith by reason and doctrine by morality. But did he realise that such a justification implies the superior authority

32. An apologetic thesis defended by Daniel Huet in his *Demonstratio evangelica* (1679).

33. 'The loss of the excuse may hurt transubstantiation, but not the Trinity. By ye excuse is meant the finiteness of our mind making it possible for contradictions to appear true to us' (Notebook B, *Works*, i.42).

of reason and the greater importance of morals? His defence of the house tended to divide it against itself, because Christianity was more than reason and morals. He took radical steps to stop the erosion of his religion by free thought and, as he saw it, by atheism. Yet he unintentionally authorised free thought by his reliance on reason for apologetic demonstration. His foregone conclusions distort Crito and Euphranor's reason when they invoke it against Alciphron and Lysicles. He also inhibits the freethinker's reason to protect his Anglicans from critical danger. The Anglicans triumph too obviously by virtue of his intervention in the dialogue. In real life, as every reader knows, the men he dismisses as minute philosophers, would offer cleverer and more determined resistance. He may persuade us to accept reason as the standard of truth, but not his version of it, whose flaws we easily detect. Although he appeals to common sense, he alters it to suit his immaterialism, a tactic that accredits the standard and discredits his use of it. A creation consisting of perceptions dependent on minds and of minds dependent on God contributes more to philosophy than to religion, despite his contrary intentions. While common sense plays an awkward role in trying to support this theory, the natural light prospers as much as ever, for immaterialism fully accommodates it. The elimination of matter makes all phenomena mental so that the universe becomes a system of thought energised and controlled by the mind of God. The perspective blesses philosophy with an opportunity that seems more exciting than the ones it owes his immediate predecessors. Perhaps this impression nonetheless stems from the continuing exploitation of the opportunity.

# Conclusion

BERKELEY was by no means the last eighteenth-century philosopher to value common sense. Among others the Scotsmen David Hume and especially Thomas Reid made it an important part of their philosophy. Yet their common sense no longer resembled Descartes's natural light, as even Berkeley's had. All of the philosophers that figure in the present study followed part of the trail blazed by Descartes. They have much in common, more in fact than meets the eye. In every case analysis begins with the mind-soul similar to God and dissimilar to matter. The relations between these three concepts hold their attention and stimulate their thought.

To them the dichotomy between spirit and matter seems the most urgent problem to solve. In spirit and matter Descartes, Malebranche, Locke and Buffier see separate substances, and Spinoza, two attributes of a unique substance, while Leibniz and Berkeley eliminate the dichotomy by declaring matter the phenomena of spirit. Only Locke and Buffier accept the Aristotelian tradition, confirmed by ordinary common sense, of spirit perceiving matter by means of the senses. Descartes suspects this perception, Spinoza and Malebranche treat it as an illusion, Leibniz and Berkeley collapse its object into its subject. To be sure, these solutions merely complicate the problem.

Each philosopher's conception of matter affects his understanding of the relations between the mind and God. Introspection confirms their belief that a superior mind exists and that it is divine. But Spinoza conceives of God as even more than a mind, since his divine substance contains an infinite number of attributes including the attribute of matter as well as that of spirit. The other philosophers' faith in the creation produces various accounts of how God made the world. Leibniz and Berkeley simplify his task by the reduction of matter to phenomena. We can imagine a divine spirit creating a world of spirits more easily than one composed of both spirit and matter. How can spirit create matter? Descartes, Locke and Buffier simply subscribe to this article of faith. According to Malebranche and Leibniz, on the other hand, God's mind contains the essences of all possible existences and these essences are coeternal as well as consubstantial with God. Malebranche makes a serious attempt to coordinate them with the existences in the material world. Intelligible extension, which he identifies with the Word, is the algebra of all the geometry that can possibly exist. From the algebraic essences in the Word, the Creator chose the ones resulting in the most efficient combination of geometrical existences possible, hence the material world. This theory of God's mind not only explains the creation, but also the natural light.

We think in God according to Malebranche and God thinks in us according to Spinoza. Leibniz's God programmes our mind to think, while Berkeley's exhibits to our minds ectypes of the archetypes in his mind. Descartes, Locke and Buffier merely assume that the Creator gave us a mind with which to think. Does it ever stop thinking? No, say Descartes, Spinoza, Malebranche, Leibniz and Berkeley. Yes, say Locke and Buffier. But all agree that thought consists of ideas, by which they generally understand a basic element of knowledge. Ideas are to spirit as atoms are to matter, even if matter does not really exist. Spinoza, Malebranche, Leibniz and Berkeley follow Descartes in limiting the origination of ideas to a spiritual source. Buffier joins Locke in his insistence on a material source as well. Descartes and Locke consider any thought that occurs to the mind an idea. Malebranche first excludes sensation and emotion, then credits ideas with the power to cause them. He views our idea as a finite portion of God's infinite idea. In defining idea, Berkeley identifies perception with the thing immediately perceived. Descartes and Leibniz advocate innate ideas in the dispositional sense, which Buffier also admits with the reservation that we are not constantly aware of them. Locke, on the other hand, rejects all innate ideas. None of these philosophers, except Leibniz, can imagine how the mind could contain an actual idea without knowing it. He promotes unconscious ideas in the form of minute and confused perceptions. This may be the most significant discovery any of these philosophers made.

The optimism over the future of mathematics, which ran from Descartes to Locke, exaggerated the extent to which ideas resemble numbers. Might ideas not serve as units in a new calculus? This illusion nourished Descartes's dream of founding a universal science on the natural light. Enthusiasm over mathematics moved Spinoza to expose his metaphysics by Euclidian procedure. Malebranche would have derived the new science from the relations between the algebra of intelligible extension and the geometry of the material world. The universal characteristic on which Leibniz worked would have established an algebra of ideas. Inspired by Boyle's quantitative analysis of matter, Locke tried in the *Essay* to devise a method for the classification of all ideas. Berkeley's hostility to abstractions finally terminated the trend. Now, however, computer language technology has revived the old illusion.

Knowledge begins with intuition: Descartes, Spinoza, Locke and Buffier concur on this point, but not on the nature of intuition. Descartes defines it as the spontaneous perception of a clear and distinct idea. Spinoza agrees except that he confines such knowledge to the second and third kinds in his system. Locke redefines intuition as spontaneously perceiving the agreement or disagreement of ideas. For Buffier, it has a similar meaning, the spontaneous perception of truths. In a more radical departure from the Cartesian definition, Leibniz conceives of intuition as the instantaneous analysis of a logical sequence, which rarely occurs in the human mind. He believes we acquire most of our knowledge without it. A series of intuitions each of which depends on the preceding one forms what Descartes calls deduction, and Locke, demonstration. Although each intuition is certain in itself, connecting them with each other in a sequence introduces the possibility of error. Again Leibniz disagrees: the logic of the whole assures the certainty of a deduction. Locke has a similar conception of judgement, a sequence of arguments tending to probability. Judgement presumes the agreement or disagreement of ideas on the strength of the intermediate arguments. Locke and Buffier assign probability to reason as well as certainty.

Spinoza and Leibniz apply the logic of cause and effect to the mind. Spinoza describes the mind both as the idea of the body and as a finite mode in a cause-and-effect concatenation of logic forming the infinite intellect of God. Every Leibnizian monad and hence every human mind contains all the predicates of its past, present and future states, each of which evolves from the preceding one in a programme synchronised with universal harmony. The author of *Siris* imagines a causal chain of faculties ascending within the mind from sensation to reason. In his earlier works Berkeley distinguishes between the passive reception of sensuous ideas and the active production of imaginative ideas by the mind. The sense of nature in Buffier's theory of mind consists of common sense as well as the intimate sense. Locke finds that experience, which stems from sensation and reflection, furnishes the mind with all of its ideas. Malebranche denies that we can know our own mind, for this knowledge would expose us to dangerous temptations. Yet he discriminates between the understanding, which receives ideas from God, and the will, which is both active and passive. Ultimately, however, the mind can neither think nor will independently of the Creator. It has three faculties: sense, memory and imagination, pure thought. Malebranche and Leibniz suppose an Augustinian society of minds. Descartes founded the philosophy of the natural light by identifying the essence of the mind with thinking.

He credits God with the creation of eternal truths, thus assigning more power to him than any of our other philosophers do. Spinoza's denial of the creation precludes such an act, which neither Malebranche nor Leibniz admits. Necessary or self-evident truths coexist with God according to all three and Malebranche even declares them consubstantial with him. He believes we learn these truths by contemplation of divine reason, the Word. He emphasises our dependence on God, and Descartes, his independence of us. Truths of fact, in

Leibniz's philosophy, differ from truths of reason, in that analysis results in an infinite regression towards identity with the final cause. Thus he tacitly agrees with Spinoza on the necessity of all truth even though, unlike Spinoza, he makes a case for human freedom too. Concentrating on first truths, Buffier distinguishes between first truths of the intimate sense, which are certain, and first truths of common sense, which are probable. He accepts universal consent as proof of self-evidence, a proof refuted by Locke and rejected by Descartes. Descartes, Spinoza and Malebranche disdain the opinion of the multitude. Malebranche defines truth as equality between ideas, and Locke, as the correspondence of relations between ideas with relations between archetypes inside or outside of the mind. The Englishman lists four kinds of self-evident truths and relegates trifling self-evidence to rebuke of absurdity. All of our philosophers concur on the intrinsic truth of what he calls simple ideas, but he also examines the extrinsic truth of both simple and complex ideas. This kind of truth, which requires the exercise of judgement, varies from case to case.

Confining knowledge to certain truth, Locke cites three kinds: intuitive, demonstrative and sensitive. Since we cannot explore all the relations of our ideas, possible knowledge will always exceed actual knowledge. Spinoza enumerates three kinds of knowledge too, but in the opposite order. Although imagination (the first kind) might deceive us, reason and intuition (the other two) never will. There are four kinds of knowledge in Malebranche's system: inner feeling, direct view of God, vision in God and conjecture. Direct view of God is a necessary condition of vision in God. Our ignorance surpasses our knowledge and we must depend on Genesis for knowledge of material existence. Divine order, which consists in the scale of perfections, sets priorities for us according to the degree of perfection. For Locke, on the other hand, the persistence of a cause-and-effect relation in nature reveals the divine order. We learn this order, Berkeley says, by experience with ideas of sense, but he restricts knowledge to reason in *Siris*. In the earlier works he divides the creation into perceptions and spirits. We learn our own spiritual existence from an awareness of perceiving ideas, and that of others from the ideas they excite in our mind. From Malebranche's viewpoint, however, only conjecture tells us that other minds exist. None of our philosophers disputes the *cogito*. Descartes, who discovered it, does not add *je sens* to *je pense* as Buffier does, because his conception of thought includes feeling. Buffier and Malebranche attribute self-consciousness to inner feeling. Malebranche, Leibniz and Locke observe that sensation triggers self-consciousness, a product of reflection in Locke's psychology. The Englishman bases personal identity on self-consciousness, which Spinoza simplistically defines as the idea of an idea. To human beings Leibniz ascribes apperception as well as perception, which they share with the other animals. Thought depends on apperception.

One strange question preoccupies all of our philosophers: do the things perceived by the senses really exist outside the mind as they seem to? Descartes says yes, because God would not deceive us; Spinoza too, because the divine attribute of matter necessarily parallels that of spirit; Malebranche too, because revelation proves the existence of the material world; Locke too, because our senses perceive the qualities of physical objects and Buffier too, because nearly all men agree on their material existence. Leibniz says no, because material things are merely phenomena founded on mutual representation by all monads. If he had committed himself to substantial bonds when he speculated on them, he would have had to change his mind and say yes. Berkeley might have said yes or no depending on how we interpret the question. The thing perceived exists inside the mind in the sense that he identifies it with a perception, but outside the mind in the sense that God perceives it even when we do not. In neither case, however, does it have material existence. Except for the dogmatic Spinoza and Buffier, moreover, the affirmers hesitate. While Descartes and Malebranche dare not deny matter, their scepticism drives them to the strange arguments we have seen. The sensuous qualities of material objects persuade the sceptical Locke that something is there he knows not what. The turtle carrying the elephant on his back lies on a mysterious substance that may even think for itself. Horrified, Berkeley eliminates matter. His analysis of the same qualities convinces him, on the contrary, that nothing is there except, as Locke puts it, a bundle of ideas conforming to a divine law. Descartes, Spinoza and Malebranche trust the senses no more than practical necessity requires and, while Leibniz has confidence in them, he limits their significance to physics. Descartes's suspicion of the senses contrasts with Buffier's trust in them. Yet Descartes emits two theories of interaction between matter and spirit. Spinoza and Malebranche adopt one, the redirection of the animal spirits by the pineal gland. Locke and the older Berkeley join them in their endorsement of communication by animal spirits between the mind and the sense organs, a part of the same theory. Together with Leibniz, they accept Descartes's other theory, the correspondence between ideas in the mind and fissures in the brain.

Despite the many elements these philosophies have partly or wholly in common, the diversity far exceeds the similarity. The resemblance between the systems of Spinoza and Malebranche, for instance, seems superficial when we consider that Spinoza advances no equivalent of intelligible extension and that Malebranche disdains Spinozan necessity and the divine attribute of matter. The differences between Leibniz and Locke are so great, on the other hand, that Leibniz wanted more than usual to correspond with him and Locke, less than usual to accept. None of the seven philosophers resigned himself to the mere refinement or elaboration of a predecessor's thought. Malebranche's admiration for Descartes did not keep him from developing his own philosophy and Buffier's respect for Locke as well as Descartes scarcely inhibited his modest originality. Nor does Berkeley's audacity need further emphasis here. This diversity came from the decline of the conformist pressures exerted by theological authority and clerical jealousy, which had been stifling Scholasticism for some time. As freedom began to generate its own power, the revolt against the old philosophies soon yielded to interaction between the new ones. Paradoxically the eroding limits imposed by Christianity constrained the clerical philosophers Malebranche, Buffier and Berkeley less than the laymen Descartes and Leibniz, while the Arian Locke and the crypto-pantheist Spinoza ignored them privately and publicly advocated toleration. Malebranche and Berkeley nonetheless exploited the right to originality as vigorously as Leibniz and Spinoza, since all four produced philosophies that transformed the nature of God and thought. Descartes, Malebranche, Leibniz, Buffier and Berkeley did not intend to challenge the traditional conception of God. The challenges by Spinoza and Locke were essentially posthumous. Yet the development of philosophy from Descartes to Berkeley encouraged and equipped the age to think independently of its religions. The pervasive influence of this elite hardly inspired subservience to theological or clerical authority. The momentum as usual carried further than the movement.

Locke distinguishes himself from the other six philosophers by admitting no direct communication between the human mind and God. Descartes, Leibniz, Buffier and the younger Berkeley affirm this communication, while Spinoza and Malebranche develop theories of the natural light. Our philosophers illustrate this concept in various ways. Leibniz and Berkeley speculate on the metaphysical equivalence of fire, heat and light. Typically Leibniz compares the rays from the physical sun with those from the divine sun. According to the author of *Siris* we judge by the unerring light from the lamp of nature. Radiation from God's mind orders the macrocosm and from each human mind, a microcosm. Locke believes in revelation by a metaphysical sunlight that tells us nothing of the divine sun itself. The candle of the Lord illuminates the moral law of nature, but not as a torch approaching a notice board, a stricture against innateness. The first rays of the natural light inspire Christianity in Buffier's opinion. Malebranche strikes out in a different direction with the *Conversations chrétiennes*, a dialogue between him and Christ.

Descartes's and Spinoza's natural light consists of intuition; Leibniz's of intuition rarely and demonstration usually; Locke's of intuition and demonstration. Spinoza limits it to reason and intuition, which produce the second and third kinds of knowledge in his system. Ideas or pure thought form the natural light in Malebranche's philosophy and, in Buffier's, first truths from common sense as well as the intimate sense. Locke and Buffier admit sense data and Buffier admits probability. Although Locke denies that we participate in God's thought, Malebranche and Leibniz consider our thought a portion of his, a drop in the ocean as Leibniz says. Like Berkeley Leibniz assumes that our mind functions in a microcosm just as God's does in the macrocosm. Leibniz and Malebranche concur on the coexistence of the eternal truths with God, the immediate source of our intelligence. Leibniz recommends that we draw eternal truths from the fountain of essence. The Creator, he affirms, sows the seeds of the highest doctrines in our minds. Though convinced that our mind has nothing in common with God's, Locke finds that the ideas of God and obedience to God conform to the natural light. Buffier declares the Christian faith a part of faith in the natural light. Berkeley describes God as the father of both natural and revealed light, the unique source of all truth. Spinoza assigns the highest authority for the interpretation of Scripture to the natural light, while Descartes prefers it to traditional authority and denies that it ever yields dangerous or perverse truth.

The semantics of the natural light and related terms like reason, common sense and good sense varies from philosopher to philosopher. Descartes and Spinoza do not use the natural light as an exact synonym of good sense or reason. Their natural light consists of intuition alone, while good sense includes demonstration as well. Malebranche does treat the natural light and reason as exact synonyms, however, and Leibniz tends to equate them with each other, but he sometimes distinguishes between reason and right reason. In this case reason may be uncertain or corrupt, while right reason is an irrefutible sequence of requisites. Leibniz defines good sense as the minimum ability to link judgements in a logical sequence tending to probability. Locke views common sense as a synonym of reason, which comprises both demonstration and judgement. It may therefore produce certain knowledge or probable information. Unlike his predecessors in this study, Locke admits sense data. To him common sense means, in particular, knowing things or thinking of them as they are in themselves (to the extent that we can). As opposed to reason, right reason, an inborn faculty, designates a moral code. Although Buffier uses common sense and the natural light interchangeably, his natural light may imply the intimate sense as well. He compares his common sense to Descartes's good sense, yet he founds it on sense data, which Descartes excludes. His common sense attains only the highest probability, while Descartes's good sense results in certainty. Berkeley ascribes his peculiar brand of common sense to ordinary men, but he adds another connotation, the improved reason of thinking men, hence his distinction between reason and superior reason. In *Siris* he eliminates sense data from reason, thus returning to Descartes's position.

Explicitly or implicitly our philosophers agree that all or nearly all men have reason, that it raises them above the animals. None would dispute Berkeley's contention that the bulk of mankind travel the highroad of common sense. From Descartes to Locke, however, they would refuse to join him and Buffier in consulting the multitude. Both Descartes and Locke criticise Herbert's appeal to universal consent, which Buffier takes as proof of his common sense. Obviously human intelligence varies, but why? Descartes gives a paradoxical answer: all minds have the same potential; few can reach this potential. Only method raises them above each other, yet most are incapable of learning a good one. Spinoza shares this opinion. As the dialogues by Descartes and Malebranche imply, one can teach an unindoctrinated young mind the highest Cartesian sciences if it has the aptitude to learn by Cartesian method. Locke attributes the light of nature to all men, but do all use it and use it properly? No, and some even dispute it. While Leibniz believes he could elicit necessary truth from a child by Socratic questions, he does not pretend that any child would do. In dialogues involving a debate with a representative of Locke, both Leibniz and Berkeley show that reason does not realise its potential without an effort that few will make. Even Buffier admits that common sense is not really common because its judgements are similar and not identical. He nonetheless proclaims the unlimited potential of common sense, which can cope with all knowledge however profound or elevated. Berkeley considers it natural in man and therefore exclusive of custom and education. Though inoperative at birth, it begins to function early in the life of every man. Whatever their stand on innate ideas, all seven philosophers and even Locke concur on the dispositional innateness of reason.

All accept Descartes's principle that reason enables us to distinguish between truth and error. This unanimity nonetheless contrasts with a diversity of interpretations, for some see truth where others see error. Spinoza, Malebranche and Leibniz affirm the truth of rational speculations that Locke, Buffier and Berkeley condemn as erroneous. The nature of error varies according to the point of view. Spinoza, Leibniz and Locke invoke reason against superstition; Leibniz and Locke against sectarianism, and Locke against enthusiasm. Neglect of common sense results in several kinds of errors listed by Buffier as if none applied to the Jesuits, an oversight that Protestants like Berkeley and Locke would gladly repair. While the Anglicans and freethinkers in *Alciphron* agree on the meaning of reason, both appeal to it when they censure the other side. Our seven philosophers do not even agree on the nature of reason, yet each relies on it to defend his position and attack those of his adversaries. They evidently envisage reason as something necessarily constant and uniform. Their analysis and use of it demonstrates, on the contrary, that there is no such thing. Fortunately, in fact, reason evolves and diversifies from thinker to thinker. Every one of our philosophers has a reason of his own and those who change their minds have two.

None of them could have ignored the religious consequences of his thought without risk, as almost any philosopher could today. Since the authority, power and vigilance of the Christian churches continued, few men dared to provoke the predominant one in their country. A loyal but superficial Catholic, Descartes tried to separate philosophy from theology and confine himself to philosophy. The crypto-pantheist Spinoza skirted dangerous issues by professing a tactful blend of respect and ignorance. An Oratorian priest, Malebranche moves in the opposite direction from Descartes by merging philosophy with theology. Leibniz, a nominal Lutheran, enjoyed the challenge of reconciling theology with his philosophy wherever an interesting conflict appeared. An Anglican Arian, Locke used much the same tactic as Spinoza, but more extensively against determined opponents. Both also complemented the avoidance of dangerous issues by the advocacy of religious toleration. Buffier and Berkeley joined their fellow clergyman Malebranche in harmonising philosophy with theology. The Jesuit insisted that his philosophy supports Catholicism. The Anglican priest designed his immaterialism to solve the philosophical problems besetting Christianity. He reviewed the ancient philosophers (*Siris*) in search of compatibility with his faith. Emancipation from control by theologians did not free our philosophers from theological constraints, but it did initiate a trend towards greater liberty.

Some of them try to reconcile faith with reason. Not Spinoza, who finds that these ideas contradict each other. Nor Descartes, who separates them and limits himself to reason. Malebranche and Leibniz attempt an elaborate reconciliation; Locke, Buffier and Berkeley, a concise one. Spinoza maintains that reason conflicts with Scripture and theology, the consolation of a majority who ignore reason. They prefer supernatural illusion to natural knowledge, which alone seems divine to him. Miracles amount to unexplained natural events. The other six philosophers acknowledge that reason cannot explain what they believe, but only why they believe it. Malebranche and Leibniz submit that faith depends on reason, which will eventually replace it. The identification of reason with the Word by Malebranche implies the necessary conformity of revelation with reason. We may examine divine mystery to the extent that reason allows, provided the results agree with dogma. A dialectic between reason and faith may well arrive at enlightenment. There is little virtue in faith without reason. Leibniz, Locke and Berkeley adopt the traditional distinction between propositions according to, above and contrary to reason. Leibniz considers that truths of reason confirm truths of fact above reason without explaining them. We cannot say why they are true, but we can refute objections to them. A mysterious truth surpasses reason because it fits into no logical sequence. Neither can reason discredit revelation nor revelation, reason. Locke condones blind faith no more than Malebranche. Believing without knowing why is neglect of the natural light. Reason has the right to verify the claim of divine origination and reject any proposition contrary to it. Buffier urges us to believe what the Church tells us God and Christ say. If Christ did not do the miracles in the New Testament, God is using the natural light to deceive us. Reason approves part of revelation, in Berkeley's opinion, and persuades us to accept the rest. We must not reject what we cannot understand, because it may be divine in origin. Except for Spinoza, therefore, our philosophers think reason supports Christianity. The six of them admit miracles. All seven state or imply that the source of the natural light would never contradict itself.

All prefer to judge by reason instead of authority. Descartes, Spinoza and Malebranche suspect Scholastic authority; Leibniz, Locke and Buffier, Cartesian authority; Berkeley, Lockian authority. This philosophical independence overshadows a theological independence evident in Spinoza's works and discreet in those of the three clergymen. Yet even the latter accept natural religion and tend to deism. In his private disregard for Anglican authority, Locke denies that divine inspiration can enable a man to impart any simple ideas to others who have never experienced them. Buffier protests against this restriction of revealed truth to empirical facts despite his sympathy with empiricism. Locke also observes that each successive transmission of testimony by witnesses weakens its probability. On the contrary, Buffier objects, the common sense and the integrity of the Christians who transmit such testimony strengthens its probability. Berkeley makes the same claim. Malebranche and Buffier stress the number of witnesses to the miracles in the New Testament. Leibniz would evaluate their testimony according to their experience. Although Locke and Buffier set standards for such evaluation, Buffier's are loose and he would settle for the satisfaction of any one out of four. He asserts the mere probability of revelation, which Malebranche considers certain. The shift from the requirement of certainty by Descartes, Spinoza and Malebranche to the tolerance of probability by Leibniz, Locke and Buffier undermined faith slightly but surely.

Only Malebranche and Berkeley believed in original sin, but Leibniz accepted part of the doctrine. Malebranche and Leibniz treated it extensively, while Locke took some interest in it, and Berkeley, less. Descartes, Spinoza and Buffier ignore it, yet Spinoza examines the fall thoroughly, along with Malebranche and Leibniz. The reasons for interest in the doctrine or lack of it vary as much as the interest itself. Descartes probably did not consider such theology worth his trouble. Buffier conformed to the Jesuit policy of neglecting theology that ran counter to the interests of the Order, in other words, that discouraged people from devotion to the Church. Berkeley seems to have viewed the fall and original sin merely as a part of the faith he had dedicated himself to defend. Locke felt obligated to revise it in the light of reason. The story of the fall provided Spinoza with an opportunity to criticise the misinterpretation of a well-known Old Testament text. Analysis of original sin, which involves far more than such exegesis, would have exposed him to Christian attacks, hence his neglect of this doctrine. The implication of divine guilt, by Bayle in particular, drove Leibniz to absolve God of responsibility for evil. The profound conviction that the fall and original sin explained the human predicament motivated Malebranche alone.

Of our seven philosophers only he advances an elaborate theory of Adam's state before the fall. He explores the details, as he sees them, of Adam's submission to God, his control of the animal spirits, his independence of the senses and his discipline of pain and pleasure. Contemplation of God inspired in him a cerebral joy effacing sensual pleasure: how could he have succumbed to temptation? Malebranche has no satisfactory answer. Still, Adam's vanity, his infatuation with Eve and his sensual appetite all contributed to his disobedience of God. Berkeley alludes rather to the temptation by Satan, while Leibniz supposes the serpent persuaded Eve that the prohibition of the fruit was not in the couple's best interest. Only Malebranche accuses the devil of perverting Adam's awareness of his resemblance to God, so that Adam tried to deify himself, a heinous crime. Malebranche speculates on the revolt of the senses and the loss of control over the animal spirits which fissured the brain irreparably. When sensations distracted reason, Adam confused sensual pleasure with spiritual joy and forgot God. The senses subverted the will, which rebelled against God. We find little of this in the works of our other philosophers.

Locke interprets God's sentence of death as the cause of our mortality, and Berkeley, as that of an early end to life and a fear of death. The story in Genesis illustrates a hypothesis rejected by Spinoza, for he reads the sentence as enslavement to fear of death, which he may have viewed as a great flaw in Christianity. Death interests Malebranche less than the psycho-physiological deterioration of Adam, which he thoroughly describes. He diagnoses a slavery of sensations and passions that reinforce each other in a vicious circle involving the animal spirits and the fissures they open in the brain. Distracted by sensations and passions, the mind misrepresents the material world and undergoes the illusions of dreams and hallucinations. Original sin is an effort, and concupiscence, the result of this effort which subverts reason. Malebranche attributes such ills as possession by demons, insanity, fever, social stratification, paganism and the hostility of wild beasts to concupiscence. To paganism Berkeley adds idolatry, wickedness, vice, injustice and violence.

Even the pagans, he observes, perceived the depravity of mankind, a symptom of original sin. He joins Malebranche in defending the orthodox version of the doctrine. Since we inherit the guilt of our ancestors, we incur the same punishment. Malebranche and Leibniz think the contagion spreads from body to body. The mother's animal spirits, according to Malebranche, make the same fissures in the foetus's brain as she has in hers, but the foetus's tender brain fissures more deeply. Thus original sin increases with every generation. During life after birth, sensations deepen these fissures. Original sin also causes a social contagion as vice proliferates throughout society. Leibniz and Locke deny that God punished Adam by corrupting him and his offspring. God condemns no one for a sin committed by someone else, in Leibniz's view, and no arbitrary majority for the sin of their original ancestors. Adam's disobedience did result, however, in a susceptibility to temptation that spread to the encapsulated germs of his entire race. The transcreation of each rational soul exposes it to immediate contamination by its body. Adam's offspring sin no less willingly than he did. But original sin neither incites them to evil nor condemns them to death, an opinion shared by Locke. He contends that they inherit the effect of Adam's sin rather than his guilt. When Adam ate the forbidden fruit, he forfeited his immortality and ours as well.

Leibniz rejects the condemnation of infidels and unbaptised infants by God, but Malebranche affirms that they receive a lesser punishment, which he thinks they deserve. Malebranche, Leibniz and even Spinoza absolve God of responsibility for evil, though each in his own way. As usual Malebranche seeks to justify dogma. Although God made Adam free to resist temptation, Adam yielded to it so that he deserved to be punished. Foreseeing that he would sin, God allowed him to do it, yet he did not coerce him and hence shares none of the blame. Leibniz makes the same point. If God had inclined Adam to resist temptation, Malebranche continues, Adam's innocence would have lacked merit. Since Adam abused his privileged status, God did not intervene to keep him from sinning. Malebranche and Leibniz deny that God should have stooped to save Adam. They concur on the maintenance by God of natural laws that enable Adam to accomplish his sin. Both applaud God for seizing the opportunity to send a redeemer. Leibniz and Spinoza conceive of evil as a deficiency necessitated by the uniqueness of divine perfection. Yet Leibniz infers Adam's guilt and Spinoza, his essential innocence. Adam abused reason, according to Spinoza, but not intuition, for evil amounts to a human prejudice. To Spinoza the story of the fall seems useful only for the ignorant majority dominated by imagination. It casts God in the role of an anthropomorphic prince who must enforce his law. Adam could not have sinned against the will of Spinoza's God who, unlike those of Leibniz and Malebranche, has absolute, though impersonal power. In contrast with our other philosophers, Spinoza rejects liberty, both human and divine. Substantial necessity implies the innocence of his God. To preserve human liberty, on the other hand, Leibniz attempts a distinction between determinism and necessity based on his juridical studies.

The Gods of Malebranche and Leibniz decided what kind of world to create on strangely economic grounds. Malebranche's God created the most perfect world he could by the simplest means conforming with divine order and general laws. Leibniz's God selected for creation the combination of compossibilities that maximised simplicity and variety. In both cases, essences coeternal and consubstantial with God determined the existences of a world inevitably flawed by evil. The Malebranchian deity preferred a fallible first man, so that the effects of his fall would necessitate a redeemer. Christ would improve the creation by restoring it. The Leibnizian deity chose the best possible world, which happens to include Adam disobeying God. In neither case can we blame God since he created a world with as little evil as possible. Malebranche and Leibniz achieve this goal, however, at the expense of limiting God's power.

God interests our philosophers more than Christ, and the superhuman Christ more than the human. Descartes neglects Christ, while Spinoza divests him of Christianity. Although Spinoza and Locke acknowledge his superiority over other men, they confine him to humanity. Aside from the traditional figure in 'Jesus am Kreuze', the Leibnizian Christ resembles a rationalist philosopher rather than a holy man. Likewise the Spinozan, the Lockian and the Malebranchian, but the latter distinguishes himself from the others by his severity. The gospel miracle worker still impresses Buffier and Berkeley or, at least, the Jesuit thinks this Jesus should impress his public. Yet even their conceptions of Christ reflect the erosion by Enlightenment reason.

None of our philosophers examines the gospel Jesus in general, not even the clergymen. Each merely discusses aspects that preoccupy him. Thus Spinoza uses Jesus to illustrate his theory of knowledge, Malebranche describes him as an occasionalist distributor of grace and Leibniz praises the founder of the most enlightened faith for raising natural religion to the status of a public dogma. Locke labours his identification of Jesus with the messiah or Son of God, by which he means a superhuman figure favoured by God. He credits the synoptic propaganda divorcing the spiritual messiah from the Jewish liberator. The Reverend Dr Berkeley tries to re-establish the authenticity of the apocryphal allusion to Christ in Josephus. Both Spinoza and Malebranche contend that Jesus adjusted his message to the mentality of ordinary men, but Malebranche says he intended to bring them to reason. The Spinozan Jesus, who intuits truths directly from God, transmits them to others by reason. Loath to admit Jesus's ignorance of God's intentions, Malebranche insists that he knew all he needed to know for the accomplishment of his mission. He could have known the time of the last judgement if he had wanted to. Leibniz argues that Jesus's ignorance of this time suits his human nature during its earthly humility. Elsewhere, however, he finds that the communication of divine qualities to Jesus's human nature includes unlimited knowledge.

Leibniz interprets Jesus's kingdom of heaven as a city or republic of God. Malebranche, Locke and Berkeley prefer another Augustinian metaphor, the mystic Church, while Buffier equates the kingdom with the historical Church. None of these writers has the faintest notion of the apocalyptic theocracy Jesus expected in Jewish Galilee. His passion attracts the special attention of Malebranche alone, who traces, back to its creation, the willingness of Jesus's soul to sacrifice itself. Reason persuaded it to offer itself for the satisfaction of God, who no longer valued Jewish sacrifice. It concurred with the divine will by submitting to a cruel and infamous death. Berkeley dismisses freethinking objections to its humiliation, which may have repelled our other philosophers. Although Spinoza and Buffier only mention the crucifixion, they comment substantially on Jesus's miracles. Spinoza denies these miracles, while Leibniz and Malebranche express no enthusiasm for them. Locke, Buffier and Berkeley certify them as historical facts established by the transmitted testimony of many reliable witnesses. Berkeley seems to interpret the transfiguration as a transfer of power from God to Christ.

Malebranche, Locke and Buffier consider the resurrection a historical fact proving that God sent Christ to us. Locke attributes the wounds probed by Thomas and the meals eaten by the risen Christ to the ignorant majority's need for empirical evidence. The resurrection convinces him of Christ's immortality, but not of his deity. It convinces Malebranche, Buffier and Berkeley of his deity. Malebranche compares the resurrection to the emergence of a silkworm from its cocoon. Buffier imagines a parallel to Christ's mission, execution and resurrection in eighteenth-century Paris. He assumes the ancient Jerusalemites would attest these events as reliably as contemporary Parisians. He finds the gospel evidence and the transmission of this evidence irrefutable. Berkeley's immaterial interpretation of the resurrection makes it seem more plausible, yet far from convincing. He not only, like Buffier and Locke, exaggerates the number and sincerity of the witnesses, but also conflates them with the Christian martyrs. Discounting these witnesses, Spinoza regrets the absence of testimony by unbelievers. Even more than Locke, he detects an appeal to the vulgar imagination in the resurrection accounts, which he compares to Yahweh's appearance on Mount Sinai. He concedes that the disciples believed in the resurrection, but he suspects them of interpreting a spiritual event materially. The similarity with Berkeley is superficial.

According to him we do not have to understand the two natures of Christ in order to believe in them and receive moral inspiration from them. We cannot reasonably doubt them, in Buffier's opinion, even though we do not understand them. When Spinoza says he cannot understand them, however, he means that he rejects them. He does not even find any evidence in the New Testament that God appeared or spoke to Jesus. Yet the younger Spinoza thinks God created an eternal Son superior to other men. Although Locke avoids the issue in his polemic, his reading notes indicate that Scripture supports the opponents of the two natures. Several modern critics refuse to take Leibniz's profession of faith in the doctrine seriously. He nonetheless defends the deity of Christ in his polemic, speculates on the communication of idioms and develops a theory of the hypostatic bond uniting the two natures. He joins Malebranche in declaring them necessary for redemption. The identification of the Word with reason by Malebranche implies so tight a union of the natures that he tends to confuse them in his conversation with Christ (*Méditations*). Malebranche and Leibniz view the incarnation as an act accomplished by the Son independently of the other two persons in the Trinity and hence an exception to the rule of collective action, a traditional exception.

Reason cannot explain the Trinity, they tell us, but it does justify faith in this doctrine. Descartes, Buffier and Berkeley share their opinion. Leibniz nonetheless admits that nature provides us with no satisfactory parallel with the Trinity. Does Scripture reveal it? Leibniz, Buffier and Berkeley state that it does, while Locke implies that it does not and Spinoza would certainly agree. Refuting the Socinian charge of tritheism, Leibniz makes several attempts to discriminate between substance and person rationally. Although Locke clears himself of confusing them, he privately disbelieves the distinction between them within the Godhead. The Father created the Son according to Spinoza and Locke; generated him according to Malebranche, Leibniz and Buffier. Malebranche and Leibniz compare the generation of the Son and the procession of the Holy Spirit to various reflexive activities of the human mind. Leibniz declares the title Father, Son and Spirit useful only as an aid to human comprehension. Spinoza alone investigates the Holy Spirit, whose evolution from the Hebraic conception of breath or wind he insinuates by means of philology.

Leibniz and Berkeley defend the ancient councils, while Locke attacks them. The councils did not dictate abstractions to Christians, Berkeley argues, but rather suppressed extremes like Sabellianism and paganism. Leibniz affirms and Locke denies that they merely confirmed established doctrines. Leibniz concedes, on the other hand, that they raised some inappropriate issues and complicated the dogma unnecessarily in resolving them. He condemns antitrinitarian heretics ancient and modern, whom he accuses of worshipping a creature. Did he penetrate the secret of Locke's Arianism? Apparently not.

Study of our philosophers therefore yields a diversity of attitudes towards Christology and the Trinity ranging from Buffier's proselytic orthodoxy to Locke's private Arianism. All nonetheless participate in a trend to deism by their common tendencies to neglect and rationalise the doctrines most vital to Christianity. The gospel Jesus appeals less to them than to us, for the age, in its reaction to previous ones, sought to insulate itself from mystery and enthusiasm. Men like Descartes and Locke need Leibniz's advice that what we cannot know or explain may nonetheless exist. Indeed Leibniz needs it himself. Deliberate in the Cartesians' case, historical ignorance impedes any attempt by our philosophers to approach the historical Jesus, whom they travesty as a philosopher of reason. They could assimilate the predominant figure in their cultural heritage only by squeezing him into their mould. Curiously, on the other hand, they feel more at ease with the superhuman Christ who, since he is more of an abstraction, suits their reason. In him a few of them even discover an opportunity for rational speculation, such as intelligible extension, the most brilliant flower in the garden. Here we encounter exceptions to the contemporary antagonism between theology and philosophy. While Christ even captivates Spinoza, the latter stops when the others proceed to consider the deity of Christ. Their treatment of the two natures and the Trinity raises the question of the priority between reason and faith. Perhaps faith persuades reason in Berkeley's and Buffier's cases, and vice versa in Leibniz's and Locke's, but which persuades which in Malebranche's? Although he would say faith precedes reason, we cannot tell. Does Descartes moreover practically ignore the two natures and the Trinity because he prefers to suspend his judgement or because they do not interest him? He may be closer to Spinoza than critics realise. Our clergymen naturally defend the Trinity, yet Buffier and Berkeley devote less energy and imagination to this task than Malebranche. Leibniz's efforts in the same area stem less from conviction than the desire for religious reunification. Our philosophers tend to weaken faith in Christ and the Trinity.

Spinoza, Buffier and Berkeley give little space to the eucharist; Locke gives more; Descartes, Malebranche and especially Leibniz give a great deal. Descartes and Leibniz emit theories to explain transubstantiation, Malebranche defends the dogma and the Cartesian interpretation of it, Leibniz adopts it and then repudiates it, Locke attacks it. Buffier approves and Berkeley disapproves of it as one might expect. Malebranche and Leibniz support the real presence, which Spinoza and Locke disdain. Malebranche subscribes to eucharistic sacrifice, but Leibniz does not. Descartes, Malebranche and Leibniz discuss the worship of Christ in the eucharist, Malebranche and Leibniz examine communion, Leibniz alone treats private mass and the lay cup.

One of Descartes's theories explains the continuing appearances of bread and wine after the consecration. The surface relief between the surrounding air and the space previously occupied by bread or wine remains unchanged, so that its contact with sense organs produces the same sensations as before. The other theory accounts for the substantial presence of Christ's body under these appearances. Christ's soul vivifies every particle of bread and wine, thus incorporating them into his body, for personal identity depends on the union of the body with the soul. This theory bears some resemblance to one advanced by the younger Leibniz: transubstantiation substitutes Christ's mind for God as the concurrent mind of the bread and wine on the altar, hence their substantial conversion into his body. For fear that Cartesian extension jeopardises the dogma, Leibniz declares energy the essence of matter. Another theory concerns real accidents or secondary powers derived from the primary energy of substance. Replacing some by others alters the nature of a body without changing its substance. Leibniz cites various ways in which God could manipulate the real accidents of bread and wine so that they inhere in the substance of Christ's body, but he does not say which one is used in transubstantiation. After repudiating the dogma, he uses it nonetheless to illustrate his philosophy. Christ for instance converts the minute structure of bread and wine into that of his body without altering their sensual appearances. Communicants misperceive them consciously and his body unconsciously in what Leibniz calls transperception. In search of a better theory, he proposes various ways of reorganising monads. If substantial bonds united the monads of bread and wine, God could destroy these bonds and transfer the monads to the bond uniting the monads of Christ's body. Or if there were no substantial bonds, God might destroy the monads of bread and wine, then put those of Christ's body in their place. Since the older Leibniz no longer believed in transubstantiation, however, he could scarcely have taken these theories very seriously. Both Leibniz and Descartes are anxious to tackle a physical and metaphysical problem that has always daunted the theologians. Concern for the integrity of the faith motivates neither profoundly.

The Council of Trent decreed that only the *species* of bread and wine remain after the consecration. Descartes interprets species as surface relief, and Buffier as accidents in a supernatural state. Buffier does not endorse absolute accidents, but he rebukes the Cartesians for denying them. Malebranche assumes that the ancient Church established transubstantiation and the real presence by something like universal consent. The Cartesian neglect of history explains his ignorance of what actually happened, the late inception and controversial development of the dogmas. Young Leibniz does not even have this excuse for affirming that the Romans needed only to translate the Greek word for conversion in order to introduce transubstantiation. Using the same argument to found opposite opinions, Malebranche and Leibniz tacitly agree that transubstantiation clashes with reason. Malebranche infers its authenticity from the number of Christians who subscribed to it anyway, while Leibniz simply concludes that it is inauthentic. The younger Leibniz not only supports transubstantiation, on the other hand, but also conflates it with the real presence. He seems to have repudiated the dogma later because he realised the Protestants would never accept it. It had also undergone more variation and resulted in more superstition than he cared to tolerate. He tried to persuade his Catholic correspondents to consider reunification without requiring the Protestants to embrace transubstantiation. In vain. How do Catholics come to believe in such a contradiction? Locke blames fear, custom and indoctrination which, according to Berkeley, convinces them gradually. Locke finds the eucharist accessible to the senses. Since we know the real essences of bread by one collection of ideas and that of flesh by another, we cannot easily confuse them. Faith in transubstantiation on the pretext that our finite mind cannot reconcile an apparent contradiction does not impress Berkeley. He objects to a doctrine unsupported by Scripture, repugnant to reason, implying a contradiction and leading to idolatry. The irrational implications of transubstantiation aggravate the traditional antagonism over this issue in the age of reason.

Malebranche defends the Cartesian theory of transubstantiation from the charge of Calvinism. Neither does Trent exclude this theory nor has the Church ever condemned it. The Cartesian reduction of Christ's body to a physical point does not imply the destruction of its biological organisation, but the Scholastic collapse of its parts into a geometrical point does. Scholastic transubstantiation would gradually destroy the creation, an objection that recalls Leibniz's strictures against the eucharistic increase and decrease of matter assumed by White. God's will, in Malebranche's view, determines the existence of Christ's body in the cradle, in heaven and on the altar. His divinity, soul and body retain their unity and identity throughout. The younger Leibniz combats deviations from the Catholic eucharist by Luther, Calvin and Zwingli. They ignore Christ's words, 'This is my body', which prove transubstantiation to his satisfaction. Although he abandoned transubstantiation, he adhered to the real presence and opposed Zwingli's symbolic presence during his entire career. He also denied that Lutherans believed in consubstantiation. Anxious to reconcile them with the Calvinists, the older Leibniz cites the Anglican eucharist as a model for compromise. He interprets the Calvinist perception of Christ's body through faith as the effect of Leibnizian energy. He tries to allay Calvinist fears of

Capernaism and denies that unworthy communicants receive the body. Dismissing Scholastic versions of the real presence, he echoes the Lutheran belief that communicants receive the body at the same time as the bread, but separately. Locke stresses the eucharistic differences between the Catholics, the Lutherans, the Calvinists, and the Zwinglians. The mind, he submits, rejects the presence of a body in more than one place at a time. He privately believes that the eucharist represents Christ's body and commemorates his death. The anthropomorphic and theophageous implications of the real presence disgust Spinoza, who scorns such superstitions unfounded in Scripture.

The physical dispersion of Christ's body, as Descartes conceives of it in the eucharist, should not detract from veneration of the sacrament. Malebranche scolds the kings and queens of England for banishing such worship and yet requiring communicants to kneel before the altar. Leibniz hopes to use the custom some Protestants have of kneeling before communion as an argument in negotiating reunification. He discriminates between the worship of Christ in the eucharist and idolatry, of which the Reformers accuse the Catholics. Early in his career he thought the Lutherans disagreed with the Catholics only on the duration of Christ's presence and hence that of the worship required. Later he rallied to the Catholic presence from consecration until digestion and later still, to the Lutheran presence limited to the moment of reception. Christ's presence in the eucharist, says Malebranche, nourishes our souls with grace, which he equates with reason. Communion unites us with God and all other Christians. Those who partake of Christ's living body fortify themselves for eternal life. The sacrament pledges that faith will one day become intelligence. Taking communion too often, however, or without a pure heart exposes the communicant to death.

Malebranche recapitulates the Catholic doctrine that Jesus initiated a continuous process of eucharistic sacrifice at the Last Supper. As priest and victim he offers his mystic body every time the sacrament is performed. Leibniz disputes the sacrificial significance of the rite, for he regards mass as nothing more than a celebration of the eucharist. Trent confuses representation with reproduction. Separating sacrifice from the eucharist, Leibniz concedes that Christ sacrificed himself once, yet offers himself perpetually for the edification of the faithful. The earlier Leibniz indulged in apology of private mass on the grounds that it provides more worship of God than ordinary communion allows. Elsewhere, however, he prefers no more than one private mass a day in every church. Private mass seems unprimitive, unnecessary and unjustified to the later Leibniz, but he described the controversy over the matter as semantic. In the *System* he observes that Jesus shared both the bread and the wine with his disciples. He nonetheless recognises the ancient precedents for restricting lay communion to

213

bread alone. If an individual had suppressed the lay cup, he would have committed a grievous sin, but we can hardly blame the entire Church. After 1698, Leibniz defended the lay right to both species and set tolerance of the lay cup as a Protestant condition for reunification.

Ideally the present study would develop as a Leibnizian series in which the coherence of the whole compensates for any weakness in the relations between the terms. In reality, however, we are not dealing with quantities, but rather qualities and the temptations of mathematics would lead only to distortion. We must strive to objectify the subjective without indulging in a naive hope of success. Malebranche's dialectic between faith and intelligence will never arrive at pure intelligence as he prophesies, yet progress usually rewards this kind of effort. After all, the reward is greater freedom. Perhaps our Christian philosophers would have made more progress if they had followed Spinoza's example and lightened the vessel by throwing useless weight overboard, the weight of traditional illusions. Instead they wasted much of their energy on impossible attempts to reconcile the natural light with revelation so-called. We have never had much patience with questions we cannot answer. Why does God allow evil? People have always assumed that at least one of us has offended him. How can we know God? People have always assumed that he sent someone to explain. Can we obtain his sympathy? People have always assumed that some kind of sacrifice would move him. Hence our theology. If our philosophers had succeeded in liberating themselves from it completely, they might have discovered that the natural light is by itself the best hypothesis. None of the others accounts for the order of being and life more plausibly.

Descartes and his successors did their thinking at a time when the prevailing theology had begun to decline and lose its authority. It no longer responded to problems by seeking solutions as it had in the twelfth and thirteenth centuries, but rather by rebuking philosophers who dared to raise the problems and seek solutions of their own. While they had reached the end of the paths along which it had guided them, it tried to keep them from blazing new ones. Thus philosophy broke away from its traditional subserviance to theology and struck out on its own, with the precaution nonetheless of speaking in theology's name. How long would it deem this precaution necessary? Not very long, for Hume soon appeared on the horizon. This phase in the evolution of the relationship between philosophy and theology provides us with the key to a theory of this evolution. Philosophy relies on reason, and theology, on faith in the search for answers to the questions asked above. As the reader of this manuscript objected, the impatience I had attributed to them has inspired an enormous patience with the search for answers.[1] 'On aime mieux la chasse que la prise,' said Pascal,[2] although he would have disapproved of the present context. Philosophy flourishes when reason deludes us with the promise of answers to those questions, and theology when faith makes the same promise. Theology declines when faith fails to keep this promise and philosophy, when reason fails to keep it. In an age of reason faith declines, and in an age of faith, reason. Nor does this cyclical evolution exclude progress, so long as we grasp this slippery term firmly. Progress need only take us somewhere else, somewhere more interesting perhaps...

1. 'The mountains of mouldering theological works that fill libraries display remarkable patience with such questions.' 'Report on W. Trapnell: *The Natural light*', p.2.
2. Blaise Pascal, *Pensées*, ed. Louis Lafuma (Paris 1962), no.136 (Brunschvicq no. 139).

# Bibliography

Aaron, Richard, *John Locke*. Oxford 1971

Acton, H. B., 'Berkeley', *Encyclopedia of philosophy*, ed. Paul Edwards *et al.* New York, London 1967

Aesop, *Corpus fabularum aesopicarum*, ed. Augustus Hausrath. Berlin 1957

– *Fables*, trans. George Townsend. London n.d.

Aguilar, Juan, *El Sentido común en las obras filosóficas del P. Claude Buffier S.I.* Barcelona 1957

Alquié, Ferdinand, *Le Cartésianisme de Malebranche*. Paris 1974

– *La Découverte métaphysique de l'homme chez Descartes*. Paris 1966

– *Malebranche et le rationalisme chrétien.* Paris 1971

Armogathe, J.-R., *Theologia cartesiana: l'explication physique de l'eucharistie chez Descartes et dom Desgabets*, International archives of the history of ideas 84. La Haye 1977

Arnobius, *Adversus nationes libri VII*, ed. C. Marchesi. Turin 1953

Augustine, *The City of God II*, trans. Philip Schaff, Select Library of Nicene and Post-Nicene Fathers. Grand Rapids 1956

Barber, W. H., *Leibniz in France from Arnauld to Voltaire*. Oxford 1955

Baruzi, Jean, *Leibniz et l'organisation religieuse de la terre*. Paris 1907

Bayle, Pierre, *Dictionnaire historique et critique*. Paris 1820-1824; rpt. Genève 1969

Beck, L. J., *The Method of Descartes: a study of the 'Regulae'*. Oxford 1964

Belaval, Yvon, *Pour connaître la pensée de Leibniz*. Paris 1952

Berkeley, George, *Three dialogues between Hylas and Philonous*, ed. Colin Turbayne. New York 1954

– *Treatise concerning the principles of human knowledge*, ed. Colin Turbayne. New York 1957

– *The Works of George Berkeley, Bishop of Cloyne*, ed. A. A. Luce and T. E. Jessop. Edinburgh 1948-1957

Bicknell, E. J., rev. by Carpenter, H. J., *A theological introduction to the thirty-nine articles of the Church of England*. London 1955

Bidney, David, *The Psychology and ethics of Spinoza*. New York 1962

Broad, C. D., *Leibniz: an introduction.* Cambridge 1975

Bronowski, J., *The Ascent of Man*. Boston 1974

Buffier, Claude, *Cours de sciences sur des principes nouveaux et simples*. Paris 1732

– *Œuvres philosophiques du père Buffier*, ed. Francisque Bouillier. Paris 1843

Burgelin, Pierre, 'Théologie naturelle et théologie révélée chez Leibniz', *Studia leibnitiana supplementa: Akten des internationalen Leibniz-Kongresses 1966*. Wiesbaden 1969. iv.1-20

Carlson, Stan, *Faith of our fathers: the Eastern Orthodox religion*. Minneapolis 1968

Collins, James, *A history of modern European philosophy*. Milwaukee 1954

Combes, Joseph, *Le Dessein de la sagesse cartésienne*. Lyon, Paris 1960

Cranston, Maurice, *John Locke*. London 1959

Dahrendorf, Walter, 'Lockes Kontroverse mit Stillingfleet und ihre Bedeutung für seine Stellung zur anglikanischen Kirche'. Diss. Hamburg 1932

Daniel, Stephen, 'Descartes' treatment of "lumen naturale".' *Studia leibnitiana* 10 (1978), p.92-100

Denziger, Heinrich, *Enchiridion symbolorum, definitionem et declarationum.* Freiburg im Bresgau 1937
Descartes, René, *Discours de la méthode*, ed. Etienne Gilson. Paris 1966
– *Œuvres de Descartes.* Paris 1966
– *Œuvres philosophiques*, ed. Ferdinand Alquié. Paris 1972-1973
Doney, Willis, 'Is Berkeley a Cartesian mind?', in *Berkeley: critical and interpretive essays.* Minneapolis 1982. p.273-82
Dufour-Kowalska, Gabrielle, *L'Origine: l'essence de l'origine: l'origine selon l''Ethique' de Spinoza.* Paris 1973

Edwards, John, *Socinianism unmasked: a discourse shewing the unreasonableness of a late writer's opinion.* London 1696
*Encyclopedia of philosophy*, ed. Paul Edwards et al. New York, London 1967

Fabian, Gerd, *Beitrag zur Geschichte des Leib-Seele-Problems.* Langensalza 1925; rpt. Hildesheim 1974
Friedmann, Georges, *Leibniz et Spinoza.* Paris 1946
Fuller, Reginald, *The Formation of the resurrection narratives.* London 1972

Gabaude, Jean-Marc, *Liberté et raison.* Toulouse 1970, 1972
Gibson, James, *Locke's theory of knowledge and its historical relations.* Cambridge 1917
Gilson, Etienne, *The Christian philosophy of saint Augustine.* New York 1960
Gouhier, Henri, *La Pensée religieuse de Descartes.* Paris 1972
– *La Philosophie de Malebranche et son expérience religieuse.* Paris 1926
Grave, S. A., 'The mind and its ideas: some problems in the interpretation of Berkeley', in *Locke and Berkeley: a collection of critical essays.* Notre Dame 1968. p.296-313
Guéroult, Martial, *Descartes selon l'ordre des raisons.* Paris 1953
– *Malebranche.* Paris 1955

– *Spinoza.* Paris 1968
Gurwitsch, Aron, *Leibniz: Philosophie des Panlogismus.* Berlin 1974
Gusdorf, Georges, *Les Sciences humaines et la pensée occidentale.* Paris 1966-1982

Hedenius, Ingemar, *Sensationalism and theology in Berkeley's philosophy.* Uppsala 1936
*Histoire de la philosophie*, ed. Bruce Parain and Yvon Belaval. Paris 1973
Hoffmann, Heinrich, *Die Leibnizsche Religionsphilosophie in ihrer geschichtlichen Stellung.* Tübingen 1903
Hume, David, *An abstract of a treatise of human nature* (1740). Cambridge 1938

Irenaeus of Lyon, *Irenaeus against heresies.* The Ante-Nicene Fathers, no 1. London 1887

Jablonsky, D. E., *D. E. Jablonsky's Briefwechsel mit Leibniz*, Acta et commentationes imp. universitatis Jurievensis. Dorpat 1897
Joye, George, *An apology made by George Joye to Satisfye (if it may be) W. Tyndale.* Birmingham 1882
Jurieu, Pierre, *L'Esprit de M. Arnauld.* Deventer 1684

Klöpel, Bernhard, *Das Lumen naturale bei Descartes.* Leipzig 1896
Körver, Helga, *Common sense: die Entwicklung eines englischen Schlüsselwortes.* Bonn 1967

Laporte, Jean, *Le Rationalisme de Descartes.* Paris 1945
Leibniz, Gottfried Wilhelm, *Die philosophischen Schriften von Gottfried Wilhelm Leibniz.* Berlin 1875-1890
– *Essais de theodicée.* Paris 1966
– *Nouveaux essais sur l'entendement humain.* Paris 1966
– *Œuvres de Leibniz*, ed. Louis Foucher de Careil. Paris 1859-1875; Hildesheim, New York 1969

– *Philosophical papers and letters*, trans. Leroy E. Loemker. Dordrecht 1970
– *Sämtliche Schriften und Briefe*. Preussische Akademie der Wissenschaften. Berlin 1923-
– *Système religieux de Leibniz*, trans. Albert de Broglie. Paris 1846
– *Textes inédits d'après les manuscrits de la bibliothèque de Hanovre*, ed. Gaston Grua. Paris 1948
– *The Leibniz-Arnauld correspondence*, trans. H. T. Mason. Manchester 1967
– *The Leibniz-Clarke correspondence*, trans. H. G. Alexander. New York 1956
Levin, Marguerita, 'Leibniz's concept of point of view', *Studia leibnitiana supplementa: Akten des internationalen Leibniz-Kongresses 1966* 12 (1980), p.221-28
Locke, John, *An early draft of Locke's Essay*, ed. R. I. Aaron and Jocelyn Gibb. Oxford 1936
– *An essay concerning human understanding*, ed. Alexander Fraser. New York 1959
– *Essays on the law of nature*, ed. W. von Leyden. Oxford 1954
– Locke. Bodleian Library, Ms. C.43.
– *John Locke's Of the conduct of the understanding*. New York 1966
– *The Correspondence of John Locke*, ed. E. S. De Beer. Oxford 1976-1982
– *The Life and letters of John Locke*, ed. Lord King. London 1858
– *The Works of John Locke*. London 1801

Mabbott, J. D., 'The place of God in Berkeley's philosophy', in *Locke and Berkeley: a collection of critical essays*. Notre Dame 1968. p.364-79
McLachland, H., *The Religious opinions of Milton, Locke and Newton*. New York 1972
McRae, Robert, *Leibniz: perception, apperception and thought*. Toronto 1976
Malebranche, Nicolas, *Œuvres complètes de Malebranche*. Paris 1958-1967
– *Malebranche: l'homme et l'œuvre*. Journées Malebranche, Paris, 1965. Paris 1967
Mandeville, Bernard de, *The Fable of the bees: or private vices, publick benefits*. Oxford 1924
Marc-Wogau, Konrad, 'The argument from illusion and Berkeley's idealism', in *Locke and Berkeley: a collection of critical essays*. Notre Dame 1968. p.340-52
Marcil-Lacoste, Louise, 'La logique du paradoxe du père Claude Buffier', *Dix-huitième siècle* 8 (1976), p.121-40
– 'The Epistemological foundations of the appeal to common sense in Claude Buffier and Thomas Reid', Diss. McGill, 1974
Mathieu, Vittorio, *Leibniz e Des Bosses (1706-1716)*. Torino 1960
Mercier, Roger, *Les Sciences de la vie dans la pensée française du XVIIIe siècle*. Paris 1963
Milton, J. R., 'John Locke and the nominalist tradition', in *John Locke: Symposium Wolfenbüttel 1979*. Berlin, New York 1981. p.128-45
Misrahi, Robert, *Spinoza*. Paris 1964
Montgomery, Frances, *La Vie et l'œuvre du père Buffier*. Paris 1930
Müller, Kurt, and Krönert, Gisela, *Leben und Werk von Gottfried Wilhelm Leibniz*. Frankfurt am Main 1969

O'Connor, D. J., *John Locke*. New York 1967
Ollé-Laprune, Léon, *La Philosophie de Malebranche*. Paris 1870

Park, Désirée, *Complementary notions: a critical study of Berkeley's theory of concepts*. The Hague 1972
Parkinson, G. H. R., 'Preface', *The Leibniz-Arnauld correspondence*. Manchester 1969
– *Spinoza's theory of knowledge*. Oxford 1954
Pascal, Blaise, *Pensées*, ed. Louis Lafuma. Paris 1962
Pichler, Aloys, *Die Theologie des Leibniz*. München 1869
Pitcher, George, *Berkeley*. London, Boston 1977

Proast, Jonas, *The Argument of the Letter concerning toleration briefly considered and answered*. Oxford 1690

Randall, John, *The Career of philosophy from the Middle Ages to the Englightenment*. New York 1962

Rescher, Nicholas, *Leibniz: an introduction to his philosophy*. Oxford 1979

Reu, Johann (ed.), *The Augsburg confession: a collection of sources*. Chicago 1930

Robinet, André, 'Grundprobleme der Nouveaux essais', *Studia leibnitiana supplementa: Akten des internationalen Leibniz-Kongresses 1963*. Wiesbaden 1969. iii.20-33

– *Système et existence dans l'œuvre de Malebranche*. Paris 1965

Rodis-Lewis, Geneviève, *Nicolas Malebranche*. Paris 1963

Rome, Beatrice, *The Philosophy of Malebranche*. Chicago 1963

Rossi, Mario, *Saggio su Berkeley*. Bari 1955

Russel, Bertrand, *A critical exposition of the philosophy of Leibniz*. London 1949

Sage, Athanase, 'Péché originel: naissance d'un dogme', *Revue des études augustiniennes* 13 (1967), p.211-48

Sardemann, Franz, *Ursprung und Entwicklung der Lehre von lumen rationis aeternae, lumen divinum, lumen naturale, rationes seminales, veritates aeternae bis Descartes*. Diss. Leipzig. Kassel 1902

Schmidt, Gerhart, *Aufklärung und Metaphysik*. Tübingen 1965

Schouls, Peter, *The Imposition of method: a study of Descartes and Locke*. Oxford 1980

Shaftesbury, Anthony, Earl of, *Characteristics of men, manners, opinions, times, etc.* London 1900

Simonovits, Anna, 'Die dialektische Einheit von Einheit und Mannigfaltigkeit in Leibniz' Philosophie', *Studia leibnitiana supplementa: Akten des internationalen Leibniz-Kongresses 1966*. Wiesbaden 1969. i.80-101

Spinoza, Baruch de, *Spinoza Opera*. Hamburg 1924

– *The Chief works of Benedict de Spinoza*, trans. R. H. M. Elwes. New York 1955

– *The Correspondence of Spinoza*, trans. A. Wolf. New York 1966

– *The Short treatise on God, man and his well-being*, trans. A. Wolf. New York 1963

Steinkraus, Warren, 'Foreword', *New studies in Berkeley's philosophy*. New York 1966

Stillingfleet, Edward, *The Works of that eminent and most learned prelate, Dr Edw. Stillingfleet, Late Lord Bishop of Worcester*. London 1707-1710

Strauss, Leo, *Die Religionskritik Spinozas als Grundlage seiner Bibelwissenschaft*. Berlin 1930

Tedeschi, Paul, *Paradoxe de la pensée anglaise au XVIIIe siècle ou l'ambiguïté du sens commun*. Paris 1961

*Theologiae cursus completus*, viii, ed. J. P. and V. S. Migne. Paris 1839

Thiele, Georg (ed.), *Der lateinische Aesop des Romulus und die Prosa-Fassungen des Phädrus*. Heidelberg 1910

Thomas Aquinas, *Summa theologiae*, trans. David Bourke *et al.* New York 1965-1975, vols. 1vi-1ix

Tipton, I. C., *Berkeley: the philosophy of immaterialism*. London 1974

– 'The "Philosopher by Fire" in Berkeley's *Alciphron*', in *Berkeley: critical and interpretive essays*. Minneapolis 1982. p.159-73

Trapnell, William, *Voltaire and the eucharist*, Studies on Voltaire 198. Oxford 1981

– *Christ and his 'associates' in Voltairian polemic*. Saratoga: Stanford French and Italian Studies 26 (1982)

Viano, Carlo, *John Locke: dal razionalismo all'illuminismo*. Torino 1960

*Vie de saint Alexis*, ed. Gaston Paris. *Romania* 8 (1879), p.163-80

Vigouroux, Fulcran (trans.), *La Sainte Bible polyglotte*. Paris 1898-1909

Voltaire, François Marie Arouet de, *Lettres philosophiques*. Paris 1964

– *Romans et contes*. Paris 1966

Wade, Ira, *The Intellectual development of Voltaire*. Princeton 1969

– *The Intellectual origins of the French Enlightenment*. Princeton 1971

Warnock, G. J., *Berkeley*. Baltimore 1969

Watson, Richard, *The Downfall of Cartesianism 1673-1712*. The Hague 1966

Westfall, Richard, *Science and religion in seventeenth-century England*. New Haven 1958

Williams, Bernard, 'Descartes', *Encyclopedia of philosophy*, ed. Paul Edwards *et al*. New York, London 1967

Wilkins, Kathleen, *A study of the works of Claude Buffier*, Studies on Voltaire 66. Genève 1969

Wolfson, Harry, *The Philosophy of Spinoza*. Cambridge 1934

Woozley, A. D., 'Remarks on Locke's account of knowledge', in *Locke on human understanding*, ed. I. C. Tipton. Oxford 1977. p.141-48

Yolton, John, *John Locke and the way of ideas*. London 1956

Zac, Sylvain, *L'Idée de la vie dans la philosophie de Spinoza*. Paris 1963

– 'Le problème du christianisme de Spinoza', *Revue de synthèse* 78 (1957), p.479-91

– *Signification et valeur de l'interprétation de l'Écriture chez Spinoza*. Paris 1965

# Index